The Shape of
Things to Come

Space Shuttle flights in the 1981–1986 time period will carry aloft military recon, surveillance, weather, and communications satellites, often several at a time in the huge Shuttle payload bay. This Shuttle is carrying three different satellites, each with an attached propulsion stage that will boost them to GEO from LEO. Courtesy Rockwell International Space Operations.

The Space Shuttle docked to an early LEO Base, which has been built from modules carried up on sequential Space Shuttle flights.
Courtesy Rockwell International Space Operations.

LEO Bases of the late 1980 and 1990 time period are likely to get large and complex, looking like they "just grew" as new modules, compartments, heat radiators, and solar electric panels are added to them. NASA.

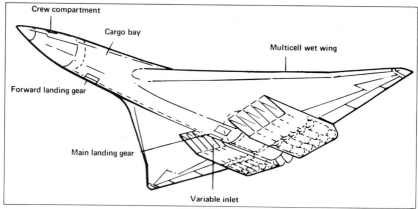

(Above) The 1990 single-stage-to-orbit StarRaker space shuttle would take off and land from ordinary airports and would be a little larger than a present-day Boeing 747. Courtesy Rockwell International Space Operations. (Below) Details of the single-stage-to-orbit StarRaker advanced space shuttle concept of Rockwell International. From DOE Satellite Power System Concept Development and Evaluation Program, see Bibliography.

Artist's concept of a manned deep space ship for operating between orbits in NEO, HEO, CLS, LSO, and TLS areas.
Courtesy Rockwell International Space Operations.

A solar-powered electromagnetic lunar surface catapult can be built horizontally on the Moon's surface because the absence of an atmosphere permits loads to be launched horizontally. The payload emerging from the muzzle of the catapult is moving at more than two kilometers per second and is just a blur.
Art by Rick Sternbach.

An artist's conception of a military base "at the top of the hill," in the Earth-Moon system: the L-5 Lagrangian Point, 60 degrees behind the Moon in the Moon's orbit around the Earth. Both a deep-space cruiser and a hypersonic space cruiser are seen. Art by Rick Sternbach.

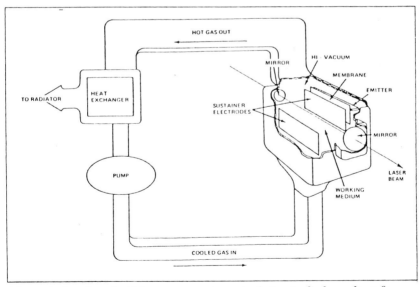

Schematic drawing of a high-energy gas-dynamic electronic-discharge laser for space. From C. N. Bain, et al, "On the Military Implications of a Satellite Power System." Prepared for DOE by Science Applications, Inc., April 1980.

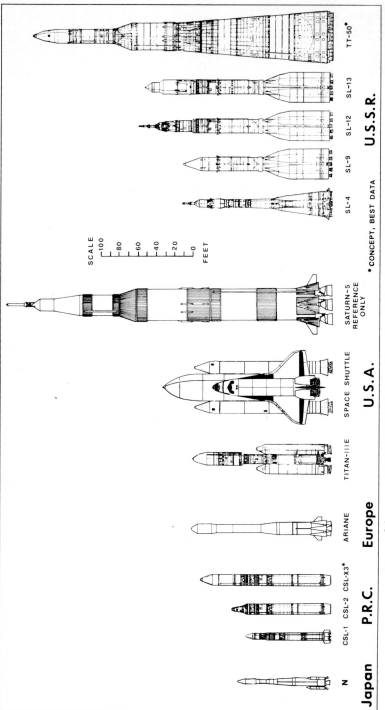

Some of the current (1980–1985) space launch vehicles shown to the same scale for comparison of relative sizes. PRC, Titan-IIIE, and USSR vehicle drawings are copyright 1980 and 1981 by Charles P. Vick and are used with permission. From The Illustrated Encyclopedia of Space Technology by Kenneth W. Gatland. Salamander Books, Ltd., London, 1981.

Confrontation in Space

CONFRON-TATION IN SPACE

G. HARRY STINE

INTRODUCTION BY DR. HERMAN KAHN

Prentice-Hall, Inc., Englewood Cliffs, New Jersey 07632

Library of Congress Cataloging in Publication Data

Stine, G. Harry (George Harry), date
    Confrontation in space.

    Bibliography: p.
    Includes index.
    1. Space warfare.   2. Space weapons.   I. Title.
UG1530.S74   358'.8   81-7346

ISBN 0-13-167437-4   AACR2
ISBN 0-13-167429-3 {PBK.}

To Captain Lewis Joseph Stecher, Jr., USN (Ret.)

Contents

Introduction
by Dr. Herman Kahn

This book on space warfare is most timely. Indeed, as I write these words, it is almost exactly twenty-four hours since the Columbia landed safely, a milestone project that many had feared would be an expensive failure. We still have to see, of course, exactly how effective the shuttle will be in cutting the cost of orbiting various objects as well as transporting men and material to satellites in space. But it now seems clear that the space shuttle program will be at least moderately successful, perhaps spectacularly so. In any case, the Columbia mission marks a new era in the exploitation of space. Such exploitation will of course not be solely American; the Soviets, Europeans, and Japanese all have plans under way, at least for mini shuttles which, even though their carrying capacity will be from a tenth to a third of the U.S. shuttle, will still be impressive. As a result, the possibility of increased military competition in space is being actively discussed, including both the concept of war in space and the exploitation of space to facilitate military operations in the air and on the ground. From now on out, the two will always be linked.

It seems that we will have to develop the concept of space war, much as we had to develop concepts of air warfare. The great model for this kind of thinking is Mahan's theory of sea warfare. As a result, the same temptation exists to make simple analogies between space and sea warfare that were made between air warfare and sea warfare. And it is quite possible that the concept of moderately effective control of space may be a more valid concept than that of moderately effective control of the air was (as opposed to almost total control of the air).

But any analogy of this kind is likely to be incomplete. While one may have to go through space in order to attack another country, much as one had to cross oceans, the use of space in warfare differs from the use of the seas in more ways than it is similar (as with air warfare concepts). Doctrines for war in space will have to be developed with more than simple analogies—and this is one of the great concerns of this book.

Some of the issues raised by the concept of war in space are brand new. Indeed, in many ways space is almost the same kind of terra incognita that Africa used to be on old maps. And yet one cannot study space without having a good background about many projects that have already been accomplished. Millions of dollars have been spent for studies on the application of space, and billions of dollars on actually exploring and utilizing space. We know a great deal about what can and cannot be done in space. While there will doubtless be as many surprises as successful predictions regarding space warfare, the study of space warfare starts from a very considerable body of knowledge.

From this point of view, Harry Stine is superbly qualified. He has been thinking about these problems since at least 1960, and has written two recent books which are relevant to these issues, *The Third Industrial Revolution* and *The Space Enterprise*. He has also collaborated on numerous articles dealing with related topics, and worked with Robert Heinlein and Daindridge Cole—two seminal thinkers on this and related subjects. This background is simply invaluable—a combination of scholarly work and serious speculation, with a certain amount of playful science fiction. He has been in close touch with appropriate individuals with whom he has exchanged and developed ideas. This kind of stimulation and concentration is necessary if one is to deal with such a new field in a constructive and responsible way. Yet, Harry would be the first to agree that this book is very much an initial and pioneering effort. But this is exactly what is most needed at this stage of the game.

The United States is now in a relatively poor position vis-à-vis the Soviets in almost every area of military preparations, including space. The usual idea that the United States and the Soviet Union have been engaged in an intense arms race is simply inaccurate for most of the last two decades. From 1963 to 1980, United States efforts can best be described by the metaphor of walking, not racing; meanwhile the Soviets at least trotted. While United States expenditures were almost level in constant dollars (ignoring the operating expenses of the Vietnamese war), the Soviets increased their expenditures by at least four percent a year. Over 17 years, this is a factor of two. As a result, the change in the relative military positions of the two superpowers is really extraordinary. From 1950 to 1963, the United States invested about 60 percent more than the Soviets did in military assets (basic equipment, bases, and infrastructure). By contrast, from 1963 to 1980, the Soviets invested perhaps 90 percent more than the United States. While such comparisons between two very different military and economic systems are inherently tricky, these data are widely accepted as giving a pretty good picture of what happened.

The United States is now engaged in a serious effort to correct critical defects and gaps and to catch up or pass the Soviets in various military areas. It seems quite clear that space will play a very important part in these efforts during the next decade or two.

Many concepts set forth in this book will be of great importance in the 1980's, and ever more so in the 1990's. Indeed, unless we start preparing now for the 1990's, we are likely to be in quite serious trouble. Given lead times for space activities and likely Soviet efforts in this area, it is already rather late to start taking space warfare seriously. At the very least, experts and the educated public should begin to understand, debate, and elaborate the ideas that are presented here.

Perhaps the most fascinating chapter of the book is one that might be called the Military Geography of Space, or the importance of the moon and the so-called Lagrangian points L1 to L5. However, I am inclined to think that Stine overemphasizes the overwhelming nature of the concepts he presents; but he may be right. While the space equivalent of what military strategists call the "high ground" and the importance of controlling and fortifying this high ground may indeed be decisive, these issues could be dominated, at least early in the game, by the relative technological capabilities of the contending parties, particularly in what is known as the measure-countermeasure competition, which will probably be at least as important as geography. However, this is the kind of issue that must be analyzed and discussed. In any case, space "geography" will certainly be important in working out the tactics and strategy of space warfare.

Many people are appalled at the very idea of having this kind of competition in space. They feel that since the military competition on earth is bad enough, it should not be exported to space. Indeed, they tend to think that it is all to the good to set up obstacles to any expansion of the arms race to any new area. Both of these propositions could be completely wrong. The real problem is to protect people on earth, and to make the cost and risks of war or appeasement as small as possible. To the extent that the arms race is a competition between the NATO alliance and the Soviet bloc, I want the United States and its allies to be clearly ahead—and transferring many activities to space could sharply improve the arms race from this viewpoint. Furthermore, doing so might allow for a certain amount of war to be fought without destroying cities or contaminating the environment of the earth. And to the extent the United States can achieve a significant lead in the arms race, this presumably means superiority for the side which is most likely to preserve the peace. United States military superiority is likely to be felt to be relatively tolerable—or even greatly desired—by most nations. The situation is somewhat like that which prevailed before World War II. At that time, Winston Churchill commented about the attitude of many Englishmen who felt that it was unfair to preserve French superiority over Germany. He noted that this was not an issue of competition between two interchangeable industrial nations: if the French were superior, peace would result; if Germany became superior, then war or disastrous appeasement would probably ensue. Thus, to take a neutral stance between France and Germany was foolish and dangerous.

I think that the world as a whole would find Soviet superiority almost intolerable and certainly very dangerous, while United States superiority of the same kind would be relatively acceptable (some Soviet citizens might even feel this way). The United States is a status quo world power; despite usually being prudent, the Soviet Union is not a status quo world power.

I thank Harry Stine for making an important contribution to the improved understanding of both military specialists and the general public of an important area. *Confrontation in Space* is likely to be an important and seminal book.

Foreword

I do not write this book because I am necessarily a militarist or a hawk, nor because I believe that the violent conflict between human beings called war is an inevitable and inescapable part of our nature.

Warfare does not produce rapid progress in science and technology to any greater degree than strong commercial competition does. Warfare may be considered a gross waste of time, effort, and resources by many entrepreneurs as well as by many ordinary people, and this may well be true. Warfare is wasteful even under conditions of extreme want.

Yet warfare exists as a reality of our world and its diverse cultures. Ignoring it does not deter it. Peaceful as most people may be, sooner or later they discover that they must defend themselves, their families, their possessions, and their social groups against coercion reinforced by the threat or use of physical violence. The choice is to resist or to capitulate, to defend one's value system or to accept the adversary's values and perhaps to do his bidding as well. Survival on all levels of existence—personal, familial, or social—does not always depend on physical surrender; survival accompanied by social and philosophical progress often depends upon resistance on the basis of such intangibles as honor, duty, and principle. If people had not fought for such intangibles in the past, our culture and our civilization today would be quite different from what it is. And we may have had no social progress whatsoever if people had not put their very lives at stake for such intangibles.

Someday, war may no longer be a constant of history. Peace is a goal worth working hard to attain. But "someday" is an indefinite period of time in the future. While working to eliminate war as an activity of the human race, we must think about war, its causes, its implications, and its conduct in *all* environments, even those such as outer space where we have only recently started to journey.

And perhaps in studying war in these ways, we may not only survive as a civilization and as a species long enough to eliminate war, but also, in the process, learn how to do it.

—G. Harry Stine
Phoenix, Arizona, 1981

List of Acronyms and Abbreviations

ABM Antiballistic Missile
ADIZ Air Defense Identification Zone
AFSATCOM Air Force Satellite Communication
ASAT Antisatellite
C³ Command, control, and communication
C³I Command, control, communication, and intelligence
CBW Chemical and Biological Warfare
CIA Central Intelligence Agency
CLS Cislunar Space
CW Continuous-wave
DEW Directed Energy Weapon
DIT Detection, Identification, and Tracking
DMSP Defense Meteorological Satellite Program
DNA Deoxyribonucleic acid
DOD Department of Defense
DOE Department of Energy
DSCS Defense Satellite Communications System
DSP Defense Support Program
EA Earth's Atmosphere
EAM Emergency Action Message
ECM Electronic Countermeasures
EEG Electroencephalograph
ELDO European Launcher Development Organization
ELINT Electronic Intelligence
EMP Electromagnetic Pulse
ET External Tank
EW Electronic Warfare
FAA Federal Aeronautics Administration
FLSATCOM Fleet Satellite Communications
FOBS Fractional Orbital Bombardment System
GEO Geosynchronous Earth Orbit
GOES Geostationary Orbit Earth Satellite
HE High Explosive
HEL High-Energy Laser

HEL(CW)   Continuous Wave High-Energy Laser
HEL(P)   Pulsed High-Energy Laser
HEO   High-Earth Orbit
HLLV   Heavy-Lift Launch Vehicle
HTOHL   Horizontal Takeoff Horizontal Landing
ICAO   Interntional Congress of Aviation Organizations
ICBM   Intercontinental Ballistic Missile
IRBM   Intermediate Range Ballistic Missile
ITOS   Improved TIROS Operational Satellite
IUS   Inertial Upper Stage
LASER   Light Amplification by Stimulated Emission of Radiation
LASL   Los Alamos Scientific Laboratory
LCM   Laser Countermeasures
LEO   Low-Earth Orbit
LIDAR   Laser Illuminated Detection and Ranging
LLRL   Lawrence Livermore Radiation Laboratory
LOS   Line-of-Sight
LSD   Lysergic acid diethylamide
LSI   Large Scale Integrated circuit
MAD   Mutually Assured Destruction
MEG   Magnetoencephalograph
MeV   Million Electron Volts
NACA   National Advisory Committee for Aeronautics
NASA   National Aeronautics and Space Administration
NATO   North Atlantic Treaty Organization
NORAD   North American Air Defense
NWS   National Weather Service
OPEC   Organization of Petroleum Exporting Countries
OTRAG   Orbital Transport-und-Raketen-Aktiengesellschaft
PBW   Particle Beam Weapon
PLV   Personnel Launch Vehicle
PRC   Peoples' Republic of China
RADAR   Radio Detection and Ranging
RAF   Royal Air Force
RI   Rockwell International Corporation
SALT   Strategic Arms Limitation Talks
SAM   Surface-to-Air Missile
SATDEF   Satellite Defense
SDS   Satellite Data System
SINS   Ship Inertial Navigation System
SMET   Sabotage, Mutiny, Espionage, and Terrorism
SPS   Solar Power Satellite

SOC   Space Operations Center
SSME   Space Shuttle Main Engine
SST   Supersonic Transport
SSTO   Single Stage to Orbit
STC   Space Traffic Control
TLS   Translunar Space
TNT   Trinitrotoluene
TRW   Thompson Ramo Wooldridge Corporation
TV   Television
UHF   Ultrahigh Frequency
UN   United Nations
USA   United States of America
USAF   United States' Air Force
USN   United States' Navy
USSR   Union of Soviet Socialist Republics
VFLSI   Very Fast Large Scale Integrated circuit
VfR   *Verein für Raumschiffahrt*
VHF   Very High Frequency
VTOHL   Vertical Takeoff Horizontal Landing
VTOVL   Vertical Takeoff Vertical Landing

SPACE: THE NEW THEATER OF WAR

Of all the activities of the human race, war is the least understood. It has been the subject of careful study for millennia. It is reviled by soldier and civilian alike during times of peace, and it is constantly resorted to for any reason that seems acceptable at the time. War has continued to be a violent consequence of failed diplomacy in spite of continual progress in military technology, which has rendered the weapons of war increasingly deadly.

In the last half of the twentieth century, efforts to understand the causes and nature of war have intensified. It is no longer considered a depraved subject of study, and it is no longer the exclusive profession of military men. Nonmilitary, civilian, academic, professional students of war and violence in all its forms now devote their full daily attention to determining the causes and nature of war.

Since war is such a ubiquitous human activity, its study has, by necessity, been compartmentalized to some degree because no one person can possibly embrace it all. Today, there are specialists in guerrilla warfare, terrorism, brushfire wars, civil wars, religious wars, chemical war, nuclear war, naval war, and so on.

The human race is now faced with a new form of warfare.

In the decade of the 1980's and beyond, the arena of war will expand to include that alien environment only recently entered by humanity and its machines: space.

Space means many things to many different people. To some, it is a

1

new area for exploration, exploitation, research, development, or utility. To others, it is a new and final physical frontier, a place to be colonized with the seed of humanity, an ecological niche to be occupied by the human race.

And to others, space is a place to conduct warfare.

Therefore, like it or not, space is a new theater of war that must be studied in that regard as thoroughly and carefully as any other lest we suddenly find ourselves confronted by the threat of physical force and violence from others who have taken it quite seriously.

In the minds of some people, space has been used for the purposes of war since 1912 when the first bombing raids from airplanes were made during the Balkan Wars. In this regard, they consider space to begin at the surface of the Earth and to proceed upward. The Earth's atmosphere is considered to be nothing but a unique part of space containing gases under varying pressures and temperatures.

To others, space begins at some undefined altitude above the Earth's surface. Definitions of space place this arbitrary boundary anywhere from 50 to 100 kilometers altitude where the effects of the Earth's atmosphere on the motion of bodies can be dismissed as trivial or "second order effects."

But regardless of where space begins, it does exist, humanity has penetrated it, and it is a theater for the conduct of warfare.

Warfare in space, or the conduct of warfare *from* space, is very real in 1981, less than twenty-five years after the Space Age officially opened with the launch of the Soviet Union's Sputnik-I on 4 October 1957. In fact, the launching of Sputnik-I was a military endeavor by the Soviet Union and was perceived as such by experts—if not by the political leaders—in the United States. However, within two years, United States political leaders had come around to accepting the fact that Sputnik-I signaled the military utilization of space by the Soviet Union.

Sputnik-I was launched by the Soviet ICBM, the Korolev R-7 *Semyorka,* designed for deployment on sidings along the Trans-Siberian Railway and capable of lofting the big and heavy Soviet thermonuclear warhead of the time to a distance of five thousand kilometers. Sputnik-I and its progeny probed the environmental conditions of orbital space through which ICBM warheads had to pass.

However, the first real use of space for the purposes of war started even earlier than that with the successful launch of the German long-range artillery rocket, the *Aggregat-4* or V-2 (*Vergeltungswaffe-2*) on 3 October 1942. This was the first man-made weapon carrier to travel beyond the Earth's atmosphere in its flight. Space became a region through which weapons had to pass.

And in common with other historic advances in technology that opened up new areas, space became a theater of war. The prime mover of space vehicles, the rocket, is first recorded in history in its use as a weapon in the battle of Pien-King in China in A.D. 1232. It was no accident that the initial steps into space in the United States following World War II were conducted by the U.S. Army Ordnance Corps and the U.S. Navy's Naval Research Laboratory.

The use of space beyond the Earth's atmosphere for the conduct of warfare is therefore not new. And it is quite likely that the next general war may be fought in space with weapons that are too powerful to be used on Earth *because* the weapons are that powerful. The weapon effects upon one's own forces are as bad as on the enemy's.

Space war is *not* "far-out *Buck Rogers* stuff" or something out of a science-fiction movie.

Space war is *not* just a game that computer buffs play for fun.

Space war is real, and it is being studied seriously today. Space war will be as deadly and decisive as any other form of general warfare, given the military doctrines of space warfare and the weapons with which space wars of the next fifty years will be fought.

The U.S. Department of Defense alone currently averages more than $1 billion worth of military satellites in orbit at any given time. The U.S. military space program's budget—which rarely sees the light of public disclosure—is many times that of the civilian National Aeronautics and Space Administration and is believed to be in excess of $10 billion per year.

The Soviet Union is also active in the military utilization of space, and even less is known about the Soviet military space budget and projects. The Soviets do not artificially separate their civilian and military space programs as the United States attempts to do. In fact, there is little separation between military and civilian activities in any area of technology in any of the Warsaw Pact countries. Sport aviation, amateur radio, automobile racing, and all the activities called hobbies in the United States are taken quite seriously in the Warsaw Pact countries, where they are all under the control of quasi-military organizations linked directly to the military services. The primary use of technology in the Warsaw Pact nations is for military purposes.

Other nations either have the capability to conduct military operations in space or will have such capability before the end of this century.

The People's Republic of China (PRC) has an impressive space launch capability, including a large ICBM whose rocket booster is also capable of placing more than a ton of payload in orbit—and it has done so. The PRC has the capability to launch military satellites now, may have already done so, and plans to possess a manned space capability before the year 2000.

France has an active rocket program that includes both land- and sea-launched ballistic missiles. The French have orbited their own satellites with launch vehicles they have developed themselves. They are planning their own manned space capability with a small shuttlelike vehicle called *Hermes*. The French have military space capability now and will have manned space capability within twenty years.

Japan is a quiet spacefaring nation. Thus far, it has launched only nonmilitary satellites. But with both indigenous and imported technology, Japan also has the potential to conduct military space operations in the future. Although it possesses only a Self-Defense Force, Japan is a nation with a culture in which militarism runs so deeply that it cannot and has not been eliminated in the few short decades since 1945.

In the near future, other nations are certain to join the ranks of spacefaring countries that also possess military space capabilities because military and "peaceful" space activities go hand in hand, with a very thin line separating them.

Only the United States and the Soviet Union are known to be currently conducting military activities in space.

Reconnaissance and surveillance satellites are real; they are in orbit now.

Both the United States and the Soviet Union now find that military communications satellites are absolute necessities in order to conduct communications, command, and control (C^3). Most military communications now go through communications satellites stationed in space. The United States depends upon military communications satellites to relay orders to strategic bomber and missile forces, in particular the "go codes," or Emergency Action Messages (EAM), that activate the nuclear deterrent.

Killer satellites are real; the Soviet Union has tested them in orbit. The United States is working on two different types of antisatellite interceptors (ASATs).

High energy laser (HEL) space weapons are real. In the United States, HEL research is going on at Los Alamos Scientific Research Laboratories, at the Sandia Laboratories, at White Sands Missile Range, and at other secret government military research labs and testing grounds.

Particle beam weapons (PBW) are real; the Soviet Union appears to be working on such devices in a very large building near Semipalatinsk, a building so large that U.S. intelligence analysts have had no trouble finding it on American reconnaissance satellite photos.

We know about these things because there have been tantalizing peeks and glimpses of them and other military systems in various magazine and newspaper articles over the past several years. The SALT II testimony given before Congress is both revealing and frightening, because the military activities of several nations now include orbital space.

A top secret military security clearance isn't needed to learn of these things because far too much has appeared in the open literature and news media. One takes the time and trouble to watch for them, and there they are.

Most people haven't looked for a number of reasons. First of all, space war isn't a pleasant thing to contemplate, and most people would rather spend time on more peaceful pursuits and studies. As George Catlett Marshall wrote in his final report on World War II on 1 September 1945, "We finish each bloody war with a feeling of acute revulsion against this savage form of human behavior, and yet on each occasion we confuse military preparedness with the causes of war and then drift almost deliberately into another catastrophe." Marshall was referring to the three great fundamental mistakes of United States' military policy: (a) the United States has entered every war without effective military forces or plans for providing them; (b) the organization and development of the military forces were accomplished during the war; and (c) the military forces were broken up immediately following the war.

And because there have been several United Nations' conventions (treaties) covering aspects of military operations in space, most people feel secure in the belief that no nation would dare abrogate a UN treaty. But these UN treaties relating to space war are extremely vague, were written long before scientific know-how and technology could even consider such things as orbital beam weapons, and can be interpreted in many ways. Some UN treaties are mere statements of principle and have no binding effect upon any signatory nation. Other UN treaties are totally unenforceable, depending upon the principle of reciprocity to command adherence.

There are only two UN treaties that presently have a bearing upon space warfare. The first of these is the 1963 Nuclear Test Ban Treaty, which prohibits the testing of nuclear weapons in the Earth's atmosphere or in outer space. The second is the 1967 Treaty of Principles that sets forth in seventeen articles the fundamental character of the rights and responsibilities for space-using peoples. One of its major points states that nuclear weapons and weapons of mass destruction should not be stationed in outer space, on the Moon, or on other celestial bodies. Another states that military operations, maneuvers, and bases should not be permitted on other celestial bodies.

But modern directed energy weapons—high-energy lasers (HEL) and particle beam weapons (PBW)—are not necessarily weapons of mass destruction and can pinpoint [with great accuracy] individual targets as small as an automobile.

And the 1967 Treaty of Principles is only a statement of principles, of high ideals rather than a pragmatic agreement hammered out on the basis of previous experience. It is not binding, and it cannot be enforced.

The 1963 Nuclear Test Ban Treaty is not observed by either France or the People's Republic of China, both of which have tested nuclear weapons in the atmosphere since 1963. No other nation or group of nations has taken any action whatsoever to react to this atmospheric nuclear activity by France and the PRC, and the United States and the Soviet Union are observing the Treaty only on the basis of reciprocity. In actuality, neither the USA nor the USSR *needs* to conduct atmospheric nuclear tests because both nations possess all the data they need from their tests made prior to 1963 and can now comfortably live with data obtained from contained underground nuclear tests.

Thus, the common belief that international law and UN treaties will prevent the development of space weapons and protect the world against the effects of space warfare is not based upon fact or history.

The world is nakedly vulnerable to space warfare.

Space war must therefore be identified as the reality it is. And, in common with other areas of international diplomacy and military doctrine, it must be subjected to careful study and public discussion based upon facts.

Even recognizing the importance for national secrecy of actual hardware programs for space warfare, the implications of the military use of space are of such importance that they must be discussed and debated openly. In the same way, Dr. Herman Kahn initiated public consideration of thermonuclear warfare in 1962 when it was considered a *verboten* subject for discussion outside a circle of experts and when the exact details of the hardware were—as they still are—national secrets.

Once Dr. Kahn brought the subject of thermonuclear warfare into the open in his classic book, *Thinking About the Unthinkable* (New York: Horizon Press, 1962), people could discuss its implications and work out options should another thermonuclear confrontation occur as it did during the Cuban missile crisis in October 1961 when, basically, World War III was averted.

At this point, one must squarely face the question, "Why do we even have to think about taking our internecine struggles into the Universe with us?"

As Robert A. Heinlein remarked through his character, entrepreneur Delos D. Harriman, in *The Man Who Sold the Moon* (Chicago: Shasta Publishers, 1949): "Damnation! Nationalism should stop at the stratosphere!"

But it hasn't.

Why?

In fact, why do humans fight at all?

A caveat must be made at this point and should be remembered throughout this book: *Not every human being wants to fight or likes to fight.* Psychological studies by the United States Army have indicated that among Regular Army personnel, only 56 percent could be classified as "fighters." Among draftees, about 48 percent were "fighters." Even among the "fighters," the most intelligent ones manage to avoid getting shot at and cluster in the safer jobs away from the front lines. During World War II, only about 15 percent of the men in the average infantry company actually pulled the trigger against the enemy; in the Korean War, this rose to about 50 percent.

With these percentages, why do people fight wars at all? Why can't people be mature enough to settle their differences by negotiation, by arbitration, or by adjudication?

The human race is trying. For the past several millennia, human beings have been hard at work developing what may turn out to be their greatest invention, a way to keep people from killing each other most of the time. It's called politics.

But it doesn't always work. It is still an imperfect invention. Like all inventions, it demands refinement and fine-tuning as more information becomes available. Refusal to look at the new information or denial of the new information once looked at does not help improve the invention.

It is probably possible to trace the aggressive tendencies of human beings to the fact (which our ancestors learned eons ago) that it is easier to take something than to make it. This is certainly true in a world of scarcity, where there isn't *quite* enough to go around. Until recently there have only been brief periods of localized abundance. Scarcity has been the lot of 99 percent of all human beings in the past and is still the norm throughout most of the world today.

The biological Law of Least Effort therefore led to the Attila Syndrome: take it from others rather than go to the greater effort to make it.

When some people gave up the nomadic life and settled down to raise seasonal cereal crops in the Tigris-Euphrates River Valley of Mesopotamia about 10,000 years ago, a new philosophy slowly developed to protect them against the Attilas of the time: the Neolithic Ethic.

This Neolithic Ethic was highly successful in a world of scarcity and has been succinctly stated by anthropologist Carleton S. Coon as follows:

You stay in your village, and I will stay in mine. If your sheep come to eat our grass, we will kill you. We may kill you anyway to get your grass for our sheep if we run short.

Any one who tries to make us change our ways is a witch, and we will kill him. Stay out of our village!

This is a definitive statement of why people fight even today.

Until this Neolithic Ethic is changed—by continuing application of technology to create relative abundance for everybody in the world—disagreements arising from this Ethic can lead to armed conflict, the coercion of others through the use of physical force.

It will take a long time to change the Neolithic Ethic, because in a world of scarcity it works very well indeed. (Anything that has been around and useful for a hundred centuries *must* be viewed pragmatically as a workable rationale.) It arose from the peasant economy, in which everybody has a little bit of everything, but nobody has very much of anything. But the Neolithic Ethic has resulted in the deaths and suffering of billions of people throughout time and has created human conflict situations instead of smoothing them out.

The Neolithic Ethic is the reason why conflicts build up slowly for a long period of time, explode in an orgy of violence, and end up in a very messy situation that is often worse than the original one.

The Neolithic Ethic worked reasonably well for hundreds of centuries. It permitted the human race to build civilization against those who would destroy it through greed and covetousness. And it permitted the human race to progress to the point where it's now obvious that humanity can't go on using it and must therefore begin to develop a new way to get along.

We're working on it. But we haven't got it yet.

While we're working on it, we must also plan for war.

We must defend against the Attila Syndrome or risk not having the opportunity to develop the new ethic and eventually eliminate war—if that turns out to be a true survival goal, which it may not.

Bertrand Barère: "The tree of liberty only grows when watered by the blood of tyrants."

Some people may argue that this is a highly simplistic presentation of why people fight. But a dictionary is the most simplistic of all books and among the most useful. The purpose of this book is not to investigate why people fight. It assumes that people do and will continue to do so. It is based on the fact that people are waging war as this is being written and that they will continue to do it for some time to come. It is only by looking at "why" that it is possible to get a firmer grip on "how" the violent form of human conflict known as warfare will be extended into outer space.

The human race has already taken the seeds of warfare into space and will continue to do so because it is simply not possible to change the Neolithic Ethic overnight.

It will take centuries of worldwide education—using near-Earth space as a location for communications satellites capable of beaming information to any spot on Earth for the education of humans everywhere—before the Ethic can be changed, before the memories of past wrongs are erased by time, and before the fires of vengeance can be damped.

A new ethic for a world of abundance and a universe full of life can be developed. But for the next century or so, on Earth and in space, people are going to fight—not all people, but enough people with enough weapon power that space warfare can have a profound effect upon life on Earth.

It would indeed be a wonderful thing if nationalism stopped at the stratosphere and if all future wars could be prevented or averted. But this condition and situation is not yet realistic.

To quote Will and Ariel Durant: "War is one of the constants of history, and has not diminished with civilization or democracy. In the last 3,421 years of recorded history only 268 have seen no war. . . . Peace is an unstable equilibrium, which can be preserved only by acknowledged supremacy or equal power. . . . In every century the generals and the rulers (with rare exceptions like Asoka and Augustus) have smiled at the philosopher's timid dislike of war."

Therefore, if we are to heed the warning of these and other esteemed historians, we must prepare for space war, be thinking about it, and have some options worked out concerning what to do when other nations make military use of space.

If the true and real nature of space war now and in the future is grasped by planners, the United States and the rest of the Free World can develop and put into place the necessary space weapons, counterweapons, and safeguards as these devices and systems become technologically feasible. The best way to avoid space war appears to be to continue the pragmatic policy of mutual deterrency—a policy which has worked since 1945 in preventing general thermonuclear war.

It appears that it will be absolutely necessary to do these things. There are a wide variety of nonmilitary space activities currently being planned and even in the initial stages of development—activities that are not basically military in nature, design, or function, but which possess potent military implications as a result of the facilities or technologies that make them possible. We *must* begin thinking about safeguards now before the potential dangers materialize.

These nonmilitary space developments cannot and should not be stopped or prevented because they may possess military consequences. They hold the promise of great benefits to all humanity and the solutions to most, if not all, of the world's problems today. We would be seriously shortchanging our children and grandchildren in terms of communications, energy, raw materials, new materials, pharmaceuticals, and a better life altogether if we were to prohibit human activities in space that might pose problems because of military potential.

There isn't very much that we can do about current military activities in space. But there may be a great deal that we can do regarding the space war of the future.

2

CURRENT SPACE MILITARY ACTIVITY

There is considerable military utilization of space today.

A great deal of this activity is under security wraps, but an amazing amount of information about it is available in the open literature, such as trade magazines, professional society publications, Congressional testimony, and scientific and engineering papers.

The accidental landing of the Soviet Cosmos-954 nuclear-powered naval surveillance satellite in Canada on 24 January 1979 was greeted with indignant surprise by the American press. This incident awoke many people to the fact that space was being used for military purposes and led some—including the incumbent American President who should have known better—to demand a cessation to such activities. In view of the historic American naive idealism regarding military operations and preparedness, this was not unusual. Nor was it surprising that most people did not know the extent to which their own nation was involved in military operations in space.

Not all of this public awareness and attitude can be blamed on native naiveté. The space activities of the United States since 1958 have been carried out in the glaring light of publicity, leading to the assumption that the space programs of the United States have all been peacefully oriented and based on the optimism and idealism of scientific exploration of this new frontier. The highly visible NASA space shots were accompanied by quiet, unannounced launches made by the Department of Defense (DOD) not only from the openly visible beaches of Cape

Canaveral but also from behind the tight security of Vandenberg Air Force Base near Lompoc, California.

A whole family of classified military space programs was started in the late 1950 decade and has never ceased to operate and grow in size and number of satellites of different types launched. The launches were dutifully reported to the United Nations, the orbits of the satellites were carefully listed in the annual Aeronautics and Space Report of the President, and the subject was quietly dropped. It was almost as though the open nature of the NASA civilian space program was designed to permit the maximum visibility of US achievements in space while allowing DOD space operations to proceed with a very low profile and extremely limited attention by the press.

However, in contrast to the roller-coaster nature of the NASA space budget, the DOD space budget has grown consistently since 1959 to the point where it now exceeds the NASA space budget.

Since the Soviet Union does not operate under the limitations of the 1955 Eisenhower space policy of distinct separation of military and civilian space programs, it is impossible to determine the precise space commitment of the USSR, to say nothing of the funding being applied to the military portion of the overall Soviet program. The USSR never made any distinction between its military and civilian space programs, and it's doubtful if such a distinction would be valid in any event since *every* aerospace activity in that nation appears to possess military significance and potential. (It is only recently that Soviet airliners no longer come off the production line without hard points on the wings and fuselages for the installation of weapon loads and without the typical Soviet design feature of a transparent bombardier's station in the nose ostensibly occupied by a navigator.) The entire Soviet space program is operated by the Soviet *Raketnaya Voiska Strategisheskogo Naznacheniya* (Strategic Rocket Forces), a completely separate service from the Air Force, Navy, Ground Forces, or Air Defense Forces that was formed under the regime of Nikita Sergeevich Khrushchev in 1960. The only way that space watchers without top-level security clearances and a "need to know" can estimate the level of Soviet military space activity is by studying the orbits and lifetimes of the ubiquitous Cosmos satellites, most of which are military satellites launched under the "Cosmos" cover name.

To date, both the USA and USSR military space programs have been used to conduct reconnaissance and surveillance of military activities on Earth and to conduct C^3 activities for their own military forces. To some extent, the USSR has also used its military reconnaissance satellites to monitor agricultural activities in other nations and through this program of crop evaluation has managed to manipulate the world's grain markets to their advantage.

Table 1 UNITED STATES OPERATIONAL MILITARY SPACE SYSTEMS

Name	Function	Number of Satellites in orbit	Inclination	Period	Perigee (km)	Apogee (km)
AFSATCOM	High-priority Communications with strategic forces using transponders on "host" satellites	?	varies	varies	varies	varies
SDS	High-priority Communications link in polar regions	3	63.3	12 hrs.	300	39,000
DSCS	Long-haul communication	4	0	24hrs.	35,800	35,800
FLSATCOM	Navy Fleet communication	4	0	24 hrs.	35,800	35,800
TRANSIT	Navy navigation	6	90	95 min.	350	1,000
DMSP	Weather data	2	90	101 min.	800	800
None	Navy ocean surveillance	4(?)	63	107 min.	1,100	1,100
DSP	Early warning	3	0	24 min.	35,800	35,800
Big Bird	Hi-resolution photo recon	1	96	92 min.	150	250

Table 1 UNITED STATES OPERATIONAL MILITARY SPACE SYSTEMS (*continued*)

Name	Function	Number of Satellites in orbit	Inclination	Period	Perigee (km)	Apogee (km)
None	Search and find photo recon (real time?)	1	110	89 min.	130	400
Ferret	Electronic and communications intelligence	1	96	95 min.	500	500

Table 2 SOVIET OPERATIONAL MILITARY SPACE SYSTEMS

Name	Function	Number of Satellites in orbit	Inclination (degrees)	Period	Perigee (km)	Apogee (km)
Molniya	Communications	16	63–66	12 hrs.	600	40,000
Stationar	Communications	11	0	24 hrs.	39,000	39,000
Cosmos	Communications	24(?)	74	115 min.	1,400	1,400
Meteor	Weather	(?)	81.2	102 min.	850	900

Cosmos	Navigation	12	83	105 min.	950	1,000
Salyut	Manned recon	1	51.6	90 min.	250	350
Cosmos	Photo recon	30/year	varies	varies	160 (varies)	210 (varies)
Cosmos	Electronic Intelligence (System I)	8	74	95 min.	550	550
Cosmos	Electronic Intelligence (System II)	2(?)	81	97 min.	600	600
Cosmos	Ocean Surveillance (System I)	2	65	90 min.	260	277
Cosmos	Ocean Surveillance (System II)	(?)	65	104 min.	900	1,000

The basic operational military space systems of the USA and the USSR are shown in Tables 1 and 2 respectively. This data has been gleaned from USA and European aerospace trade publications and from other unclassified material in the public domain. As such, it is probably incomplete and may, in some cases, also be inaccurate albeit the best data available. It should also be noted that some systems operate in multimode fashion, having several functions other than the primary one that is listed.

Although the USA launches far fewer missions per year than the USSR, this is no indication of the level of activity. By and large, Soviet military space systems have shorter in-space lifetimes than US space systems. This is exemplified by the average thirteen-day orbital lifetime of the Soviet reconnaissance satellite system, which requires up to thirty launches per year if the Soviets are to maintain one satellite on station at all times. In contrast, the United States appears to launch three to four such satellites per year, the reduced launch rate made possible by the longer lifetime of the space segment of the system. In addition, all indications are that the Soviet military space systems are far less complex, are smaller, and depend upon large numbers of individual satellites operating in space at a given time. This conjecture is supported by what is known of the general Soviet philosophy of aerospace design and systems operation. It has not only been extensively used and abundantly evident in their aircraft for more than fifty years, but it was also discovered to be the primary design philosophy behind their space systems, spacecraft, and launch vehicles, since the initial unveiling of the Korolev R-7 *Semyorka* launch vehicle in its uprated version at Le Bourget Aerodrome near Paris in May 1967. The general Soviet approach of simplicity, engineering overdesign, and lack of redundancy or fail-safe backup in their aerospace systems was further confirmed by the close look at these systems afforded United States experts during the Apollo-Soyuz Test Program that culminated in 1975.

Current military space activities of both the USA and the USSR fall into several general categories: communication, command, and control (C^3) satellites, weather satellites, navigation satellites, surveillance satellites, and reconnaissance satellites. Intercontinental ballistic missiles (ICBM) and other ground-to-ground ballistic missiles that travel through space during part of their flights are not considered to be space systems in this context.

Military space programs known to be under development in the United States and believed to be under similar development in the Soviet Union include antisatellite (ASAT) interceptors, directed energy weapons (DEW) such as high-energy lasers (HEL) and particle beam weapons (PBW), and electronic warfare (EW) techniques.

A brief look at each category will help in evaluating the current "state of the art" of military space technology which, in turn, will assist consideration of rational space weapons systems of the future.

Because of the paucity of information on the exact nature of the various Soviet space systems, it will not be possible to discuss them in detail. However, since the technology of similar space systems currently utilized by the United States cannot differ significantly from that available to the Soviets, one can reasonably assume that the Soviet systems have similar capabilities and military functions.

At this time, communications satellites are absolutely crucial to the operation of United States military forces around the world. Command, control, and communication (C-cubed or C^3) functions are vital to US military operational doctrine and practice. The nature of US forces deployed around the world is such that a very large amount of C^3 traffic is in existence. Without military comsats, it would be difficult, if not impossible, to exercise the high level of C^3 currently required. Thus, the military comsat networks are vital nodal points for long-haul communications as well as for tactical purposes. And the dependence upon military comsats is growing constantly, especially with the explosive growth in minicomputer and large-scale integrated (LSI) circuit technology, which permits even the soldier in the field to have access to enormous computer networks to provide him with information on local troop dispositions and capabilities, updated local maps, and other tactical information. The support of the Department of Defense (DOD) for advanced electronic technology is indicated by their massive funding of Very Fast Large Scale Integrated (VFLSI) circuit technology, which promises to increase computer switching and gate times by several orders of magnitude.

A perusal of Table 1 will indicate the extent of DOD's involvement with military comsats. However, the table does not list the circuits leased by DOD from Comsat for dedicated military use of noncritical, unclassified data processing.

An example of this last is DARPANET, a DOD computer network of astounding complexity and enormous computer power. In order to keep this net exercised constantly, DOD has permitted a number of nonmilitary computer users to have low-priority access to DARPANET through local telephone exchanges. DARPANET permits the possessor of a small home minicomputer to link in with the net and have access to large multipurpose computers in such places as MIT, CalTech, the Pentagon, NATO-Brussels, and so on. Most of DARPANET's links are through commercial comsats.

DSCS (Defense Satellite Communications Systems) is DOD's dedicated general purpose long haul communications program. It provides a communication relay for all US military users. It even permits intratheater communications between small portable ground sets—backpack radios—so that commanders will be able to maintain communications with their units in the field down to and including infantry platoons. DSCS satellites are military equivalents of commercial comsats in many respects; four of them are maintained in geosynchronous orbit 35,800 kilometers in space, where they go around the Earth once in twenty-four hours and therefore appear to stand still in the sky from a given spot on Earth. The use of four such satellites permits worldwide communication, since the satellites can relay signals received from a ground station to another ground station, and so forth.

FLSATCOM provides a similar capability for the United States Navy. Along with leased services of commercial MARISAT satellites operated by Comsat, FLSATCOM satellites are visible to naval ships and facilities between latitudes 70 degrees N. and 70 degrees S. This satellite system is the Navy's primary C^3 network.

To cover areas of high latitude that are not visible to the DSCS, FLSATCOM, or other comsats stationed in geosynchronous orbit, SDS (Satellite Data System) consists of three satellites placed in high inclination orbits that are also highly eccentric orbits. They are the only DOD communications satellites that are not positioned in geosynchronous orbital slots over the Earth's equator. As a SDS satellite swings up over the north pole of the Earth, it is at apogee and is moving quite slowly. It is then used to provide communications and data relay from DOD polar facilities such as the Air Force base at Thule, Greenland. A SDS satellite will remain visible to north polar stations for about eight hours before it swings in toward perigee over the South Pole, where it moves very fast. Three SDS satellites properly phased in orbit therefore provide a continuous twenty-four-hour coverage of the north polar region.

AFSATCOM is a system of small UHF (ultrahigh frequency) radio repeaters placed upon other host satellites such as DSCS and especially the SDS spacecraft. The primary purpose of the AFSATCOM system is to relay orders to the USAF Strategic Air Command bomber forces aloft. AFSATCOM uses the UHF frequency spectrum, especially on the SDS satellites, because the auroras and electromagnetic disturbances in the north polar regions render VHF and lower frequency communication channels difficult to use or often totally unusable. This capability of communicating at any time, even under the most difficult conditions, is extremely important because AFSATCOM is the system that is used to transmit the Emergency Action Message (EMA) or "go code" to USAF Strategic Air Command bombers at their turnaround points.

The TRANSIT navigation satellites represent the oldest United

States military space program. The first of these satellites was launched on 13 April 1960. The system was designed to support the Polaris (and later the Poseidon) missile-launching submarines by providing them with extremely accurate positioning data so that the missile guidance systems and the Ship Inertial Navigation System (SINS) could be continually updated. A missile-launching submarine and its load of missiles must "know" at all times where it is in relationship to the missile targets.

Because a ballistic missile submarine's defense lies in stealth, it cannot break radio silence to interrogate a satellite. Therefore, TRANSIT is an active system that continually sends out a coded radio signal with a known frequency accompanied by a time-reference signal. Ground receivers pick up this signal, and the shipboard computer processes the data to provide the ship's latitude and longitude. Accuracies of the TRANSIT system are said to be on the order of one part in a billion (10^9).

Naval vessels have used the TRANSIT system extensively. Since 1968, the TRANSIT system has been available to nonmilitary, commercial interests, who have put it to work on a wide variety of navigational uses.

A new system called NAVSTAR will be orbited in the 1980 decade and be usable by both military and commercial interests. NAVSTAR will consist of twenty-four satellites, eight in each of three inclined orbits at an altitude of 20,400 kilometers to cover the entire globe with continuous time and position signals. The accuracies of the NAVSTAR system provide a clue regarding the precision with which current military space technology operates. The signals from NAVSTAR satellites will allow a receiver on the ground to compute its location within 8 meters (26.2 feet) horizontally and to within 10 meters (32.8 feet) vertically. The velocity of the receiver can be determined with an accuracy of 0.185 kilometers per hour (0.115 miles per hour). DOD developed the NAVSTAR system primarily for improving the accuracy of tactical battlefield missiles, and it will also be used by tanks, trucks, ships, aircraft, and even individual soldiers with NAVSTAR positioning backpack receivers/computers.

TRANSIT and NAVSTAR solve one of the most vexing problems of any military commander: "Where am I?" In the haze of battle, precise data on location is often very important information to have. Military navigational satellites also make possible highly accurate maps and charts without which military engagements cannot be conducted today. In fact, the navsats may be far more accurate than the available maps for many years to come, which poses other serious problems for both theater and field commanders.

In addition to the US National Weather Service (NWS) of the

National Oceanic and Atmospheric Administration of the Department of Commerce, the Department of Defense operates its own dedicated Defense Meteorological Satellite Program (DMSP) to provide weather data from satellites. Weather data from satellites has become a vital part of meteorology and has permitted the National Weather Service and the Federal Aviation Administration to issue weather observations and forecasts of great accuracy, especially to civil aviation interests but also to such diverse activities as outdoor rock concerts and oyster harvesting. The importance of accurate and current weather information and reliable weather forecasts to military and naval commanders should require no emphasis. In spite of modern military systems involving radar, lasers, and infrared sensing and imaging, foul weather can strongly impact any military operation. Temperatures, precipitation, cloud cover, and winds have important bearing on how an operation can be most successfully conducted.

Therefore, although relying on the NWS meteorological satellites already in orbit, the Department of Defense maintains its own exclusive series of metsats, DMSP. These are two satellites in polar orbit at an altitude of 800 kilometers in a sunsynchronous orbit—i.e., they pass over all points on Earth at local sunrise and sunset times or at local noon and midnight. One DMSP is phased in the sunrise-sunset orbit, the other in the noon-midnight orbit. Thus, a commander can obtain a weather update every six hours with considerably higher resolution than from the NWS satellites—notably GOES, ITOS, Nimbus, and others whose sensor resolution is often a mile or more.

Again, DMSP is an active system working with passive receivers on the ground. No unit need reveal its location by having to interrogate the satellite to receive information. Data is continually transmitted from the satellites.

The ability to operate highly sensitive sensors on orbiting satellites has led to the development of a series of spacecraft with dedicated functions of detecting discrete activities on the ground and in the atmosphere below. The most obvious sensor to place on a satellite is a camera with a long-focus lens to carry out reconnaissance in the classic manner of aerial photography, albeit from a much higher vantage point. When this was first done with balloons, then aircraft, and finally rockets (to a limited degree for experimental purposes), the vehicles were immune to interception and destruction. This is the best of all possible worlds for a scout, because scouts are usually considered expendable and liable to be destroyed either during the opening moments of a conflict or when their location is pinpointed by the enemy. However, balloons and aircraft soon became prey for antiaircraft guns, armed scouting airplanes, and surface-to-air guided missiles. Until recently, the reconnaissance and surveillance satellite has been immune to interception and destruction, but this is changing rapidly as one might expect it would, with the development of antisatellite interceptors (ASATs).

There are two basic types of military sensing satellites: reconnaissance (recon) and surveillance. Reconnaissance is normally used in its classic military sense of scouting or taking a quick look when desired for certain activities suspected of being conducted by the adversary. Surveillance is watching, often for a wide variety of activities, in order to provide an indication of change in the adversary's activities, to detect new activities, or to give early warning of a military operation.

Camera-carrying recon satellites faced many problems early in their development, not the least of which was the perfection of a suitable and reliable means for returning the photographic data back to Earth. The USAF Discoverer program was the first to test out and perfect the most obvious method of doing this: eject the film and let it land on Earth where it could be picked up and developed. Discoverer-1 was launched 28 February 1959, but it wasn't until Discoverer-13 was launched (10 August 1960) that its entry capsule was successfully recovered from the ocean after being ejected from the satellite on the seventeenth orbit. Today, both USA and USSR recon satellites use the film return capsule technique, the Soviets to a greater extent than the US. However, photo techniques have progressed significantly over the years to the point where now the film can be processed in the orbiting satellite, scanned electronically, and the data sent back to the ground on a radio signal.

Photo recon satellites also take pictures in other portions of the spectrum than visible light. Today, they are equipped with infrared sensors capable of penetrating clouds as well as being able to provide sensing data when viewing the night side of the Earth.

Recon satellites are necessarily orbited as low as feasible in order to provide the greatest possible sensor resolution. There is very little information available concerning the actual resolution obtained by US recon satellites—and none from the Soviet Union, of course. However, from such USAF recon satellites as Big Bird 150 kilometers up, it is said that individual vehicles can be identified. Whether it is true or not, someone once remarked that it is possible with modern optics, photo emulsions, and recon techniques to read from orbit the poker hand in that friendly little game played on top of the oil drum in the motor pool at lunchtime.

DOD has several recon satellite programs. Big Bird is the only one actually named. It is a high-resolution photo recon satellite in sun-synchronous orbit. There is another program, unnamed, that is a system designed for rapid launch to search and find, a scout in the classic sense; it is said to be able to report in real time—i.e., probably through some manner of television camera and satellite-to-ground radio link.

Surveillance satellites that orbit and watch, waiting for their sensors to be activated from below or keeping continual watch with their sensors, are in higher orbits where they can keep a very large portion of the Earth in view. One of the first surveillance satellite programs of DOD was Midas, standing for Missile Defense Alarm System, which was intended to detect Soviet ICBM launches and signal the alarm. The first Midas satellite was successfully orbited on 24 May 1960. Another early surveillance satellite program was Samos (Satellite And Missile Observation Satellite) successfully orbited for the first time on 31 January 1961. By far the most successful announced USAF surveillance satellite program was the Vela Program, which began in 1959 and placed the first pair of Vela satellites in orbits 113,000 kilometers up on 16 October 1963. The Vela satellites were designed to detect the brilliant fireball produced by a nuclear explosion in the atmosphere as well as X rays, gamma rays, and neutrons released by nuclear explosions.

The Midas and Samos satellites have been superseded by a new series of surveillance satellites known as the Defense Support Program (DSP) Code 647. These DSP satellites, built by TRW and weighing about 1000 kilograms, are launched into geosynchronous equatorial orbit by the Titan IIIC, the biggest expendable launch vehicle currently in the United States stable. The DSP satellites use infrared sensors to detect ballistic missile launches. The first of these DSP satellites was orbited on 5 May 1971.

Keeping track of electromagnetic signals from radio transmissions and radar is the job of the Ferret (Code 711) satellites, the first having been built by Lockheed and Sanders Associates while the new generation is being built by Hughes Aircraft. These Ferret satellites operate in sunsynchronous orbits at 500 kilometers altitude to provide world coverage on a daily basis.

Enormous amounts of data come back to Earth from these spacecraft every day. If it were not for computer analysis and highly trained personnel capable of detecting significant changes in the data flow, the sheer volume of this information would completely swamp the facilities and people involved, resulting in long delays between data acquisition and presentation of the "reduced" or "massaged" data to the National Command Authority, the National Security Council, the Joint Chiefs of Staff, the CIA, the Defense Intelligence Agency, and others to whom it is valuable. Delaying the transmission of vital intelligence data is almost as bad as not obtaining it in the first place because there is always a time factor involved in military intelligence work.

However, as might be expected, very little is said about DOD payloads. The launches are announced afterward, the orbital elements are proclaimed, and the report ends with the words "Classified payload."

Even less is said about Soviet military payloads and launches, and the only glimpse anyone has had of a Soviet military spacecraft was the remains of Cosmos-954, an ocean recon satellite that landed by mistake in Canada. But the missions of Soviet satellites—most launched under the cover name of "Cosmos"—can often be deduced by their launch sites and their orbits.

However, the Soviet Union possesses one important military space system that the United States does not: the Salyut manned military recon and surveillance station. The importance of human eyes and brains in space cannot be overrated. Had there been people aboard the Vela satellite that reported a flash of light, there would be little question whether this was a large meteorite or a clandestine nuclear explosion set off in the Indian Ocean by the Republic of South Africa; we would have known immediately. The Soviets have used their manned Salyut space station for military purposes, regardless of their claims to the contrary. The Salyut on-board telescope is claimed to be a "solar research telescope" but has all the attributes of a reconnaissance instrument capable of a ground resolution on the order of a half-meter (18 inches) *or less.*

As the United States Space Shuttle begins operation, some flights will involve military missions and will be flown with military crews. Separate mission control facilities have been constructed at Johnson Space Center in Houston, Texas, and extreme measures have been taken to insure the absolute security—physical as well as electromagnetic—of this military mission control center. Thus, to some extent, the United States will be following the Soviet practice of dual-use of space facilities and will probably exhibit the same extreme reluctance to discuss these activities openly.

What is known of the state of the art in both the USA and the USSR indicates that the Soviet military satellites are smaller, lighter, less complex, and shorter lived than those of the USA. However, from all indications, the Soviets can achieve similar results in spite of their different approach. Much information about satellite recon and surveillance capabilities can be inferred from the Congressional testimony on the SALT II Treaty as well as from the extreme extent to which the USAF proposes to go in the new MX missile program to insure that the Soviet recon satellites can verify the number of missiles emplaced, but not *where* they are emplaced.

Current recon satellite technology, it has been said, is so sophisticated and advanced that it is possible to determine whether an ICBM missile silo, covered with concrete and "hardened" against a direct nuclear blast, contains a real ICBM with warhead, a dummy of the same mass, or nothing. In order to deceive successfully a modern recon satellite, a dummy missile in a silo would have to be so similar to the real ICBM that it is not worth the cost or the effort to install the decoy.

If a general war between the NATO nations and the Warsaw Pact nations were to break out today, the space activities of the USA and USSR would involve only passive military activities—C^3, scouting, reconnaissance, surveillance, intelligence gathering, and weather depiction. By and large, the military systems deployed in space are not offensive in nature today.

This will not be the case in the future as space launch and transportation vehicles become larger, more efficient, and more numerous.

And as the state of the art in technology applicable to true space weapons matures.

SPACE TRANSPORTATION: THE STATE OF THE ART

The extent of military activity in space depends totally upon the space launch vehicles that are and will be available to transport military payloads into and around space now and in the future.

At this time, the rocket-propelled vehicle is the only workable space transportation device, and it has its roots deep in military history. In fact, the modern rocket vehicle owes its existence to military requirements. There would be no space flight without rockets developed for military uses. This holds true in nearly every nation in the world.

Although rockets were usually considered only as recreational and display devices such as fireworks intended to impress the populace with the political power and might of their rulers, rockets were developed by the Chinese as military weapons. The first description and illustration of a *Huo yao pien chien* or fire arrow appears in a book *Wu-ching Tsung-yao* (Complete Compendium of Military Classics), published in China in A.D. 1045 twenty-one years before the Norman conquest of England. We do not know whether the early Chinese "arrows of flying fire" were ordinary archery arrows to which tubes of burning black powder had been attached for incendiary purposes, or if they were indeed rocket-boosted arrows.

Because military technology was a pragmatic, cut-and-try endeavor until less than a hundred years ago, other weapons were developed at the expense of the rocket and achieved greater accuracy, reliability, storability, efficiency, and cost-benefit ratio (to use a modern military term that means, in essence, "more bang for the buck").

For a brief period from 1804 to 1850 in the interim between the development of large smooth-bore cannons and accurate rifled artillery pieces, the war rocket developed by Sir William Congreve, William Hale, and others provided acceptable barrage artillery. The use of Congreve rockets by the British in the battle of Bladensburg was decisive, causing the rout of the United States' forces and resulting in the British capture of the city of Washington. Hale rockets were extensively used by US Army troops in Mexico in 1847 and 1848. '

However, since these rockets were solid propellant units using black powder as a propellant, there were limits to their sizes and storability. Their reliability was never as good as it should have been and certainly far below that required by military commanders in the field who count on weapons to perform as expected. Black powder is a perfectly fine solid rocket propellant, as millions of model rocketeers around the world will attest. But Congreve, Hale, and their contemporaries lacked the technology to utilize it properly as a rocket propellant. The manufacture of black powder rocket motors demands precision loading equipment because the propellant grain must be "dead pressed" in such a manner that it possesses nearly constant density throughout. This can be done easily and repeatably today and will produce highly reliable black powder rocket motors with up to 125 grams (2.2 ounces) of propellant and internal diameters up to 25 millimeters (about an inch). Beyond this size, the structural limitations of dead-pressed black powder—its brittleness, for example—render it susceptible to cracking, which usually causes the rocket motor to overpressurize and split its casing upon ignition. Thus, large black powder artillery rockets were often more lethal to the fusiliers (as the rocket troops were called) than to the enemy.

Modern composite solid propellants, however, have physical characteristics quite different from the classic black powder propellants. Solid propellant rocket motors today are eminently practical propulsion devices for military rocket vehicles up to and including ICBMs in size. Solid propellant rocket motors have also found utility in large manned space transportation systems such as the Space Shuttle, which uses two solid propellant booster rockets on each flight; each booster is 3.7 meters in diameter and 45.46 meters long containing 503,627 kilograms of propellant and producing a thrust of 12,899,200 newtons (2.9 million pounds). These Space Shuttle Solid Rocket Booster rockets are the largest solid propellant rocket motors ever built.

The modern rocket vehicle used to place military payloads in space stems directly from the weapon restrictions placed upon Germany by the Treaty of Versailles in 1919. The German Army was prohibited from developing or operating long-range artillery guns. German prowess in large-caliber fieldpieces was a very recent memory to those who met in Versailles for the purposes of restructuring the European map after World War I.

In actuality, the Treaty of Versailles prevented Germany from doing nothing that the German General Staff wanted to do; if necessary, the projects were carried out in other countries. For example, German officers and soldiers were trained, and some equipment was developed and tested in the Soviet Union under secret agreement.

However, because of the international nature of the armaments industry, it was practically impossible to embark at that time on any new secret development of a large weapon without foreign countries becoming aware of it. Therefore, the Waffenprüfamt (Weapons Testing Department) of the German Army went looking at what inventors were doing—and came away appalled and disenchanted. In 1930, Professor (later General) Becker, Captain von Horstig, and Captain Dpl.Ing. Walter Dornberger of the Waffenprüfamt investigated the work being done on rockets by a group of space enthusiasts known as the Verein für Raumschiffahrt (VfR or Society for Space Travel) at an old Army munitions storage area in Reinickendorf on the north edge of Berlin. They were impressed with what they saw. On 1 October 1932, the Ballistics and Munitions Branch of the Waffenprüfamt established Versuchstelle Kummersdorf-West (Experiment Station Kummersdorf-West) some twenty-seven kilometers south of Berlin under the command of Captain Dornberger and hired a young student member of the VfR named Wernher von Braun as the chief engineer.

By March 1936, the Dornberger-von Braun team at Kummersdorf-West had developed reasonably reliable liquid propellant rocket motors and had flown two sequential rocket vehicle designs, the *Aggregat-1* (A.1) and the *Aggregat-2* (A.2). They were working on an improved model, the A.3, when Dornberger was told that the big money needed for future work hinged on developing rockets capable of throwing really big loads over long ranges with good prospects for hitting the target. Dornberger sat his enthusiastic young rocket engineers down and told them that their new design, the proposed A.4 rocket, would be designed to have twice the range of the World War I Paris Gun with a hundred times the warhead weight and with greater accuracy than the fabled *lange 22, 2 Zentimeter Kanone in Schliessgerust* (as the Paris Gun was officially called). The new rocket would be capable of being transported on a standard railway flat car through any railway tunnel in Europe. Armed with these military specifications, Von Braun and his colleagues went to work. The rocket called A.4 that was subsequently developed was 14.3 meters long and 1.65 meters in diameter with four tail fins spanning 3.555 meters. It carried a warhead of 750 kilograms of amatol explosive, weighed 4008 kilograms empty and 12,805 kilograms at takeoff, and was propelled by a 25-ton thrust liquid rocket motor using liquid oxygen and ethyl alcohol/water propellants. It was launched vertically, was guided by either a self-contained inertial guidance system using gyros or by a radio beam, and had a range of 250 kilometers. Accuracy was better than long-range artillery by a factor of two.

The world knows this rocket as the *Vergeltungswaffe-2* (V-2) or Vengeance Weapon Two, the appellation given to it by Dr. Goebbels at the Propaganda Ministry.

On 3 October 1942, the first successful test version of the A.4 rocket rose to an altitude of 100 kilometers, traveled 193 kilometers, and landed 4 kilometers from the intended target.

At a celebration that evening, General Dornberger told his team of engineers, "The following points may be deemed of decisive significance in the history of technology: we have invaded space with our rocket and for the first time—mark this well—have used space as a bridge between two points on the earth; we have proved rocket propulsion practicable for space travel. To land, sea, and air may now be added infinite empty space as an area of future intercontinental traffic, thereby acquiring political importance."

Following the collapse of the Third Reich in May 1945, rocket technology split into two camps: the United States and the Soviet Union. Whereas the USA obtained Dornberger, Von Braun, and the remainder of the A.4 development team from Peenemünde, the Soviet Union occupied what was left of the Peenemünde rocket development station on the Baltic Sea, obtained a large number of German rocket production engineers and technicians, and eventually occupied the Mittelwerk underground A.4 assembly plant near Nordhausen in the Harz Mountains—but not before American troops occupied it and stripped it of enough components to assemble about a hundred A.4 rockets.

The United States program proceeded with excruciating slowness and lack of money under Von Braun and his colleagues, who were stationed at the US Army's Redstone Arsenal in Huntsville, Alabama, in 1950 and who all eventually became naturalized American citizens. The US Army Ordnance Corps set up White Sands Proving Ground in New Mexico and proceeded to launch a total of sixty-eight V-2 rockets from White Sands, Cape Canaveral, and the deck of the US Navy's aircraft carrier *Midway*. No attempt was made to open a production line for V-2 rockets in the United States, although Douglas Aircraft Corporation fabricated some V-2 tail sections, which were in short supply, not enough having been captured in good condition at the Mittelwerk. The Von Braun team, with the assistance of a growing cadre of American engineers and military rocketeers, developed the Redstone tactical rocket which was a big, improved, Americanized V-2. They went on to develop the Jupiter ballistic missile, which led directly to the big Saturn-I launch vehicle, which led in turn to the Saturn-5 moon rocket. German liquid propellant rocket motor know-how was acquired by the Rocketdyne Division of North American Aviation (now Rocketdyne Division of Rockwell International) and by the Aerojet-General Corporation and forms the foundation of all of today's American liquid propellant rocket motor technology. Offshoots of the Von Braun Huntsville team developments include the Titan ICBM, which was stretched and matured into the USAF Titan-II ICBM and the Titan-III series of space launch vehicles, which are today the largest US expendable space launch vehicles. Nearly all of the USA space launch vehicle stable stands on the foundation of Peenemünde, with the exception of the SLV-1 Scout solid-propellant small satellite launcher. Even the NASA Space Shuttle can trace its main engine ancestry back to the A.4 and its winged gliding recovery concept back to the experimental Peenemünde A.4b, which was an A.4 with swept wings attached to stretch its range by gliding back through the atmosphere.

The Soviet Union's rocket program is also based upon the foundations laid at Peenemünde, added to the work the Soviets had already done themselves. But the Soviet program proceeded differently. The potential of the V-2 rocket was immediately recognized by Stalin, who instigated the development of an intercontinental rocket shortly after the end of World War II. The program was put under the management of Sergei Pavlovich Korolev, a Soviet rocket pioneer who had participated in most of the extensive prewar Soviet rocket development activity. Korolev, as the chief designer of the Soviet program, was a man of the same stature, vision, and competence as Dr. Robert H. Goddard and Dr. Wernher von Braun.

Table 3 CURRENT MILITARY SPACE LAUNCH VEHICLES

Nation	Name	Payload Performance (kg) to LEO	to GEO	Remarks
USA	Titan-III B SLV-5B	3,600	-----	Titan-III core
USA	Titan-III C SLV-5C	13,200	1,432	
USA	Titan-III D SLV-5D	13,635	-----	
USA	Titan T-34D	14,955	1,900	Titan-III with Shuttle IUS 3rd and 4th stages
USA	Titan-III E	-----	3,364	Titan-Centaur
USA	Space Shuttle	29,545	-----	Payloads to GEO with IUS and other upper stages. Manned and reusable
USSR	SL-4*	7,500	-----	Soyuz launcher
USSR	SL-9*	18,182	-----	Proton launcher
USSR	SL-12*	-----	6,590	SL-9 with upper stages
USSR	SL-13*	22,727	-----	Salyut launcher Uprated SL-9
USSR	TT-50(?)	159,000 (est.)	-----	USSR "Saturn-5" but bigger
Europe	Ariane	2,755	973	
Japan	N-1	1,000	-----	License-built USA Delta
Japan	N-2	?	?	Uprated N-1
PRC	FB-1 (CSL-2*)	1,200	-----	CSS-X-4 ICBM
PRC	CSL-X-3*	-----	1,000	FB-1 with LOX-LH 2 upper stage
India	SLV-3	35	-----	First launch vehicle

(Note: Major launch vehicles used after 1980 only. *indicates US designation of USSR and PRC launch vehicles.)

The history of the Soviet rocket and space program is public knowledge but has never been completely told in print. Rocket development in Russia and the Soviet Union goes back to the beginnings of the twentieth century with Konstantin Eduoardovich Tsiolkovski, a visionary schoolteacher who stimulated and encouraged Korolev, Tsander, and the other Soviet rocketeers to develop an impressive level of rocket technology under the continuing support of the Soviet government until the Great Patriotic War (World War II) intervened and stopped most Soviet rocket development work. To a large extent, Soviet rocket and space technology has deeper roots in the Soviet Union than it does in the United States.

To recapitulate briefly Soviet rocket and space development since World War II, the Soviets put the V-2 rocket into production at the Mittelwerk and eventually moved the production facilities to the Soviet Union. The first launching site was established on the Volga River at a place called Kapustin Yar, a site equivalent to White Sands or NASA Wallops Station in the United States. Korolev, Yangel, and other Soviet engineers improved the V-2 into the Soviet Pobeda. They developed a stable of liquid propellant ballistic missiles, which Korolev also used for upper atmospheric and space research as the V-2A version of the Pobeda and the V-5V versions of his early Redstonelike ballistic missile (NATO code name SHYSTER). By 1949, the Soviets had an atomic bomb, and by 1952 they had tested the fission-fusion thermonuclear bomb. They had no long-range bomber capable of delivering this weapon at intercontinental ranges in contrast to the USA with its B-36 and forthcoming B-47 and B-52 bombers.

Korolev embarked on the first Soviet ICBM development. He adapted the four-chambered RD-107 rocket motor to a central core and attached four strap-on boosters—also powered by RD-107 motors—which were adapted from the Soviet R-4 IRBM, which in turn was built from a Peenemünde design study called the "Peenemünde Arrow" (Peenemünde *Pfeil*). Korolev's ICBM was the R-7 or Semyorka. Using liquid oxygen and hydrocarbon fuel, the R-7 achieved its first flight at intercontinental range on 27 August 1957 launched from the new Soviet cosmodrome east of the Aral Sea and north of a town called Tyuratam. To mislead Western military intelligence, the Soviets called it Baykonyr Cosmodrome, because the tiny village of Baykonyr lies under the flight path of an orbital or ICBM shot from Tyuratam. But U-2 photos and later satellite photos have positively identified the Tyuratam site. It is the Soviet equivalent of the USA's Cape Canaveral.

On 4 October 1957, Korolev used the R-7 to launch Sputnik-I into orbit. With the addition of an upper stage, the R-7 attained the capability of placing 5,000 kilograms in Earth orbit and sending 1,500 kilograms into high orbit, to Earth-escape velocity, and to the Moon. On 12 April 1961, the Korolev booster and upper stage (called the SL-4 in the United States because the precise Soviet designation is not known) launched Major Yuri Alekseyevich Gagarin into orbit.

The SL-4 booster has been the mainstay of the Soviet space program since 1957. It has been uprated and improved with a series of more powerful upper stages and has been used for all the manned space missions, including the Soyuz-T spacecraft, an obvious cover name to hide the fact that the Soviets deployed a new three-man spacecraft in November 1980. Soyuz began as a three-man spacecraft until the accident with Soyuz-11 that killed three cosmonauts, forcing the Soviets to cut the standard Soyuz crew back to two cosmonauts and use the resulting additional space and weight for an additional life support system to permit the two cosmonauts to ride in full pressure suits as insurance against future accidents of the same sort.

On 16 July 1965, the Soviets revealed a new and larger space booster known in the USA as the SL-9 or D Class Launch Vehicle with the launch of the 12,200-kilogram Proton-1 satellite. The Soviets have released no photographs of the entire SL-9 booster except the upper portion. Charles P. Vick, an astute Soviet space watcher in the United States, believes the SL-9 and the SL-12 and SL-13 derivatives were built using the same Korolev philosophy of putting strap-on boosters around an existing military missile core. In this case, Vick believes the SL-9 consists of an SS-7 (NATO code SADDLER) ICBM core surrounded by six SS-7 strap-on boosters. The SL-12 and SL-13 consist of this basic SL-9 booster with additional upper stages. The Soviets have never man-rated this big booster and had continual problems with its guidance and control system in the 1960's and early 1970's. Vick believes that the problems revolved around the slenderness of the basic SL-9 vehicle, which led to extreme dynamic bending problems.

The SL-4 Soyuz launch vehicle and the basic SL-9/12/13 Proton launch vehicle form the core of the current Soviet space program. The SL-4 is a proved man-rated vehicle that has been in use since 1957. The SL-9/12/13 has apparently had its guidance problems solved and is now in regular use as the Salyut launch vehicle. The production lines on both launch vehicles are still running and will probably continue to operate for some time to come because in a socialist economy these production lines mean continuing jobs for people.

The Soviet military space program is also supported by at least two smaller launch vehicles of the same performance as the United States Delta and Atlas class space boosters.

Some of the Cosmos satellites boosted into high inclination polar orbits are launched from a third Soviet launch site near Plesetsk south of Arkhangel'sk; this is the Soviet analogue to Vandenberg Air Force Base.

The Soviets began the development of a very large space booster in the period between 1959 and 1963. They were clearly behind the USA's development of the Saturn-5 vehicle by several years. The first intelligence data on this very large booster came from US recon satellite photos in the summer of 1966. Its existence has never been confirmed by the Soviets, and it has been known as Webb's Giant (from NASA Administrator James Webb who mentioned it in the late 1960's), the Class G launch vehicle, and the Lenin booster. Most recent data indicates its designation as "TT-50." Excellent estimates can be made of its size because the Soviets released a drawing of its gantry service structure in a book. Charles P. Vick's latest estimate places the size of the TT-50 at more than 100 meters tall with a lift-off thrust of 14.5 million tons and a capability of placing 150,000 kilograms in low-Earth orbit. The massive launch facilities for the TT-50 show up plainly on Landsat photos of the Tyuratam area.

But the Soviets have not had a great deal of success with the TT-50. Their first attempt to launch it in early June 1969 was a spectacular failure; it exploded on the launch pad during fueling operations, killing several important Soviet military men and engineers. It is reported that the explosion was photographed by a US Nimbus meteorological satellite. The disaster destroyed the launch site. In August 1971, the Soviets had rebuilt the launch facilities and attempted to fly the TT-50 again; it exploded at an altitude of about 12 kilometers. The third attempted launch of this huge rocket occurred on 24 November 1972, and the vehicle was destroyed about two minutes into the flight. Following these failures, it was obviously "back to the drawing board" since the TT-50 was no longer required for a prestige race to the Moon with the USA. In 1980, there were new indications that the TT-50 was again an active program, whose purpose had been changed. According to the latest available information, the Soviets may be grooming the TT-50 as a Heavy Lift Launch Vehicle (HLLV) for the purpose of orbiting one or more elements of a very large permanently manned space station—or perhaps several space stations. Clearly, the Soviet space program's goals since the lunar landing program was canceled in early December 1968 has been directed solely to developing a permanent manned presence in space primarily for military purposes with a number of industrial activities as second priority.

In 1980, the People's Republic of China (PRC) revealed to the world the extent of their indigenous rocket and space program.

Initially, the PRC obtained ballistic missiles of the SS-3 (NATO code SHYSTER) and modified the design by lengthening it to create the CSS-1, which can lob a 20-kiloton nuclear warhead to a range of 1,200 kilometers.

The first purely Chinese development was the CSS-2 single-staged ballistic missile, to which an additional stage was added to create the CSS-3 capable of boosting a 1-megaton thermonuclear warhead over a range of 7,000 kilometers. This became the CSL-1 (Long March-1) space booster, which launched China's first and second satellites in April 1970 and March 1971 respectively.

The CSS-X-4 is an ICBM of the Titan-II class, and its space booster version launched the next five Chinese satellites weighing up to 1,200 kilograms. The Long March-3 space booster, a CSS-X-4 with a Centaur-type third stage, is expected to be operational in 1981 and be used for placing PRC military satellites in geosynchronous orbit. The CSS-X-4 ICBM in its FB-1 space booster version is capable of placing a manned spacecraft in orbit.

The primary PRC booster factory is located in Shanghai and the PRC Cape Canaveral is at Shuangchengzi in the Gobi desert. Both sites have been visited by American space scientists and engineers from the American Institute of Aeronautics and Astronautics and the National Aeronautics and Space Administration. And, of course, there are excellent Landsat photos available of the Shuangchengzi launch site; some of these have been openly published.

The nations of Western Europe have come together to develop the Ariane booster to provide themselves with a space launch capability independent of the United States and the Soviet Union. Ariane is the culmination of many false starts as well as many successes in the individual and joint space programs of Western European nations. The British Black Arrow and the French Diamant boosters both successfully launched satellites, but the Europa-I and Europa-II launch vehicles jointly developed by a consortium of nations organized as the European Launcher Development Organization (ELDO) never were truly successful. However, in Ariane the Europeans have a launch vehicle of considerable sophistication. The Ariane launch site is at Kourou in French Guiana, South America, near the equator. The first successful Ariane flight took place on 24 December 1979 and placed its payload in orbit.

The French have proposed a five-man mini shuttle gliding recoverable spacecraft called Hermes that would be boosted by Ariane.

Japan has had a space program since February 1955, when Professor Hideo Itokawa and his colleagues at the University of Tokyo began launching miniature rockets called Pencils, smaller than many of today's model rockets, which can be purchased in American hobby shops. In 1981, the Japanese have an impressive space launch capability and are building the American Delta launch vehicle under license. This gives the Japanese access to modern rocket technology. They possess satellite launching capability and are, as of this writing, on the verge of having geosynchronous orbital capability. This implies a capability of launching a manned spacecraft. It also implies the capability of inverting the path of rocket development followed elsewhere and converting an orbital launch vehicle into a military ballistic missile by a relatively simple change of payload and guidance system commands.

India orbited the 35 kilogram Rohini satellite with its own SLV-3 booster on 18 July 1980.

In the wings, an independent German corporation, Orbital Transport und Raketen Aktiengesellschaft (OTRAG), has test-flown three of its modular launch vehicles from its new launch site in the Sahara Desert 1,000 kilometers south of Tripoli, Libya. By 1982, they plan to have the capability of placing 10,000 kilograms in low-earth orbit or 2,000 kilograms in geosynchronous orbit. OTRAG is not sponsored by a government and is building space launch vehicles for sale. Under pressure from the Soviet Union in 1979, the Republic of Zaire canceled OTRAG's $25-million-per-year lease on 100,000 square kilometers of jungle the company was using as a launch site there, forcing OTRAG to develop a new launch site in Libya. The OTRAG launch vehicle is modular in concept and is exceedingly simple to manufacture and operate. OTRAG is quoting costs of $17.5 million for a Delta class vehicle, $30 million for an Atlas-Centaur class booster, and $40 million for a vehicle with Titan-III capabilities.

This brief review indicates the state of the art that permits the launching of today's military space capabilities in C^3, reconnaissance, surveillance, weather forecasting, and electronic intelligence and countermeasures.

It should also serve notice that space technology is not stagnant but continuing to advance with more and more members being added to the Space Club all the time. Twenty years ago, only two nations—the USSR and the USA—had space capability of any sort. Today, at least seven nations have equal or better space capability to that which existed in 1961. Twenty years from now, there will be more nations in the Space Club, and there will be space activities of the scope, magnitude, and capabilities that will move military space operations from the passive mode into an active one.

Space vehicles *currently in design, development, and testing phases* will permit a vast expansion of military capabilities in space in the 1980 decade.

SPACE TRANSPORTATION: THE NEXT TWENTY YEARS

Beyond 1990, the extent of military capabilities and the rapidity with which military space systems are deployed depends to a large extent on a number of factors:

1. Will the United States undertake the research, development, testing, and in-space evaluation of elements of a solar power satellite (SPS) system in the 1980's? If so, will this lead to a 1990 program of construction and operation of an extensive SPS system, thereby developing a very large, low-cost space transportation system and a very large in-space power capability that could be useful for military systems in space?

2. Will the Soviet Union continue to expand its manned military space capabilities by reinstituting their Saturn-5 class vehicle (the TT-50) and thus establish one or more very large manned space stations by orbiting more than 150,000 kilograms per flight?

3. How rapidly will directed energy weapons (DEW) become practical (i.e., small enough and powerful enough) to be deployed in space and powered by solar electric arrays of photovoltaic cells or other on-board energy sources? Who will do it first to achieve a political and military advantage?

4. Will the Soviet Union undertake the development of a military-oriented SPS system to provide in-space power for any DEW systems it wishes to deploy in addition to making a bid to become a major supplier of electric power from space to nonaligned Third World nations?

5. Will an international consortium backed by petrodollars undertake the development and operation of an SPS system as a logical extension of the current involvement of the petroleum cartel as the major supplier of the world's energy?

6. Will political and/or economic pressures either push future space activity or act to slow it down it the point where the continuing long-range Soviet space programs eventually permit world military dominance by the Soviet Union with space weapons systems?

7. Will profitable space industrialization activities (exclusive of the currently profitable space communications industry) result in a major push into space by governments and private enterprise? Eventually this could phase out government participation as risk is reduced and return-on-investment times shorten, leaving governments the classical task of defending the facilities and citizens of their respective nations. Or does space industrialization manage to accomplish what is thought today to be highly unlikely: that nationalism stops at the stratosphere except for continued military presence in space in the same context as today?

Unless the Soviet Union opts for a military space capability far beyond their current passive systems of C^3I, or unless the United States makes a similar decision in order to enhance its current marginal military C^3 satellite activity, the development of advanced space transportation systems over the next twenty-five years will be primarily carried out for ostensible commercial (nonmilitary) purposes.

This is the announced policy with regard to the NASA Space Shuttle. Much has been made of the nonmilitary capabilities and of the scientific, developmental, and commercial payloads either already scheduled or potentially available. Very little has been said about the military utilization of the NASA Space Shuttle.

There has been military involvement of the US Department of Defense (DOD) in the Space Shuttle program almost from its inception. DOD was ordered by the White House to incorporate the Space Shuttle into all future space operational planning and to phase out the DOD stable of expendable launch vehicles in favor of the Shuttle. The Space Shuttle Orbiter has delta-shaped wings instead of the straight wings NASA favored because of a DOD requirement for maneuverability of the Orbiter upon its return to Earth for landing. The United States Air Force plans to fly the Shuttle with military crews and has even established its own mission control center at NASA Johnson Space Center in order to maintain the high security it demands for military Shuttle missions.

Because of what DOD and the USAF consider to be unreasonable delays in Shuttle development, and because the United States will have a shortfall in space launch capability in 1985 and after—more payloads are scheduled for launch than there are Shuttle flights or even expendable boosters available to launch those payloads—there has been talk in the Pentagon of "Blue Shuttle," that is, the complete takeover of the entire Space Shuttle program by the USAF, which would schedule, man, and operate all flights of the four planned Orbiters from both Cape Canaveral and Vandenberg Air Force Base. As of early 1981, there appeared to be a "65 percent chance of Blue Shuttle becoming reality," according to inside sources.

However, even though the Space Shuttle could orbit large military space payloads, these payloads can be carried only to low-Earth orbit (LEO) by the Shuttle. An upper stage attached to the payload and carried aloft with it in the Shuttle Orbiter payload bay must be used to kick the payload up to the militarily useful geosynchronous Earth orbit (GEO). The Inertial Upper Stage (IUS) is behind schedule and incurring large cost overruns as of early 1981.

However, with the NASA Space Shuttle alone a vastly expanded manned space capability can be achieved by the United States with a minimum of investment while work proceeds on more advanced systems.

The United States historically has an aversion to true long-range programs that require more than four years from announcement in Washington until some sort of results are shown. There have been notable recent examples of this, such as the Boulder Canyon Project which built the complex now known as Hoover Dam. The Swing-Johnson Bill was signed by President Calvin Coolidge on 21 December 1928; the first appropriation of $165 million was approved by President Herbert Hoover on 3 July 1930. Initial excavation began on 16 May 1931, and the Boulder Dam was dedicated by President Franklin D. Roosevelt on 30 September 1935. There have been other long-term projects, but most of them have been low-budget and low-profile affairs. Very few programs survive if they cannot show significant progress or achievement within the four-year term of a President.

The Apollo manned lunar landing program survived three Presidents because of one man, Lyndon Baines Johnson, whose idea it was in the first place. Johnson had been a staunch space supporter in the US Senate and was chairman of the National Space Council while he was Vice-President under John F. Kennedy. It was Kennedy who asked Johnson to come up with a space spectacular to overwhelm the Soviet lead in space and to cover the Bay of Pigs fiasco. Johnson presented Kennedy with the Apollo manned lunar landing goal. It survived Kennedy's assassination because it was Johnson's program. By the time Johnson left office in 1969, the die had been cast, the goal had been publicly trumpeted from all the bastions of Washington to the American public and the world, and the momentum of the program was such that, even in the face of NASA budget cutbacks, there was no way Apollo could have been wound down. However, President Richard M. Nixon inherited the Apollo program, and he was no champion of it because it wasn't his. Space Shuttle was his, but not to the extent that Apollo was to Johnson. In retrospect, the Space Shuttle was Nixon's with great reluctance, and the project was stretched out over a decade in a funding program that depended upon success and left no margin for error. Hence, the Shuttle was delayed because the engineers were pushing technology to its limits without sufficient budgetary cushion for failures, and failures exist in *any* technical endeavor.

Reflecting on these historic facts, space advocates have presented the Reagan administration with a series of long-range space goals that are supported by short range goals which can be achieved within four years. Among the most attractive of these is Project Starbase One, which offers a number of civilian and military opportunities.

The NASA Space Shuttle carries the liquid hydrogen and liquid oxygen for its three main engines in a large External Tank (ET) strapped to the belly of the Orbiter. The External Tank is *big*: 47 meters long and 8.38 meters in diameter. The standard Shuttle mission plan calls for the ET to be dropped from the Orbiter at an altitude of about 100 kilometers and with a velocity slightly less than orbital velocity. On launches eastward out of Cape Canaveral, the ET will enter the atmosphere and break up over the southern reaches of the Indian Ocean; on polar flights out of Vandenberg Air Force Base, the ET will land in the South Pacific vastness. The ET could just as well be orbited with each Shuttle flight, but the presence of hundreds of ET's in LEO would not only constitute a potential Skylab-type hazard but also create problems for other Shuttle and unmanned missions. The ET was considered to be a liability and had to be gotten rid of by dropping it off short of orbital velocity.

However, for any sort of space goal that involves the permanent presence of people in orbit, any large orbiting structure capable of holding pressure becomes a valuable resource.

An additional velocity of between 25 and 100 meters per second (orbital velocity is approximately 7,680 meters per second) is all that would be required to place the ET in space permanently on any Space

Shuttle mission with an extremely small penalty in terms of payload weight. In fact, in common with other aerospace programs, the entire Shuttle is now on a diet; once the initial units are built—all being overweight because of the inevitable accumulation of small design errors inherent in any large system—a program of weight reduction is undertaken. The ET has already had its weight shaved by almost 3,000 kilograms, an amount which can be put into additional Orbiter payload or toward orbiting the ET itself.

The ET would provide the USA with a *free* series of space facilities each capable of holding up to 1.5 atmospheres of pressure and with an internal volume of at least 1,961 cubic meters, a volume equivalent to about four average homes or a medium-sized manufacturing plant. Add to it the 25-kilowatt power module currently under development to increase the Orbiter's electrical capacity, make a few minor additions, and the ET becomes a perfectly acceptable manned space facility capable of housing up to a dozen people in space at a time. It would be used as a headquarters for space operations such as tending nearby free flying satellites and modules testing out new space manufacturing processes, beam building machine development leading to perfection of methods for constructing large space structures such as an SPS, long-term human space factors research, and other research, development, testing, and evaluation projects that require a manned presence in space for a long period of time for their completion.

The Space Shuttle Orbiter was designed to stay thirty days on orbit if required for scientific or technology development purposes, but the current traffic model and the growing shortage of payload lift capability will render such long stays of the Orbiter in space completely impractical, because, since there are only four Orbiters, it will have other work to do carrying things to and from orbit.

Starbase One can be achieved within four years and provide the foundation for the follow on Space Operations Center (SOC).

The fact that an ET in orbit may also have military uses has not escaped the consideration of space planners, either.

Therefore, although the Space Shuttle program with its four Orbiters could provide a large payload to orbit capability for both military, scientific, and commercial users in the 1980 decade, and although these Shuttle missions could be used to establish a manned space station currently known as the Space Operations Center (SOC) to develop space technology, it's already becoming apparent that the Space Shuttle has shortcomings and that new and more advanced space launch systems will be required by 1990 or before.

If the United States opts for a phased development, construction, and deployment of a Solar Power Satellite (SPS) system, the resulting space transportation system that must be developed and deployed to meet the requirements of such a program will have profound impacts on military, scientific, and commercial utilization of space before the year 2000.

The SPS is a concept initially developed by Dr. Peter E. Glaser of Arthur D. Little, Inc., in 1968. Basically, the SPS system involves one or more very large satellites located in GEO. Each satellite would have a large array of photovoltaic cells (solar batteries) approximately 10.4 kilometers long by 5.2 kilometers wide. This array would be exposed to sunlight 24 hours a day in GEO and would collect 10 gigawatts (10 billion watts) of electricity. This solar-generated electricity would be converted to radio-frequency energy operating in the radar wavelengths at approximately 2.45 gigahertz. The radio power beam would be directed toward a receiving antenna on the Earth's surface below. This ground antenna would be designed not only to receive the power beam but also to convert the 2.45 gigahertz frequency to direct current; therefore, this "rectifying antenna" is known as a rectenna. A single rectenna receiving the 10 gigawatts (gW) from an individual SPS would be large as well—at 35 degrees north latitude, it would cover an elliptical area 13 by 10 kilometers in extent. At the rectenna, the SPS electric power would be converted to the local electric standard voltage and frequency and switched onto the existing power grid. The energy density of the power beam at the rectenna would be 23 milliwatts per square centimeter, which is well below the US standard limit of 100 milliwatts per square centimeter for industrial exposure to radio frequency energy. The power beam is held in boresight alignment with the rectenna by a pilot beam sent up to the SPS from the rectenna; the pilot beam is coded so that the SPS recognizes its dedicated pilot beam. The pilot beam controls the phasing of the SPS transmitting antenna to hold the power beam in columnation and direction. If the SPS loses the reception of the pilot beam from the rectenna, the power beam automatically defocuses in a fraction of a second and spreads out to an energy density of less than 0.005 milliwatts per square centimeter, which is far below anything that could possibly be considered to be harmful to the environment.

The United States Department of Energy and NASA completed a four-year study of all aspects of an SPS system in December 1980. This extensive Satellite Power System Concept Development and Evaluation Program considered the technical, economic, social, environmental, financial, management, and military implications of an SPS system. This study revealed no "program stoppers," nothing that would render an SPS system unworkable, uneconomic, or hazardous. If the US builds two

10-gW SPS units in orbit every year starting in 1991, more than 45 percent of the United States baseload electric power requirements could be satisfied by the SPS system by the year 2025 *or before.* Of all the future energy options thus far studied by DOE, the SPS system appears to be the most economical, have the least impact upon the terrestrial environment, and require less in terms of resources to construct and place in operation.

Furthermore, the SPS system could be built at a cost identical to that required to build equivalent capacity in coal-fired or nuclear power plants on Earth in the same time period. This cost is about $2,000 per kilowatt installed, to use the terminology and reference standard of the electric utility industry.

One of the most important elements of this cost analysis is that, unlike terrestrial energy options, the construction and deployment of an SPS system includes the cost of development and operation of a *very large* space transportation system.

Both this space transportation system and the SPS system itself have profound military implications both in terms of threats and vulnerabilities.

Table 4 indicates some of the potential future space launch vehicles that have been discussed as part of the SPS program, that are known to be under consideration or development in other countries, or that are considered to be likely realities by the year 2000 given the momentum of space programs in the individual countries.

The USA vehicles would be developed to support the SPS program. Although the SPS system development and test phase could be started with the Space Shuttle and SOC—which would be engaged in testing the construction of very large space structures, details of the radio power beam system, and human factors—a Heavy Lift Launch Vehicle (HLLV) capable of orbiting 77,300 kilograms in support of SOC and perhaps a pilot SPS satellite can be developed directly out of Space Shuttle technology. This Shuttle HLLV involves replacing the recoverable Orbiter glider with a simple payload container; a propulsion module using the three Space Shuttle Main Engines would be attached to the rear of the payload container and would be deorbited and reused along with the Solid Rocket Boosters. A further 1980 decade modification of Space Shuttle technology creates a seventy-five-passenger Personnel Launch Vehicle (PLV) to provide personnel support at SOC for construction and development work both on the SOC and on the pilot SPS. The Shuttle PLV amounts to a standard Space Shuttle with a seventy-five-passenger module inserted into the Orbiter payload bay; such a module has been designed by Rockwell International's Space Operations Division, builders of the Orbiter.

Table 4 POTENTIAL FUTURE SPACE LAUNCH VEHICLES
(1981–2000)

Nation	Name	Payload (kg) to LEO	Remarks
USA	Shuttle HLLV	77,300	Payload in place of Shuttle Orbiter (UM)
USA	Shuttle PLV	88,730	Boeing concept
USA	Star Raker	91,000	Rockwell winged advanced shuttle
USA	HHLV	228,000	Boeing Big Onion (UM)
USA	Winged HLLV	424,000	Two-staged shuttle HLLV Boeing concept
France	Hermes/Ariane	(?)	Minishuttle on Ariane
USSR	Shuttle	9,000 (?)	Minishuttle
PRC	CSL-X-3M*	2,000 (?)	Manned capsule on CSL-X-3*
Japan	(?)	3,000 (?)	Manned capsule on new vehicle

NOTE: (a) New vehicles in addition to continued use of vehicles in Table 3. (b) Listed vehicles based only on announced concepts as of early 1981 or upon advanced programs known to be under consideration with exception of Japan, which is speculative. (c) All vehicles Earth-to-orbit; direct ascent to GEO (geosynchronous earth orbit) probably via orbital transfer vehicles of space tugs from LEO (low earth orbit) staging bases to GEO or with HLLV with upper stages.)

Legend:
HLLV = *Heavy Lift Launch Vehicle*
PLV = *Personnel Launch Vehicle*
(UM) = *Unmanned. All others manned.*

Thus, using straightforward engineering "stretches" of the Space Shuttle, the USA can obtain a 1980 decade space capability that includes a 77,300 kilogram payload space cargo vehicle plus a seventy-five-passenger personnel vehicle.

The basic problem with stretches of Shuttle technology is cost per pound to orbit. Although the Space Shuttle represents a significant cost reduction in comparison to the expendable launch vehicles of the Saturn class, the lift costs for Shuttle in 1980 dollars amount to $700 per kilogram. This is an order of magnitude too large to permit truly economical domestic space operations although it might be justified in terms of military requirements, where cost may not be a primary consideration.

Constructing, manning, operating, and maintaining the space segment of an SPS system will require a space transportation system with lift costs in the order of $50 per kilogram. Such lift cost reductions would also strongly affect potential military operations.

These lift cost reductions can be achieved with technology that is either currently in hand in 1981 or that can be forecast with reasonable assurances to be in hand in 1990. The DOE-NASA SPS study considered the nature of the launch vehicles that would be required to achieve this lift cost goal, because the mass of an SPS built according to the DOE-NASA baseline design is on the order of 25,000 metric tons. Each kilogram of this will have to be lifted up from Earth, at least during the first decade of SPS system construction; once the space transportation capability has been developed, a stretch of the SPS transportation system permits use and exploitation of extraterrestrial materials, which promise an overall cost reduction by a factor of four because of the reduced energy requirements of obtaining the raw materials from other sources than the Earth with its strong gravity field.

Out of the DOE-NASA study, two Earth-to-orbit space vehicle concepts emerged that offer the best promise of low cost, routine operation, reasonable stretch potential, but perhaps somewhat advanced technology. In other words, these concepts appear to possess more favorable characteristics in all areas except the technology base; the USA would have to begin development of this technology within the near future in order to incorporate it into the SPS space transportation system.

Rockwell International's Space Operations Division has come up with a highly advanced personnel shuttle concept called Star Raker, which is a large delta-winged vehicle of the same size as the Boeing 747 airliner or the Lockheed C-5A Galaxy, heavy military logistics transport aircraft. It would be powered by ten advanced technology turbofan/ramjet engines with a combined thrust of 6.23×10^6 newtons (1.4 million pounds) and three Space Shuttle SSME rocket engines with a total thrust of 1.424×10^7 newtons (3.2 million pounds). The Star Raker would use the Earth's atmosphere during ascent to orbit by taking off horizontally from an airport runway and climbing initially under the thrust of its ten advanced air-breathing engines. As it began to leave the atmosphere, the three SSME rocket engines would be phased in for propulsion. The Star Raker is a single-stage-to-orbit vehicle capable of orbiting a 91,000 kilogram payload and returning to land on the runway at the launch site. The RI Star Raker thus becomes both a personnel launch vehicle and a light cargo launch vehicle. The SPS construction program would require a minimum of two Star Rakers.

Boeing has designed a large HLLV for SPS support. Its appearance has earned it the appellation of "The Big Onion." It, too, would be a single-stage-to-orbit vehicle that throws away nothing and reuses everything except rocket propellant. The Big Onion design is a vertical lift-off, vertical landing design 76 meters tall with a payload diameter of 23 meters and a base diameter of 41 meters. Utilizing liquid oxygen and liquid hydrogen—the most efficient and energetic chemical rocket propellants known—the Big Onion would have a total thrust of 1.602×10^8 newtons (36 million pounds) and be capable of placing 228,000 kilograms in orbit. The big blunt rear end of the Big Onion is the reentry heat shield to protect it when it deorbits and descends through the atmosphere for landing in a recovery pond at the launch site.

Boeing has also designed a two-staged fully reusable winged HLLV capable of placing 424,000 kilograms in orbit. This HLLV looks like two very large Space Shuttles stacked one atop the other to a height of 164 meters. Lift-off weight would be 11,040 metric tons and the first stage booster would produce a thrust of 1.37×10^8 newtons (30.8 million pounds) while the second orbital stage produces 2.926×10^7 newtons (6.575 million pounds) of thrust. Wing span on the first stage booster would be 79.9 meters. The payload diameter available in this concept is 18.5 meters. This is a very large and heavy aerospace vehicle but well within current design and construction capabilities; aircraft designers in 1981 are already laying plans for cargo aircraft with million pound payloads.

A fleet of ten Big Onion HLLV's or five two-staged shuttle-type HLLVs will be required for the SPS program.

Therefore, if the USA proceeds with an SPS program in the 1990 decade, space transportation activity can be expected to increase to include at least one HLLV flight per day and a PLV flight every five days. This is an immense space transportation effort in view of 1981 activity. Undoubtedly, the volume of air traffic and the wide-bodied jets such as the 747 and DC-10 would have seemed equally implausible to airplane planners in the DC-3/DC-4 era of 1945—and the DC-3 was a far-out dream to the aviators of 1914. In view of the fact that the costs of the space transportation system development and operation are included in the overall cost of $2,000 per kilowatt for the SPS system, it is well to keep this sort of perspective in mind when thinking about the space transportation effort that will be required.

It is highly unlikely that any United States' space program of any sort—whether it is merely a slow runout of Space Shuttle capabilities to 1991 (an unlikely possibility) or a commitment to an SPS program—will proceed in a vacuum of noncompetition from other nations.

The Soviet Union would obviously regard any US program to construct and operate an SPS system as a partial military threat as well as commercial competition. The US intelligence agencies already have recon satellite and other photos of the Soviet TT-50 HLLV which, if the pressure were applied via a regenerated US space program, the Soviets would accelerate to operational status to give them a 159,000 kilogram orbital lift capability for their *own* SPS system. And it would cause the Soviets to accelerate their winged reusable shuttle program.

It has been hinted for a number of years that the Soviet Union has its own reusable winged shuttle program, and a few details have surfaced concerning it. The Soviets have recently confirmed that they have such a program. Charles P. Vick has thoroughly analyzed all available information and has concluded that the Soviets have indeed made unmanned tests of their shuttle vehicle. The Soviet shuttle is smaller than the NASA Space Shuttle and seems to bear some similarities to an earlier US winged spacecraft, the Boeing/USAF X-20 Dyna-Soar. The Soviet shuttle is apparently unpowered, a delta-winged orbiter with a maximum gross weight of approximately 11,000 kilograms, making its payload in the range of 2,000 to 6,000 kilograms. The apparent utility of the Soviet shuttle appears to be as an Earth-to-orbit personnel carrier with a possible payload of five to ten cosmonauts.

Initially, the Soviet shuttle would be launched with an expendable booster of the SL-9 or SL-13 type. As the program progressed, the Soviets might deploy boost systems of increasing reusability.

These figures for the Soviet shuttle are based upon the fact that the Soviets have been launching two of their shuttles atop a single SL-13 booster, thus getting two test flights for the price of one booster. Only five SL-9/13 boosters are produced per year at current rates.

With the 159,000 kilogram payload capability of the TT-50 and the capability to shuttle up to ten people back and forth to orbit in the 1980 decade, the Soviet Union can possess a space transportation capability in excess of that of the USA in the 1980's. Whether or not they can maintain this margin of capability in the 1990 decade depends upon how hard they're pushed by any SPS program and its attendant space transportation system in the USA.

Since there are obvious military implications inherent in large and extensive space transportation systems, the Soviets may continue to hold and expand their current lead in manned LEO programs where, because of continued use of Soyuz and an apparent commitment to manned space presence in Salyut, they currently have a five-year head start on the rest of the world.

France is looking at the possibility of building a five-passenger reusable winged shuttle payload for an uprated Ariane. It is likely that this Hermes shuttle could become operational in the 1980 decade. Ariane technology plus Hermes manned reusable shuttle technology can provide France and Western Europe with a respectable LEO capability in the 1990 time frame, a capability that can be expanded if it is based upon exported US space technology or, as is currently under way, additional space capability via French links with the Soviet space program. (French astronauts are training in Star City in 1981 for participation in Soviet Soyuz flights.)

The recent revelations of the rocket and space capabilities of the PRC also point toward a reasonably firm forecast of a Chinese manned presence in space within the next twenty years. They currently have the CSL-X-3 booster with a capability to orbit a two-man capsule. They could develop the capability to orbit a Hermes class manned winged reusable shuttle within the next two decades and probably before 1990. Thus, as recent history indicates, the PRC does have the technical and industrial base to deploy manned systems in LEO by the 1990 time period.

Japan will not stand idly by while either the USA, the USSR, or especially the PRC deploys large space transportation systems. It is certainly not outrageous to assume that Japan will develop a manned orbital capability before this century is out.

This forecast expansion of manned space activity on the part of at least five nations by the 1990 time period presages some radical changes in current military space activities. The passive role played by the military in space can change to an entirely different operation once people have ready access to LEO and to GEO and once true heavy-lift capability at reasonable costs becomes available through continued development in space transportation systems and the operational deployment of new vehicles based upon recent technology. The larger payload lift capability combined with the potential of obtaining very large quantities of electrical power from an SPS type of satellite brings a rather large number of highly advanced weapons into the realm of reality. This includes the various directed energy weapons (DEW) which may not only be the strategic weapons of the future but which find in the space environment the ambient conditions most conducive to effective operation.

THE BASIC
MILITARY DOCTRINES
OF SPACE

All military space systems currently deployed are utilizing an ancient doctrine of warfare known as the high ground. Since organized military forces were first used in warfare, there has been a significant military advantage to being able to occupy the high ground—the top of a prominent hill, a ridge of hills, a mountain range. The high ground provides an opportunity for surveillance of the battleground or the defense perimeter. It allows scouts, sentries, and guards to keep watch over a large area.

In the past two hundred years, technology has provided commanders with new means for extending the concept of the high ground. The first extension was into the air above the area. Manned balloons were the first military aircraft. Captive manned balloons were first used by the French army in 1794 when five were constructed in Paris by M. Coute. Captain J. M. Coutelle was the first military aviator (aeronaut). At the battle of Maubeuge in May 1794, he conducted five days of aerial observation of the movement of Austrian troops until the enemy brought up a 17-pounder gun and initiated the use of antiaircraft artillery. The balloon was hauled down until the gun was captured, and then balloon observation was begun again. At the battle of Fleurus on 17–26 June 1794, Captain Coutelle remained aloft in an 8-meter balloon positioned at 400 meters altitude far enough behind his own French lines to be out of range of enemy fire; thus positioned, he reported on the movement of Austrian troops to his commander, General Jourdan. The surveillance balloon had a demoralizing effect upon the Austrian troops, one of whom remarked, "How can we fight against these republicans who, out of reach, see all that passes beneath?"

As a result, a company of *aérostiers* was formed in the French army. But the balloons were clumsy and difficult to handle. More than fifty hours were required to inflate it at a new location. Once inflated, ten men were required to walk the balloon on the ground. Although field equipment was devised that could inflate a ten-meter balloon in about four hours, the difficulty of field deployment of balloons overcame the surveillance advantages they offered, and ballooning was abandoned by the French army in 1798.

Napoleon Bonaparte was a balloon advocate. In 1812, he proposed a fleet of balloons to transport his troops across the English Channel to attack England. Each balloon was to carry 6,000 troops. The scheme never materialized, being beyond the technology of the time.

Observation balloons were used by the Union Army in the Civil War. T. S. C. Lowe was the first military balloon pilot in the United States and used his balloon, the *Great Western,* to carry out observation duties for General McClellan with the support and encouragement of President Lincoln. Although General Grant believed that aeronautics were of little practical value on the battlefield, Lowe conducted reconnaissance of enemy positions and reported on the accuracy of artillery fire.

When the airplane made its debut in the Balkan Wars of 1912, the first military use to which it was put was the same as that of the balloon: scouting, reconnoitering, artillery spotting, and observing. It was only through the development of long-range strategic bombing that the airplane moved military aeronautical utilization out of its passive roles into that of an active offensive weapon. It required the development of strategic doctrines of air power by General Giulio Douhet in Italy after World War I and the advocacy of these by General William Mitchell and Major Alexander P. de Seversky to produce the only strategic bomber of World War II, the Boeing B-29 *Superfortress,* with which Generals Arnold, Eaker, Spaatz, Doolittle, and LeMay burned the industrial heart out of the islands of Japan in 1945.

The development of military space systems and military space doctrines appears to be following the same well-trodden historical path as ballooning and aviation: initial deployment of systems *not* as weapons but in the classic roles of spies and scouts making use of the "high ground" or "high view" of the surface of the Earth from orbital space.

To the normally conservative mind of a military planner, the concept of space warfare may appear to be bizarre and naturally raises a number of questions.

Except for the known use of space for the "high view" of Earth for reconnaissance, surveillance, communications, command, and control, how can space possibly be an arena for warfare?

Does this mean the sort of thing seen on movie and TV screens in *Star Wars* and *Buck Rogers* with space fighters engaged in dogfights with laser cannons? Death stars? Space forts?

How would space warfare be conducted and why would it be conducted that way?

What are the basic military doctrines that will govern space warfare?

Outer space seems to be overwhelmingly large. The distances in space are considered by our earthbound minds to be tremendous. The difficulty of getting there, living there, and going from one place to another in space are considered by most people in 1981 to be problems so large and so difficult that they must be dismissed out of hand as visionary.

This is not the case at all.

It is perceived as such by the layman because space technology is yet new and primitive, and is also unreliable and expensive. "All rockets blow up" has been the shibboleth that was implanted in American minds by the news media on 6 December 1957 when the US Vanguard rocket blew up on the launch pad, thereby "dealing a severe blow to American efforts to overtake the Soviets in space." Since "all our rockets blow up," as pointed out by author Tom Wolfe, people are absolutely amazed when modern space vehicles work as designed.

Early aviation suffered from the same stigma: airplanes always crash, and even seventy years after the Wrights first flew at Kitty Hawk, most people still believe this to be true in spite of the fact that in 1979 570,589,000 passengers flew 277,307,460,000 passenger miles in airplanes in the United States alone. In accomplishing this feat, there were only 1,660 fatalities in comparison to 51,083 automobile deaths. It is difficult to convince people of the progress in technology over the span of a quarter of a century.

All new and primitive technologies are crude, difficult, and expensive, but they do not remain that way very long. Nor will space technology be any different, as the previous chapter pointed out. Twenty-five years ago, the orbiting of a simple satellite was one of the most difficult of technological problems; today, it is done routinely, and the technology has been so developed that the feat of orbiting a satellite has been accomplished by seven nations with their own indigenous space launch vehicles. Manned space flight has been accomplished at great expense and with great difficulty by only two nations; but at least three other nations are preparing to accomplish it in the 1980's. Building large facilities in space and living and working in them for long periods of time is today a very difficult thing to do because it is yet at the leading edge of space technology. This will not be the case by the year 2000.

Long before the year 2000, human beings will be working in space and producing products and services of value to human beings on Earth.

The doctrines of space warfare are based upon the same two foundations as the doctrines for warfare on Earth, as it has been conducted for centuries.

One of these is the fact that space and the things in it are slowly being recognized by people as having value.

Anything having value is a suitable target for ownership or control. Since it has value, others operating with the Neolithic Ethic and the Attila Syndrome will be covetous of it. The thing of value must therefore be protected by both institutional safeguards such as laws, treaties, and other agreements *and* by the threat of the use of physical force—military action—should the institutional safeguards break down as they have far too often in the past.

Lawyers, who are trained specialists in the resolution of human conflicts, are perhaps most aware of these facts and in some ways appear to other people to be extremely cynical. Lawyers have good reason to appear to be so cynical; they see human conflict on many levels as an everyday occurrence. And a good lawyer will try to arrange things for a client to eliminate as many areas of conflict as possible in relationships with other people, based upon his own experience coupled with the recorded experience of other lawyers.

However, even the best-drawn agreement can break down and lead to conflict requiring the application of jurisprudence and, in the extreme, coercion through the use of physical force.

The second of these doctrinal foundations for space warfare is the simple fact that certain locations in space possess military value if military people are to adequately perform their job of reenforcing with the threat of the use of physical force the nonviolent institutional safeguards of laws and agreements.

These facts were recognized as early as 1963 by the pioneer technological forecaster, the late Dandridge M. Cole. His outstanding creative contributions to space industrialization and colonization have been largely overlooked by the most vocal proponents of these activities today. However, Cole recognized and often discussed with the author the military implications of space industrialization and colonization that would follow these activities into space as surely and certainly as they have historically done on Earth.

In 1963, Cole proposed his "Panama Theory" of astropolitics.

The choice of Panama as an earthly analogy to forecastable political and military doctrines in space was an excellent one.

The American Midwest has a unique geographical feature: it is a broad plain with fertile soil and abundant natural resources. It has a natural outlet to the oceans of the world via the Mississippi River, which is fed by the Missouri River, the Ohio River, and the Arkansas River. All of these rivers are navigable almost to their headwaters. These rivers provide an inexpensive natural transportation system to the sea for the products of this great American heartland, which is both the breadbasket of the world and the site of one of the planet's most developed and advanced industrial complexes.

The markets for the output of this American heartland could move easily and quickly by sea to Europe provided that the US Navy could control the Gulf of Mexico and the Caribbean Sea. This control was firmly established as a result of the Spanish-American War of 1898. There are a string of naval bases on Cuba, Puerto Rico, and the Virgin Islands that assure the right of passage of American ships from the Mississippi River ports to Europe.

But Europe is a limited market. In the early twentieth century, most European nations were still operating under the colonial system, in which their own colonies provided them with many of the products of the American heartland.

So Americans looked westward across the Pacific Ocean to the Orient as they had for nearly a hundred years.

The most common reason given for the building of the transcontinental railroads was to link the West Coast with the rest of the United States. This was only part of the reason. The development of these railroads was undertaken to help increase the trade with the Orient, an area which has become a growing marketplace for American goods over the past 150 years.

But railroads provided a relatively costly link between the American heartland and the Pacific Ocean. Transportation by railroad is expensive compared to transportation by ship. And transcontinental railroad transportation required an additional transfer node at West Coast seaports, which increased the costs.

What was needed if the Orient was to help absorb the tremendous output of the American heartland was a seagoing route as short as that to Europe.

To get from New Orleans at the mouth of the Mississippi River to the Orient by sea meant sailing almost 13,000 kilometers around Cape Horn at the southern tip of South America. Even in 1981, this is still a long and arduous journey that is both costly and hazardous.

A strip of land less than fifty miles wide—the Isthmus of Panama— required that long ocean voyage around Cape Horn.

If a ship canal could be built across the Isthmus of Panama, thousands of miles of travel could be eliminated and the relatively high risk of shipping around Cape Horn could be reduced.

The French under Ferdinand Marie, Vicomte de Lesseps, completed the most recent canal across the Isthmus of Suez on 17 November 1869, thus eliminating the need for a similar long journey from Europe to the Orient via the Cape of Good Hope at the southern tip of Africa. (This is the most recent canal across that isthmus because the first was built 4,000 years ago from the Nile delta to the Red Sea by Pharaoh Sesostris I; it has been abandoned and restored several times since then.) Lesseps began the construction of a canal across the Panamanian Isthmus in 1879 and failed because of lack of planning, bankruptcy, and disease. John F. Stevens succeeded for the United States, however, and the Panama Canal was officially opened 15 August 1914.

When the Panama Canal was opened, the military significance was stated to be of secondary importance. The primary importance lay in the fact that the Canal cut 13,000 kilometers off the distance between the American heartland and the Orient and permitted the tremendous output of the American heartland to be economically transported to these markets in Asia.

Thus, Panama became a location of great geopolitical and therefore military importance to the United States of America.

Dandridge M. Cole spotted the similarity between this and the coming situation in space. That is why he labeled his principle the Panama Theory.

It can be stated simply·

There are strategic areas in space—vital to future scientific, commercial, and military space programs—which could be excluded from our use through occupation and control by unfriendly powers. This statement is based on the assumption that in colonizing space, man (and other intelligent beings) will compete for the more desirable areas. . . .

When the Panama Theory is applied to military operations in space in the Earth-Moon system, there are two doctrines that govern the military utilization of space. The prime strategic doctrine is that of the "gravity well."

The gravity well is a concept first published by Dr. Robert S. Richardson, then an astronomer at the Mount Wilson Observatory, in a science-fact article entitled "Space Fix" in *Astounding Science Fiction* magazine, April 1943. (In those days, especially during World War II, the only place one could get a speculative science article about space flight published was in a science-fiction magazine. However, the *type* of publication the article appears in should not detract from its scientific or technical importance—although it usually does. To some extent, the top science-fiction magazines are still the only places where a speculative article about any field of science can be published.)

The gravity well concept becomes easy to understand if Figure 1 is referred to in connection with the text.

Because of the Earth's gravity field, our planet can be considered as being at the bottom of a tapering, funnel-shaped well about 6,500 kilometers deep. Near the bottom of the well, the walls of this gravitational funnel are very steep. Near the top of the funnel, the gravity well walls become less and less steep until they become a nearly flat plane that merges into the gravity well of the Sun.

At a distance of some 390,000 kilometers from the Earth, the flat plane or top of the terrestrial gravity well has a dimple in it. This is the shallower gravity well of the Moon.

(It is possible to draw a gravity well diagram for the entire Solar System, but this simplified model of the Earth-Moon gravity well serves to illustrate the gravity well doctrine of military space operations. In fact, Richardson's original diagram included the gravity wells of the entire Solar System because he was using the concept to illustrate how one navigates a space ship around the Solar System.)

To climb up the walls of the gravity well from Earth requires energy in the form of velocity. For example, to throw a ball up and out of the Earth's gravity well, one would have to impart a velocity of slightly more than 11.5 kilometers per second to the ball so that it would climb up the wall of the gravity well, slowing down as it did so until it reached the nearly flat plane where, in the Solar System, the gravity of the Sun would predominate.

If one threw the ball at exactly the right velocity and in precisely the right direction, it would climb up the gravity well of the Earth, roll over the flat plain, and then fall into the gravity well of the Moon. This is an analogy of the sort of thing that is done to get a rocket to the Moon.

Partway up the gravity well, it is possible to maintain the position of the ball in the gravity well funnel by making it spin around the surface of

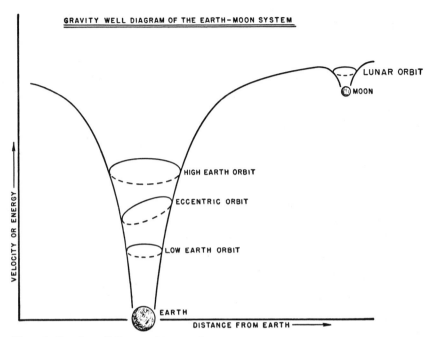

Figure 1. Gravity well diagram. Not to scale.

the funnel rapidly enough so that the centrifugal force tending to make it go up the funnel exactly balances the gravity force pulling it down the funnel. The ball then becomes a satellite of the Earth.

On the nearly level plain at the top of the gravity wells of both the Earth and the Moon, *very little* energy or velocity is necessary to get a ball to fall into either gravity well. Once the ball enters the gravity well, it picks up speed and falls down the gravity well until it hits the bottom—the Earth or the Moon. Or the ball can be given some sideways velocity as it enters the gravity well; this will cause it to spin around the walls of the funnel and become a satellite of the Earth or the Moon, depending upon which gravity well it's in.

The military implications of the gravity well concept should be obvious from the following analogy:

Put one person at the top of a well and another person at the bottom of a well. Give them both rocks to throw at one another.

Which person is going to have more time to see the opponent's rocks coming, more time to get out of the way, and more room to maneuver?

Which person has the best opportunity to dodge rocks?

Which person has the greater opportunity to do something?

Which person stands the greatest chance of being hurt the worst?

The strategic military implications of the gravity well concept require that one be at the top of the gravity well or at least higher up on the gravity well than the opponent.

The historic equivalent of the gravity well on Earth is the doctrine of the high ground. In naval tactics during the age of sail, it was the "wind gauge" or getting upwind of the enemy. In aerial warfare, it is the altitude advantage during the attack and the attendant defensive advantage when under attack from below.

The salient features of the gravity well doctrine in military operations in space include both an energy advantage and a maneuvering advantage to the person on the high ground of the gravity well.

Far less energy in the form of rocket propellants is required to operate and maneuver high on the gravity well. A military spacecraft having a base of maneuver high in a gravity well or in a shallower gravity well has a definite military advantage over an opponent in terms of the energy required to make a strike, the energy required to use countermeasures, the energy required to maneuver, and the time available to make decisions.

The logical consequence of the military doctrine of the gravity well leads inevitably to the most important military fact of the next fifty years:

With improvements in space transportation currently forecastable, with the technology in hand to maintain long-term military positions in space, and with the weapons technology of the foreseeable future, (a) the control of the Moon means control of the Earth, and (b) the control of the L-4 and L-5 lunar libration or Lagrangian points means control of the entire Earth-Moon system.

Control means the ability to permit or deny passage of space traffic, to deny the use of other military or commercial orbital areas to others, to launch strikes against _any_ target on Earth, on the Moon, or in Earth-Moon space, or to detect and take action against any threat originating anywhere in the Earth-Moon system.

On the Moon, a military commander has a solid base from which to operate and a celestial body some 3,480 kilometers in diameter into which he can burrow for safety or concealment. But he is still at the bottom of a gravity well and therefore open to attack from anyone atop that shallow well only about 2 kilometers per second deep.

It was once thought that the Moon was the primary military site in the Earth-Moon system. But this was before the importance of the Earth-Moon libration points was recognized.

A libration point is a special solution to the "three body problem" of celestial mechanics. Sir Isaac Newton in his classic dissertation on the laws of motion and gravitation, the *Philosophiae Naturalis Principia Mathematica,* called the *Principia* for short and published in 1687, gave the solution to the problem of the gravitational interaction of two bodies. But there is no known general mathematical solution to the behavior of three celestial bodies of sizes such that their individual gravitational fields affect the other bodies in the three-body system.

There are, however, five special solutions to the three-body problem.

Figure 2 shows the Earth-Moon system drawn to scale. The location of geosynchronous orbit is shown so that some perspective on distances can be obtained. There are five points in the Earth-Moon system where a third body could *theoretically* retain its position with respect to both the Earth and the Moon because the gravity fields of all three bodies would be in balance.

These five locations are libration points. They are also known as Lagrangian points in honor of Joseph Louis Lagrange (1736–1813), the French geometer and astronomer who first suggested this special solution to the three-body problem.

The First Lagrangian Point, L-1, is located on a line between the Earth and the Moon and approximately 76,000 kilometers from the Moon. The Second Lagrangian Point, L-2, is also located on a line from the Earth to the Moon but is about 71,000 kilometers outside the orbit of the Moon. The Third Lagrangian Point, L-3, is on the Earth-Moon line but located in lunar orbit 180-degrees away from the Moon on the other side of the Earth.

The first three Lagrangian Points are "unstable"—i.e., any object placed at any of these will eventually wander away because the orbit of the Moon isn't precisely circular and because the gravitational pull of the Sun adds a fourth body to the system, albeit one whose gravity field is much weaker in comparison to that of the Earth and Moon in this system.

But this isn't true at the Fourth and Fifth Lagrangian Points, L-4 and L-5. The Fourth Lagrangian Point is located in the lunar orbit 60 degrees ahead of the Moon; the Fifth Lagrangian Point is in lunar orbit 60 degrees behind the Moon. L-4 and L-5 are *stable* libration points and are also known as Trojan Points. L-4 and L-5 are known to be stable because of the Trojan planetoids (named after the heroes of Homer's *Iliad*) at the L-4 and L-5 points in Jupiter's orbit about the Sun. The Trojan planetoids have been there for a long time.

But the Trojan Points are not the only orbital locations in the

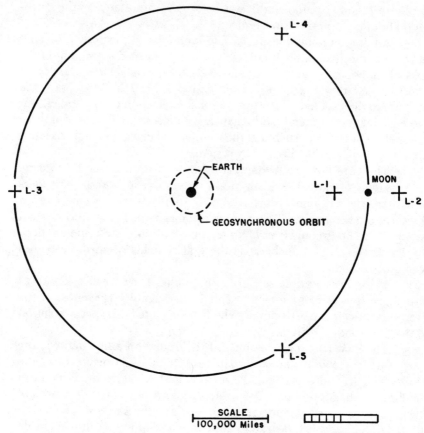

Figure 2. The Earth-Moon lunar libration or Lagrangian points, drawn to scale.

Earth-Moon system where another body can remain in a reasonably predictable orbit. Technically, it is possible to put any number of objects in any orbit and have them stay in place for a long period of time—hundreds of years or more in some cases—with only minor orbital adjustments with electric rocket thrusters. Any number of satellites can occupy a given orbit; the rings of Jupiter, Saturn, and Uranus are proof of this. (Earth has no rings; Dr. Clyde W. Tombaugh proved this as part of his extensive search for small natural satellites of the Earth in 1953–1959.)

The important military reality of either L-4 or L-5 is that the military commander there sits atop the hill of the entire Earth-Moon system. He has no gravity well to worry about. He is at a point in space without a gravity well. He can maneuver at will. He is "uphill" from both the Earth and the Moon. He controls the Earth-Moon system unless somebody else occupies the other Trojan libration point.

The military implications of the L-4 and L-5 libration points make it unlikely that they will be used as the sites for large space colonies as envisioned by Dr. Gerard K. O'Neill. No politician or diplomat on Earth could tolerate a large space facility with a population of 10,000 people that occupies such a militarily strategic place in the Earth-Moon system. It's a threat that cannot be ignored.

It is analogous to positioning a terrorist with a machine gun atop every tall building in town and hoping that business will go on as usual.

Dandridge M. Cole had more than the Earth-Moon system in mind when he worked out his Panama Theory. But Cole's Panama Theory coupled with the gravity well concept provides the foundation for military thinking in and the conduct of space warfare for the next fifty years.

The second doctrine that governs strategic doctrine for the military utilization of space is the "atmospheric interface."

The Earth possesses a thick atmosphere. Fifty percent of this atmosphere is below an altitude of 5,500 meters above sea level. The remaining 49.999999999 percent extends upward to an altitude of approximately 100 kilometers. The upper portion, called the ionosphere, consists of atoms of oxygen, nitrogen, argon, helium, xenon, and a few other gases that have been ionized or had their outer electron shells stripped off by radiant energy from the Sun.

Because of this atmosphere, the bottom 100 kilometers of the Earth's gravity well not only affects potential offensive military activities of the surface-to-space and space-to-surface categories, but also offers a radically different regime for the operation of military aerospace vehicles.

Viscous drag and high velocity heating effects predominate upon any body passing through this zone.

The presence of the atmosphere with its very small "mean free path" between atoms and molecules, a factor which decreases markedly closer to the Earth's surface, plus the dielectric constant and other electrical characteristics of this mixture of gases places limitations on the type of directed energy weapons that can be used in military operations within and through this atmospheric interface.

What is militarily workable or usable on either side of the atmospheric interface may not be workable or usable *across* it. Thus, the atmospheric interface governs military activities to as great an extent as the gravity well, especially when military space activities and terrestrial military activities merge or depend upon one another.

These two doctrines—the gravity well and the atmospheric interface—totally govern both strategic and tactical military operational doctrines in space warfare and dictate the type of weapons systems that is feasible as well as its operational deployment and use.

WEAPONS:
AN ANALYSIS

Over the next fifty years, it is a reasonably safe forecast to assume that most military activities in space will be largely confined to the Earth-Moon system.

However, because of the potentially exponential growth of space transportation capability and progress in the state of the art of deep space technology, there may be some military space operations that extend beyond the Earth-Moon system. This progress in space transportation technology hinges on the potential use of solar power satellite outputs to provide energy sources for advanced deep-space propulsion systems via the use of laser or microwave power beams, concepts that appear to be well within the state of the art in the time period under consideration. But these Solar System military operations will probably be divorced from the geopolitics of the Planet Earth and will by and large be as different from Earth-oriented space warfare doctrines as the British naval operations of the eighteenth and nineteenth centuries in the Orient were from the day-to-day politics of Europe at the time.

Since the primary consideration of military activity in space will center on the impact of the atmospheric interface and the gravity well doctrines upon current terrestrial strategic military operations and upon military activity in the Earth-Moon system as it affects terrestrial politics and diplomacy, first priority should be afforded the discussion of the Earth-Moon theater of operations.

The Earth-Moon theater can be thought of as consisting of a series of definite military operational zones.

A better mental picture can be obtained by considering these zones as a series of concentric spheres with the Earth at their center since the Earth possesses the deepest and strongest gravity well of any body in the system and also possesses an atmosphere.

These zones cannot be defined with hard boundaries although they will be considered as beginning or ending at certain distances from the Earth. They must be considered as regions that fade into one another with indistinct boundaries. In a sense, they resemble the energy levels of electrons around an atomic nucleus.

Briefly, the Earth-Moon military operational zones may be defined as follows:

Earth Atmosphere (EA): This zone extends from the surface of the Earth to an altitude of 100 kilometers and contains most of the gaseous atmosphere of the planet. Military activities in this zone have been carried out for almost two hundred years.

Low-Earth Orbit (LEO): This zone extends from the top of the sensible atmosphere of the Earth at about 100 kilometers altitude to approximately 500 kilometers altitude. This zone is below the Van Allen Belts.

High-Earth Orbit (HEO): This second zone is higher up on the gravity well and extends from 500 kilometers to geosynchronous Earth orbit (GEO), approximately 40,000 kilometers up where a satellite goes around the world in twenty-four hours, making it appear to stand still in the sky when seen from the ground below.

Cislunar Space (CLS): This zone extends from GEO at 40,000 kilometers to lunar orbit 390,000 kilometers from Earth.

Lunar Orbit/Surface (LOS): This is a zone moving with the Moon within CLS as the Moon moves in its orbit around the Earth. It extends from the lunar surface up to an altitude of 100 kilometers above the lunar surface and is the lunar equivalent of LEO.

Translunar Space (TLS): Beyond lunar orbit at 390,000 kilometers to a distance of about a million kilometers from the Earth is the last Earth-Moon system military operational zone. Beyond 1 million kilometers from the Earth, the Earth's gravity well becomes considerably less predominant than the solar gravity well, in which the Earth-Moon system

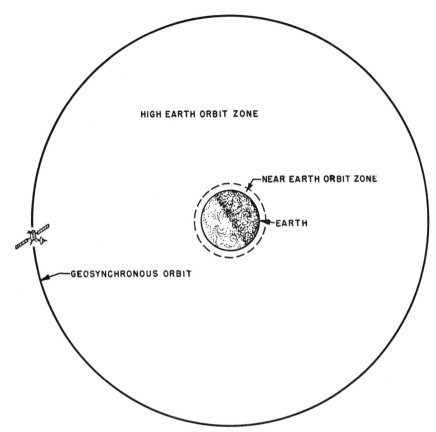

Figure 3. Military Space Operational Zones, near-Earth view to scale.

moves in its joint orbit around the Sun. Beyond a million kilometers, a wholly different set of military operational zones and rules of operation take effect, but the Earth and the Moon no longer predominate these Solar System military operational zones.

Figure 3 shows the close-in zones to scale, while Figure 4 is a scale representation of all six zones.

These six military operational zones in the Earth-Moon system have not been established at random. Each zone has unique military considerations that effect the military doctrines, tactical operations, useful weapons systems, and effective countermeasures that are optimum for each. Each zone also contains or will probably contain specific and unique types of unmanned and manned space facilities. And each zone will have

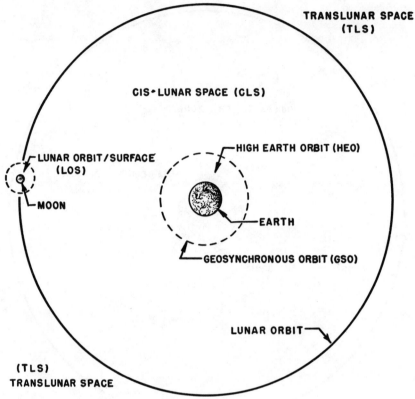

Figure 4. Military Space Operational Zones, overall view, Earth-Moon system, to scale.

its own unique Panama Points. This last term is used to indicate critical positions within each zone that conform to the locations spoken of in Cole's Panama Theory.

The basic characteristic of the EA zone that makes it unique in space warfare is the presence of atmospheric gases in sufficient quantities and under pressures high enough to allow fluid dynamic principles to govern the movement and propulsion of military vehicles as well as to affect strongly the deployment and operation of nearly all types of weapons. The atmospheric interface doctrine dictates that there will be some weapons that can operate only on one side or the other of the interface between the Earth's atmosphere and space as well as some that can operate across the interface. This interface therefore makes the EA zone

one of physical significance because its presence dictates the physical design and operation of military weapons, vehicles, and facilities.

Nearly every nation in the world possessing a military department has the capability to conduct military operations in this zone.

EA is already a theater of war and has been since World War I. It is primarily used at the present time to support tactical military activities on the Earth's surface. It is not in active use for strategic warfare at present, although the weapons for conducting such strategic military activities exist under the doctrines of deterrence and Mutually Assured Destruction (MAD). However, with increasing performance capabilities of modern military aircraft and with the potential military applications of Space Shuttle and space transportation technology to produce very high altitude hypersonic bombers and reconnaissance aircraft as well as hypersonic space-based craft capable of leaving LEO to dip into EA for strike and recon and then return to LEO, EA takes on new meaning in the age of space warfare.

EA is also that zone through which a surface-to-surface ballistic missile must pass during two portions of its flight: ascent and reentry. It is also the zone through which any vehicle launched from the Earth's surface to orbit must pass during ascent. The presence of the Earth's atmosphere has profound effects upon the design and operation of these devices. The characteristics of their operation also have an effect upon the Earth's atmosphere, which permits detection of their operation at very long distances by suitable sensors.

LEO is the zone where a considerable level of true military space activity can take place in the 1980 decade and beyond. Currently, LEO is a valuable military operational area because it is technically easy to reach with any one of a number of launch vehicles capable of achieving a velocity of 8,000 meters per second. In the 1980 decade there are at least six nations capable of conducting military operations in LEO, and some have already done so. These activities have mostly involved the passive operation of unmanned reconnaissance and surveillance satellites in LEO and meteorological and communications satellites up at GEO as discussed previously. Both the US and the USSR have the capability in 1981 to conduct limited manned operations in LEO, but the USSR is far ahead of the USA in this regard. The Soviets have developed a fractional orbit bombardment system (FOBS), which consists of ballistic missiles launched into orbits that carry them only partway around the Earth to their targets, where they deorbit their warheads on preselected ground targets. They have kept men in space longer than the United States. They have successfully refurbished and reused their Salyut-6 space station, and they have transferred supplies from unmanned cargo spacecraft to Salyut-6. Once the US Space Shuttle becomes operational, the manned situation in LEO may change.

LEO is an operational area that is useful for earth-launched and earth-oriented activities. In the years to come, LEO will continue to be used for improved quick-look and high-resolution earth reconnaissance and surveillance. It is also an Earth-oriented tactical scouting zone.

LEO is a transit zone for surface-to-surface military operations, where part of the mission passes through LEO. It is the zone through which ICBMs must pass during the ballistic portion of their flight above the Earth's atmosphere and therefore the zone in which they are most vulnerable to intercept by ABMs or targeting by space-based DEWs.

Since it is near the Earth and requires less energy/velocity to reach, LEO is a location that offers little security to orbital military facilities. LEO is easily and quickly reached by antisatellite (ASAT) weapons. Any military vehicle, facility, or system based in LEO is highly vulnerable to Earth-launched attack.

LEO is an area where it is difficult to respond to any attack because the times involved for vehicle flights are short, thereby reducing the time available to detect, track, identify, and react. The nearness of counter-measures and weapons on the Earth's surface or in orbit plus the large amount of energy required to maneuver effectively in LEO make it necessary to site some critical military space systems in other zones further out.

Military operations in HEO are different because HEO is higher on the side of the gravity well. It is a far more valuable military operational zone with greater protection because of the ability of space vehicles to maneuver more easily within it. Since HEO goes out to GEO, it is already a zone in which military activity is taking place.

HEO military facilities are less vulnerable because it takes longer for any Earth-launched space vehicle to climb up the walls of the gravity well to this zone. It is only fair to point out, however, that military facilities in *all* zones are necessarily somewhat vulnerable to ASAT systems em-placed and waiting in those zones. These orbital ASATs are also known as killer satellites. The Soviet Union appears to have tested several of these and may already have some killer satellites waiting on station in orbit disguised as something else under the Cosmos satellite program cover.

The GEO locations in the HEO zone that have been used for military space systems thus far are all above the Earth's equator where they appear to remain stationary in the sky when seen from the Earth's surface. There are more than a hundred unmanned satellites in equatorial GEO as of early 1981. GEO is not only the prime location for domestic communications satellites and meteorological satellites but also the preferred location for the forthcoming solar power satellites (SPS) of the 1990 decade. GEO is becoming crowded as of 1981, and domestic comsat firms are beginning to jockey for the preferred positions there. The political importance of GEO has been brought to world attention in the United Nations by several equatorial nations who have laid claim to these preferred GEO positions directly over their territorial boundaries. Since the right of passage over territorial airspace above the atmosphere was tacitly granted by the failure of all nations to react in this regard to the Soviet launch of Sputnik-I on 4 October 1957, the settlement of these claims of the equatorial nations seems to be a moot point. However, the validity of Cole's Panama Theory becomes evident with the consideration of the "preferred" locations in equatorial GEO that are already the subject of controversy between nations.

It is really not necessary to put a satellite in equatorial GEO to take advantage of most of the characteristics of a geosynchronous orbit. It can be placed in an *inclined* GEO, which would make it appear to swing north and south in the sky. This sort of behavior can be perfectly acceptable as long as the satellite's position is known in advance so that ground-based tracking systems can either locate it or be programmed to follow it in the sky. Such a satellite in an inclined geosynchronous orbit can also be provided with a radio beacon transmitter to permit it to be tracked, provided that such a beacon doesn't compromise the security of its position. Figure 5 shows satellites in inclined geosynchronous orbits. Viewed from the Earth's surface, they appear to trace a vertical figure-eight in the sky.

Properly phased, numerous satellites could be placed in these inclined GEOs as shown in Figure 6. To an observer on the Moon, these inclined GEO satellites would appear to wrap around the Earth in the classic "ball of yarn." However, to an Earth observer, they would appear to be several satellites moving in the same vertical figure-eight ground track.

Inclined GEO is a preferred place to put any military orbital facility at geosynchronous altitude because a little more velocity is required to effect an orbital plane change (assuming an Earth launch into a nearly equatorial transfer orbit) and to reach it with an ASAT and because it is clearly separated from valuable nonmilitary space targets most of the time. To some, this may be viewed as a disadvantage, but the valid question remains: How will domestic users react to having their expensive nonmilitary satellites become vulnerable targets because military facilities

Figure 5. The path of an inclined geosynchronous satellite. The figure-8 path is the way three satellites would appear to move in the sky as seen from the surface of the Earth. The elliptical orbits are the actual paths through the sky that the satellites in three different inclined geosynchronous Earth orbits would take in space.(NASA)

mingle with them in equatorial GEO? This question has not yet arisen but will become significant once ASATs can reach GEO.

The illustrations indicate that there is a good deal of room in GEO for many satellites and facilities if inclined GEO orbits are used.

An interesting orbit, which has not received wide attention and which traverses both LEO and HEO, is the Soviet Molniya orbit. This is a highly inclined and highly eccentric orbit that has been used for the USSR's communications and weather satellites. (See Table 2.) The Molniya orbit comes to within a few hundred kilometers of the Earth at perigee and

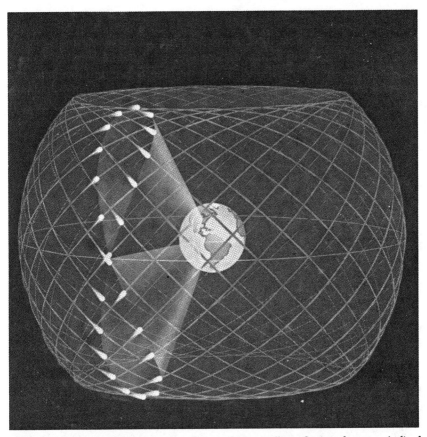

Figure 6. This drawing shows twenty-four separate satellites sharing the same inclined geosynchronous Earth orbit. From the Earth's surface, they would appear to be moving in the figure-8 path in the sky, but in actuality they would be weaving that "ball of yarn" trace of satellite orbits around the Earth in space.

goes out beyond GEO at apogee. The orbit is phased so that the high altitude portion occurs over the USSR, where the satellite moves very slowly and can therefore be tracked easily; the fast-moving portion near perigee occurs on the other side of the world from the USSR where the Soviets don't use the satellite. The Molniya orbit requires that several satellites be placed in the same orbit so that one is available at or near apogee over the ground stations at all times.

Molniya orbits are also excellent for military reconnaissance and surveillance satellites that take their data during the fast sweeps through perigee at low altitudes to improve resolution and then play back the data during the slow passage through apogee.

There are currently no manned operations in HEO. If the USA opts for a solar power satellite program, there will be nearly a thousand people living at the GEO Construction Base building the SPS units in the 1990 decade and beyond.

Cislunar Space (CLS) is perhaps the most important of all the military operational zones to the year 2025. CLS includes the L-4 and L-5 lunar libration or Lagrangian points, the top of the hill for the Earth-Moon system. The extreme importance of the Panama Points at the L-4 and L-5 libration points in terms of gravity well doctrine has already been stressed. They are the two most important military locations in the Earth-Moon system.

Very little energy is required to maneuver in CLS, and there is a great deal of volume in which to maneuver in this distant zone. Activities in CLS are relatively immune to Earth-launched ASATs. But because of the increased distance from Earth, the real use of CLS for military purposes will have to wait for the further development of deep-space manned transportation systems and facilities that may be the spin-off of the SPS program in the 1990 decade. Exploitation of the military capabilities of CLS will require manned orbital transfer vehicles (OTV). Many of these will be designed, built, and used during the buildup of the SPS program where both materials and personnel must be transferred from LEO to GEO.

Lunar Orbit/Surface (LOS) has military operational characteristics that are quite different from the other zones. Because of the mass of the Moon, this celestial body is a stable platform for a military base and offers the possibility of protection by burrowing deep within it. The Moon is therefore an important Panama Point in the Earth-Moon system, albeit of secondary importance to the L-4 and L-5 libration points because of its gravity well 2 kilometers per second deep.

Out beyond the Moon in Translunar Space (TLS) there will be nothing but copious amounts of space for maneuver, at least for the next twenty-five years. TLS is too far from Earth for suitable recon and surveillance activities, which can be done better in LEO and HEO. TLS is not on top of the hill the way L-4 and L-5 are in CLS. So it is probable that TLS will be used militarily only as a place to maneuver or to rendezvous. In addition, TLS could be used as a staging area, provided the zone is not under thorough surveillance at all times. There is, after all, a rapidly increasing amount of volume in which to operate as one gets further away from Earth and the view of radars and other sensors.

There is one Panama point in TLS that deserves mention: the L-2 lunar libration point, which lies on the opposite side of the Moon from the

Earth and on the imaginary line connecting the Earth and the Moon. (See Figure 2.) It is an "unstable" libration point, which is to say that anything placed there will not stay there very long. But it will stay there for several years before it begins to wander away, and station keeping can be carried out with minimum applications of low-thrust attitude control rocket burns. This libration point cannot be seen from the Earth or from GEO, and it cannot be seen from the side of the Moon facing the Earth. It can be seen only from the back side of the Moon or from the L-4 and L-5 lunar libration points.

With these Earth-Moon military operational zones now defined, what are the potential space weapons that can be used in each zone?

Space weaponry may turn out to be quite different from some of the concepts of science-fiction writers and military planners who are not aware of the atmospheric interface and gravity well doctrines or who have not thought about the different operational zones in the Earth-Moon system. The technology of space weaponry ranges from the absurdly simple to the most complicated and advanced technology.

As technology has progressed over the ages, weaponry based on progressing technology has shown a tendency to become more complex and varied. It's no longer possible to conduct land warfare in the twentieth century with just an infantry soldier and a rifle.

The rifle itself has changed greatly in this century. The single-shot, magazine-fed Mauser-type bolt-action rifle firing a copper-clad bullet about 7.6 millimeters in diameter has given way to semiautomatic or fully automatic assault rifles and light infantry rifles firing high-velocity bullets with calibers as small as 5.5 millimeters and cyclic rates as high as 800 rounds per minute.

Not only must the infantry soldier be equipped with a modern rifle equal in performance and field characteristics to the enemy's but he must now have other weapons to use under differing battlefield circumstances— grenades, a bayonet, a night vision scope and sight, various types of ammunition—and he must be supplemented with other specialized infantry soldiers such as light machine gunners, mortar crews, antitank crews, and antiaircraft missileers. These must be supported in turn by artillerymen, chemical engineers, military engineers, ordnance specialists, armored vehicle and tank crews, communications specialists, and tactical aircraft pilots. Considering the speed with which modern land warfare can move and the extended nature of battlefronts—prior to the American Civil War and the Franco-Prussian War, there were no real battlefronts per se; rather, wars were conducted through isolated battles between armies with minimum force contact between these major battles—rapid and reliable communications between various levels of command down to the smallest field unit must be established and maintained in order to coordinate overall battle strategy properly.

The soldier's deployment in Europe is different from his deployment in Asia. He requires different weapons, equipment, and support, depending upon the characteristics of the theater of operations, the battlefield, and the tactical situation.

In space warfare, the problems are of a different kind but not degree.

Weapons, military personnel, and the principles of utilizing them to the best advantage to prevent or to win a conflict will be different in the different operational zones of the Earth-Moon system.

The sort of weapons that could be used in space warfare in the next fifty years must be analyzed before consideration is given to the impact of both the gravity well and atmospheric interface doctrines and the safeguards that could be implemented in military space operations.

It is not presumptuous to consider potential future space weapons out to as far as fifty years in the future, because if a weapon can be defined with sufficient breadth and accuracy, the technology used to bring the weapon to reality can probably be developed within the time period forecast, physical laws permitting.

It is therefore necessary in considering space war of the future to be able to define what a "weapon" is.

A "weapon system" is almost superfluous wordage. A weapon usually is a system, meaning that it is a collection of mutually operable devices working in synergism, which is another term meaning that the whole is greater than the sum of its parts. Therefore, "weapon" and "weapon system" have equal meaning in this discussion.

A weapon has been defined by Robert A. Heinlein as a machine for the manipulation of energy, but the definition is broader than that.

A weapon can be generally defined as a means for imposing one's will upon another by coercion or action.

Thus, a weapon does not need to have a physical reality. The *threat* of the possible use of a weapon, real or imagined, may in itself be a weapon. But the opponent must *believe* that the weapon is real and that it will be used against him.

As a matter of fact, even a real weapon can be ineffective if the adversary believes it will not be used and therefore constitutes no threat. This amounts to a very dangerous game of military bluff in which, if the adversary has miscalculated or obtained misleading intelligence, can result in his defeat.

In order to determine the sort of weapons that can be anticipated in the next fifty years in space warfare, the following categorization may not only be useful but may also provide some insight into new and unique weapons that might be developed and deployed anywhere if the technology were available or could be developed to permit them.

Mass manipulators: These produce physical damage by the use of the basic inertial characteristics of mass. They convert the mass energy of position (potential energy) to the mass energy of motion (kinetic energy) which, upon direct physical impact with the target, converts kinetic energy into the other forms of energy such as heat, compression, and so on. They may simply provide mass to serve as decoy weapons. They include mass projectors, penetrating weapons, mass detectors, and mass decoys or deceivers.

Energy manipulators: Weapons of this sort are relatively new, the first of them being black powder. They produce damage by means of the application of a large amount of energy on a small area or by the rapid release of large amounts of energy in a small volume. This category includes the general classes of energy projectors, concentrators, releasers (explosives), screens, and detectors.

Chemical/biological manipulators: These produce damage through chemical action to nonliving entities (chemical weapons) and living organisms (biological weapons). They include various gases, diseases, poisons, corrosives, and dissolvers. They may be active against specific materials or organisms.

Psychological manipulators: These weapons produce a change in the mental state of the enemy in a desirable fashion to reduce his will or capability to resist without necessarily causing physical harm. In this weapon category are propaganda, counterintelligence, brainwashing, manipulation of the news and information media, mood-altering drugs, and consciousness-altering drugs.

Some of the weapons in these four broad general categories require a vector or delivery device to transport them to the point of intended action.

Some weapons are an ingenious combination of one or more of these categories or one or more groups within a category.

Generally it can be said that any weapon that has been used, is currently in use, or will be conceived in the future will fall into one of those four categories. With a minimum of effort, one can assign a category to almost any weapon that comes to mind.

It is also possible to discover that some weapons exist and have been used that were unsuspected at the time of their use. An example of this is the use of various forms of tetrahydrocannabinol (THC) and other chemical agents affecting the central nervous system as a weapon against US forces in Southeast Asia from 1965 to 1973. Although some observers may argue the point, it cannot be denied that these psychological warfare agents did get into the hands of the troops and did strongly affect the outcome of the conflict.

It may be surprising to discover that, under this definition and these categories, a suspected weapon turns out upon analysis not to be a weapon at all. Or, in the worst case, a proposed weapon may turn out to be more effective against one's own forces than those of the enemy, given a specific application, environment, and situation.

Using the definition and categories of weapons, it is also possible to conceive new weapons or modifications of existing weapons capable of being used not only in existing and known environments on Earth but also in the space environment, especially in the six operational military zones of the Earth-Moon system. Careful analysis will reveal unsuspected weapons, as well.

With this foundation and background, it is now possible to synthesize a reasonable armory of space weapons, doctrines for their use, rules of engagement, safeguards, and countermeasures.

MASS MANIPULATOR SPACE WEAPONS

Probably the first weapon in the mass manipulator category was a rock either thrown by a warrior or used to increase the mass and hardness of the human fist holding it.

In spite of more than a million years of progress and the most advanced technology available today, the most effective weapon in space war of the future will probably be the rock.

But there will be other weapons of equal power, some of them merely extensions or further developments of many of today's weapons in the mass manipulator category.

The basic characteristic of this weapon category is the basic nature of matter itself: mass and its inertia. The effectiveness of mass manipulator weapons lies in their ability to convert the energy of motion and the energy of position back and forth with very little required in the way of human manipulation necessary.

Some definitions are required.

Inertia is that property of mass defined in Sir Isaac Newton's First Law of Motion—i.e., a mass at rest tends to remain at rest and a mass in motion tends to remain in motion unless acted upon by an outside force.

On the surface of Earth, humans are not fully aware of the reality of this basic law of nature because they were born and brought up on Earth surrounded by its atmosphere and continually under the persistent pull of its strong gravity field. It seems ridiculous to claim that once a ball starts rolling along the ground—say, on a very large, flat billiard table—that it will go on rolling forever. This would be true if it were not for the fact that the ball is indeed being subjected to outside forces that Newton spoke of— in this case, rolling friction caused by gravity holding it to the table and to a certain extent depending upon its speed, the frictional drag of the air around it. In space away from the effects of gravity and the atmosphere, a baseball, golf ball, tennis ball, football, or billiard ball hit by even the worst duffer or beginner would take off and go forever in an absolutely straight line.

Just as it takes energy in the form of a force applied from outside the ball to get it moving, so it theoretically takes the same amount of energy to change the path of the ball. To stop the ball, the energy of the ball's motion, which was put into it to cause it to begin to move, must be taken out of the ball in some manner, usually by impact with another object.

Energy may best be defined as that elusive entity which creates change. There are many definitions of energy and many physicists who would define it differently according to their particular universe view. But this definition will suffice for this discussion.

There are two basic forms of energy: (a) energy of position, called potential energy, and (b) energy of motion, known as kinetic energy. A rock resting on the top of a high hill has potential energy. The same rock can have its potential energy of position atop the hill converted to kinetic energy of motion by rolling it down the hill. At the bottom of the hill, it will have acquired a speed determined basically by the height of the hill. If it were to be stopped, energy would have to be expended to overcome its kinetic energy. Or if it impacted a very solid wall at the bottom of the hill, its kinetic energy would be converted into other forms of energy such as heat, shock waves, deformation waves, and so on.

The ball or rock also possesses *momentum,* which is a product of its mass times its velocity. When it's stopped after being in motion, or when its motion is changed, there must be an exchange of momentum. The heavier the rock and the faster it travels, the greater its momentum. Momentum has absolutely nothing to do with gravity; an object will have the same momentum in the weightlessness of orbit as it does on the surface of the Earth, and it will require just as much energy or transfer of momentum to stop it in space as on Earth.

All of these very basic principles of physics lie behind every mass manipulator weapon made and used by human beings since the dawn of time. These principles work equally well in space and can therefore form the foundation for an entire series of space weapons.

A cannon would be a perfectly acceptable space weapon useful for space-to-space and space-to-surface applications. It could also be a highly accurate weapon because, in space, there would be no aerodynamic factors to take into consideration, only gravitational ones. Instead of moving in the highly modified parabola/ellipse of a long-range artillery shell fired on the surface of the Earth, a space-fired cannon shell would move in the highly predictable and classic ellipse that is shaped totally by the gravitational field in which it's fired and the velocity with which it's sent on its way from the gun muzzle.

A space cannon would require a space vehicle or facility many times as massive as the shell it fires because, according to Newton's Third Law of Motion, there will be a reaction force generated by firing the shell, and this reaction force will tend to propel the cannon and its mount in the opposite direction with the same momentum as the fired shell. Anyone who has fired a gun is well acquainted with this reaction force: the recoil of the weapon.

Recoilless cannons would eliminate this problem, and a large number of these weapons have been deployed with armed forces around the world since World War II.

The common, garden-variety artillery shell will be an excellent weapon useful in space-to-space operations not only for close-in engagements but also at very long ranges because of the ability to predict its trajectory accurately in the absence of the atmosphere.

A guidance and target homing system in such a space projectile is not required but would, if circumstances such as the value of the warhead and the need for accuracy dictated, improve the effectiveness of space artillery in the space-to-space mode. The ability of a projectile—whether gun-launched or rocket-powered—to identify, track, and home in on its intended target eliminates the need for someone or something to monitor it constantly during its trajectory. "Fire and forget" is an attractive operational mode, especially during the haze of battle or when the location of the gun or launcher must remain unknown to the enemy and not revealed by its mission monitoring activity.

Warheads in projectile-type weapons are really not required in space if the target is soft enough or if the impact velocity is high enough.

Most manned space vehicles and facilities are and will be extremely fragile and thin-skinned—i.e., "soft"—for some time to come because (a) every gram of their mass will have to be lifted up the Earth's gravity well at a definite cost per unit mass in terms of rocket propellant required, and (b) except for space facilities beyond the Van Allen Belts in HEO and above (excluding under the lunar surface), they will be built with external walls just thick enough to hold the internal pressure (plus a safety factor) and keep ultraviolet radiation from the Sun out. Like the old Skylab (and perhaps the Salyut-6), they may carry thin micrometeorite shields. These shields were designed in the past to protect space facilities from penetration by micrometeoroids, tiny meteors less than the diameter of a grain of sand. While there are measurable numbers of micrometeors in the Earth's vicinity, there have been no indications of any meteors of larger sizes. A micrometeoroid shield will not prevent the penetration of a space facility by something as simple as the round from an M-16 rifle. Many people have no concept of the extremely fragile nature of most orbital equipment designed to work in a vacuum without aerodynamic drag and to maintain their structural integrity only against the accelerations produced by their own change of motion, not that of gravity. Space equipment looks and is *flimsy* in comparison with things people are used to on the Earth's surface.

The major elements of most satellites and manned space facilities can be holed by 4-millimeter BB shot traveling at 1,000 meters per second. A cloud of such pellets can do irreparable damage to the solar array panels, heat radiator panels, or even the main structural components of most space facilities. While it is unlikely that such projectiles would cause major damage to space vehicles that were designed to cross the atmospheric interface, they will certainly raise havoc against most orbiting objects.

The larger the projectile and the faster it moves with respect to the target, the greater damage it can produce upon impact and the conversion of its kinetic energy (one-half the mass times the square of the velocity). Double the velocity, and the damage potential increases four times.

While flimsiness may be a hallmark of space equipment in LEO and unmanned facilities in GEO, what has been said thus far may not hold true for manned facilities orbiting above the Van Allen Belts. These regions of trapped space particles mostly originating from the Sun provide facilities in LEO with protection against the constant stream of charged particles—protons and electrons—produced by the Sun as the solar wind. In times of increased solar activity, the Sun experiences flares on its surface, which generate not only a greatly increased quantity of charged particles but also X rays and, to some extent, gamma rays. The intensity of the radiation produced by a solar flare can be lethal to human beings outside the protection of the Van Allen Belts. All of the Apollo lunar missions were scheduled during periods of greatly reduced solar flare activity, thereby eliminating the need for extensive (and heavy) radiation protection of the three-man crews. However, if people are to live and work above the protection of the Van Allen Belts, they will need some protection against the radiation and charged particles produced by a solar flare. This will require shielding, which amounts to mass between the living quarters and the Sun.

Therefore, most manned space facilities above LEO will include at least a massive "storm shelter" into which the facility's crew can retreat during solar flare activity, which produces radiations and charged particles at a level that can cause biological damage. What has been said about the flimsiness of space facilities does not hold true of the storm cellar portions that will be an integral part of manned facilities in GEO and at the lunar libration points. This does not mean that such high-orbit facilities will not be vulnerable to attack and damage by simple mass manipulator projectile weapons; it means that these high-orbit facilities can't be totally put out of action by such attacks.

The ordinary artillery piece or recoilless gun may not possess the capability to impart a muzzle velocity to any projectile that would be high enough to produce real damage to a space facility in a space-to-space encounter. The legendary Paris Gun of World War I, which could fire a shell weighing about 10 kilograms to a range of 130 kilometers, had a muzzle velocity of about 1,000 meters per second. The best high-velocity artillery pieces today have muzzle velocities in the neighborhood of 1,300 meters per second. In orbital space, satellite velocities are in excess of 8,000 meters per second and meteor velocities are measured in kilometers per second, 8 kilometers per second (8,000 meters per second) being considered as "slow."

Therefore, the best of the early projectile throwers for space-to-space, Earth-to-space, and space-to-Earth military use will probably turn out to be rocket propelled for a very simple reason and basically the same reason that rocket artillery has in some cases replaced gun artillery on Earth: the mass of the launching device for a rocket-propelled projectile is considerably less than that required for an artillery shell.

Rocket propulsion will be required in any event if a projectile possesses a capability to identify, track, and home in on its target, the fire-and-forget characteristic.

Exceedingly modest-sized rocket vehicles are required for hundred-kilogram nonexplosive payloads in the Earth-Moon system. This is particularly true for antisatellite (ASAT) weapons which are primarily mass manipulator weapons.

Current development work known to be under way in the United States involves two different types of ASAT weapons.

One is obviously a large ASAT with an active energy-manipulator payload (nuclear or conventional HE) to be silo-stored and launched like an ICBM. It is likely to be very large with a heavy payload and thus capable of attacking and destroying very large satellites, probably up to and including in GEO although, as will later be discussed, it need not have an altitude capability of more than 200 kilometers if it delivers a thermonuclear warhead to that altitude.

The other is a smaller ASAT under development by Ling-Temco-

Vought in Fort Worth; it is designed as an air-launched ASAT to be released from under the wing of an F-15 fighter plane at high altitude. This air-launched ASAT is reported to be capable of reaching GEO altitudes. This indicates small size and highly restricted payload capabilities. It will probably be a self-guided penetrator.

An Earth-launched ASAT need not be this complex if the target is any facility in LEO. Any sounding rocket capable of lifting a payload of 100 kilograms to an altitude of 500 kilometers makes an amazingly effective ASAT. In 1981, there are several US made off-the-shelf scientific sounding rockets that will lift 100 kilogram to 500 kilometers with very simple launching equipment and requirements because these vehicles are solid-propellant, unguided, fin-stabilized rockets—shoot-and-forget types.

The "poor man's ASAT" could be launched from anywhere, including the deck of a ship on the high seas, directly under the orbital path of a facility in LEO. The sounding rocket would rise vertically and at apogee, in the incoming path of the satellite, deploy its payload: 100 kilograms of sixpenny common iron nails, each about 5 centimeters long. This would fill a volume of 70 × 70 × 35 meters, assuming a 3-meter separation between nails in the cloud. The ASAT does not have to be aimed at the target, nor does it have to intercept the target. It must merely deposit its deployed payload in the path of the oncoming satellite. Closing velocity with the target satellite would be approximately 8.5 kilometers per second. Such a payload would literally shred any but the most heavy-armored satellites or space facilities, carrying away solar panels, antennas, and heat radiators as well as penetrating the light walls of the satellite proper. It would have "killed" Skylab, which had an external hull on the workshop and living units consisting of milled aluminum with an average thickness of 3 millimeters, a 25-millimeter core of foam polystyrene, and an inner coating of 1 millimeter of epoxy. Even if the Skylab micrometeoroid shield had been in place, a sixpenny nail traveling at 8.5 kilometers per second would have blasted through the thick aluminum shield and through the pressure vessel wall as well. The nails also would have riddled the solar arrays and the aft heat radiator.

This simple ASAT uses 1969 technology and can be assembled from surplus guided missile and rocket engine components readily available on the open market with no questions asked. (There will be no description given here of the components, their performance, their availability, or where they can be found.) In the hands of a sophisticated terrorist group, the "poor man's ASAT" becomes a potent antispace weapon, available to anyone with basic technical skills and enough money to purchase the components. There are no federal or state laws in the United States prohibiting the possession, shipment, or use of the components provided the applicable federal regulations are assiduously followed. No permission is required to launch this vehicle in most states. There are no aspects of international law that prohibit the launch of the vehicle in the United States or upon the high seas.

Every space facility in LEO is extremely vulnerable to such a simple ASAT.

This example provides an indication of the effectiveness of very simple mass manipulator weapons against space targets, especially those in LEO. Explosive warheads—either HE or thermonuclear—are not necessary. The basic laws of physics make that plain.

Space-to-Earth mass manipulator weapons can be as simple, uncomplicated, and straightforward as Earth-to-space types.

For eons, the Earth and all the other planets of the Solar System have been bombarded by smaller masses. This has become increasingly evident from the photographs sent back by unmanned spacecraft such as the Mariners, Vikings, and Voyagers. Most of the other rocky planets of the Solar System resemble the Earth's Moon, and the Earth is unique in not displaying a large number of meteorite impact craters. This is not to say that the Earth has not been struck by meteorites—and some exceedingly large ones—at various times in its past; it has, but the crater scars have been obliterated over the ages by the effects of weather and erosion.

Earth-impact mass manipulator space weapons need be no more sophisticated than large rocks traveling at velocities of 20 kilometers per second or more. (If one were simply to drop a meteorite down the Earth's gravity well funnel, the velocity it would attain from the gravity well alone on its journey down to the Earth's surface would amount to 11.6 kilometers per second, the same velocity required to toss a rock up *out* of the Earth's gravity well.)

The bigger the meteorite and the faster it's moving when it impacts the Earth's surface, the more energy it releases upon impact and the more devastating its effects to the point where the impact and its aftermath produce disturbingly profound effects on the entire Earth.

The evidence of the severity of such meteoroidal impacts can be seen in the Barringer Meteor Crater in north-central Arizona. About 25,000 years ago, a nickel-iron meteorite approximately 25 meters in diameter and weighing about 800 tons struck the Mogollon Rim of Arizona with a velocity that has been estimated to be on the order of 40 kilometers per second. It left a crater that exists to this day and is 1,200 meters in diameter and 170 meters deep.

The amount of energy released by the impact of the Barringer Meteorite was equivalent to a 2.5-megaton thermonuclear bomb.

But the only nuclear radiation released by this impact was that caused by the ultrahot plasma sheath created ahead of the meteorite during its plunge into the atmosphere. There was a brief pulse of X rays from that plasma entry sheath, but no nuclear radiation released upon the impact and explosion of the meteorite.

Literally thousands of meteorites enter the Earth's atmosphere every day. Most of them are small—the size of a grain of sand or less—and they are consumed by ablation and vaporized 50 to 100 kilometers up. In short, it appears that most of the natural meteorites left over from the formation of the Solar System have already found planetary homes or are continuing to orbit in the planetoid belt between the orbits of Mars and Jupiter.

However, even though most of the *natural* meteorites have already been swept up by the motions of the planets in the Solar System, this does not mean that the Earth, the Moon, and human facilities in space won't experience the effects of meteorite impact in the future, because it is technically possible to throw large rocks around in space and even to move planetoids more than a kilometer in diameter.

The Moon is an extremely sensitive Panama Point in the Earth-Moon system in spite of its gravity well 2 kilometers per second deep, because it is already being considered as the optimum site for a different kind of space transportation device intended to launch lunar materials off the Moon and into GEO or to the lunar libration points for purposes of space industrialization and colonization. This device is the space catapult. It has been discussed in science-fiction for at least thirty-five years and is just what its name implies: a means for catapulting loads of material from one place to another in space.

Early space catapults were considered (as well as being designed in considerable engineering detail) as a means for launching manned spacecraft off the surface of the Moon and even off Earth. Heinlein envisioned an Earth-launch catapult built up the side of Pikes Peak in Colorado in his 1947 *Saturday Evening Post* story "Space Jockey" and later in his book, *The Man Who Sold the Moon* (Chicago, Shasta, 1949).

However, in the past decade, catapults have been given a new lease on life by being considered one of the primary means of launching lunar materials off the Moon.

A lunar cargo catapult could be built horizontally along the surface of the Moon because there is no sensible atmosphere to contend with and no atmospheric interface. On Earth, because of the atmospheric interface and the desire to get a spacecraft *out* of that atmosphere as quickly as possible to eliminate efficiency-robbing aerodynamic drag effects, a launch catapult would have to be built up the side of a mountain or nearly vertical.

These space catapults are conceived as being nothing more than linear electric induction motors. On the Moon, the lunar catapult would be powered by solar arrays. On the Earth, a launch catapult would probably use the output of a solar power satellite and its ground rectenna.

Modern space catapult design no longer considers slinging large loads weighing several tons at widely spaced intervals. The modern "mass driver" is envisioned by Dr. Gerard K. O'Neill and his colleagues at Princeton and MIT as a constant-use device continually launching a stream of small kilogram-mass loads from a series of buckets running down an electromagnetically accelerated portion of the track and then returned after launching the load to receive another load in a sort of endless chain of buckets.

Technically, the Moon is an ideal site for either the large catapult or the smaller mass driver because (a) the Moon provides an ample supply of material for the mass driver to toss, (b) there is abundant sunlight fourteen days of the month at any given site on the Moon so that the mass driver can be adequately powered, and (c) the lunar mass provides a very stable base for the mass driver, a factor that greatly improves its inherent accuracy.

The lunar mass driver is a critical system for the overall commercial industrialization of the Earth-Moon system because, utilizing lunar materials, the cost of a solar power satellite can be reduced by a factor of four. Therefore, at some time during the next twenty-five years, one or more lunar mass drivers are certain to be built and operated to improve the basic economics of space industry.

Large lunar catapults may also be built and operated to reduce costs of personnel and cargo transport from the Moon. There may even be a few built on Earth where their operation, energized by solar power satellites, would eliminate any possibility of polluting the upper atmosphere with rocket exhaust effluents.

However, the catapult is an old military weapon, and it takes on new meaning in space war of the future.

A lunar mass driver can be quickly converted into an incredible ASAT with minimal changes only to the computer program that tells the mass driver when and at what velocity to launch its payloads so that they arrive at the intended location in GEO or the lunar libration points.

Lunar mass drivers or even small mass drivers emplaced in GEO or at the lunar libration points for use in space commerce are almost instantly convertible to military use as rock throwers. Since a mass driver throws only a few kilograms per load but throws these small loads in rapid succession, a mass driver *anywhere* in the Earth-Moon system above the atmospheric interface becomes a space Gatling gun. The impact of a one kilogram mass traveling at 20 kilometers per second is capable of creating major damage to almost any space facility, even the ones with storm cellars above the Van Allen Belts. Lunar mass drivers also have a nearly unlimited supply of ammunition.

The large space catapults capable of hurling masses of several tons or more become space-based heavy artillery and can function as a deadly and accurate Earth bombardment system without violating *any* existing UN treaties of principle or placing nuclear weapons anywhere in space.

The impact of one ton of lunar rock at 12 to 20 kilometers per second would produce an impact explosion equivalent to 500 tons of TNT. This is a spherical piece of rock approximately 3.7 meters in diameter. It is about one-fourth of the TNT equivalent the Japanese dropped on Pearl Harbor on 7 December 1941. The largest HE bomb dropped during World War II was the 10 metric ton RAF Grand Slam.

But it is probable that a large lunar catapult will be able to launch more than one-ton loads. When the load approaches 1,000 metric tons, the impact potential on a terrestrial target increases greatly. A 1,000-ton rock would be approximately 15 meters in diameter. Upon impact on Earth, it would release the energy equivalent of almost 2-megatons of TNT, which is equivalent to a middle-sized thermonuclear warhead. But the energy release is not accompanied by nuclear radiation (except from the superheated plasma of the atmospheric entry sheath).

Furthermore, these lunar-launched rocks can be targeted with great accuracy—probably to the same accuracy as an ICBM which means a "circular error of probability" of about 40 meters. Precise control over the launching time and the catapult exit velocity is required, and both of these factors can be precisely controlled with 1981 computer technology if an electromagnetic lunar catapult is used.

There is no practical limit to the ammunition supply for the lunar catapult, and its operation depends upon a renewable energy source, the Sun. Even after lunar sunset, electrical power could be provided to the catapult(s) from solar power satellites at the lunar libration points.

Retaliatory attack against the lunar catapults and mass drivers would be extremely difficult from any location other than the Moon or the L-4/L-5 libration points. The Moon sits atop the gravity well of the Earth. From the Moon, it is possible to detect, track, identify, and launch an interception rock against any vehicle launched from orbits up to and including GEO.

The only places in the Earth-Moon system that dominate the Moon are the L-4 and L-5 libration points. While the Moon would be the strategic location for a large catapult, the L-4 and L-5 points provide optimum locations for mass drivers whose purpose it is to protect the lunar catapult through being able to throw intercept rocks and to provide power from solar-power satellites for the lunar catapults when they are on the night side of the Moon.

For any nation occupying a lower position in the gravity well complex, it becomes very difficult to defend against the lunar catapults converted to military uses or against the L-4 and L-5 mass drivers.

Whoever manages to control a lunar catapult and to occupy both L-4 and L-5 will be able to exercise complete and total military control over the entire Earth-Moon system *without a single thermonuclear weapon* or a single piece of advanced weapons technology beyond the know-how of being able to build and computer-control the linear induction motors that are the basic catapults and mass drivers themselves.

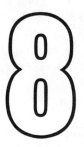

EXPLOSIVE WEAPONS IN SPACE

The use of the energy manipulator weapon category is almost as old as the use of mass manipulators. Somewhere in the dim recesses of past history, some warrior used fire as a weapon to demolish enemy facilities or as a tactical assist by setting a grass fire. There have been numerous combinations of mass manipulators and energy manipulators. The fire arrow is an example of this.

Perhaps the most famous of all ancient energy manipulators was Greek fire, which may not have been Greek in origin but which was certainly used by the Byzantine Greeks during the siege of Constantinople in A.D. 673. Greek fire may have been created by the ignition of naphtha, pitch, charcoal, sulfur, or any combination of these. It was a jealously guarded secret then, and it remains a secret today. Whatever it was, it could not be extinguished by the application of water.

The most common energy manipulator and the one that caused the most drastic change in the conduct of warfare was black powder. It is often called gunpowder, but this term is a generic one that can be applied to any gun propellant. Black powder is a very definite composition of potassium nitrate (saltpeter), sulfur, and carbon (charcoal). Black powder can be easily ignited at a temperature of 288 degrees Celsius, burns on the surface of each particle of powder with a temperature of about 588 degrees Celsius, and produces about 285 cubic centimeters of gas at this temperature for every gram of black powder burned. A stick of solid black powder burns at a rate of about 29 millimeters per second at atmospheric pressures and temperatures; confined, its burning rate increases drastically.

Thus, black powder converts chemical energy into heat energy at a very high rate and undergoes a very rapid change of state from a solid to a gas in the process. It also produces a very high temperature as it does so. When confined in a tightly enclosed container, there is no practical limit to which it will continue to generate gas from its solid form because it contains both a fuel (something to burn) and an oxidizer (something to burn the fuel in) and because it exhibits what is known as a positive pressure coefficient. This last is a technical term meaning that as the surrounding pressure increases, so does the burning rate of the black powder. Eventually, the gas pressure generated by the burning of the black powder exceeds the structural limits of the container, and the container ruptures suddenly. This all takes place in thousandths of a second, releasing a large amount of kinetic and heat energy in a very small space in a very short period of time.

In short, an explosion is created.

Black powder was perhaps the first explosive whose use was brought under control in cannons and hand guns, where the rapidly expanding gases were used to propel a projectile down a closely fitting tube, ejecting the projectile at a high velocity and therefore with both great momentum and great kinetic energy.

But black powder itself can be exploded as a weapon because the sudden release of large amounts of energy in a small volume is the hallmark of the category of weapons known as energy manipulators.

There have been many explosives developed and used since the advent of black powder, which was probably invented by the Chinese in the tenth or eleventh centuries A.D. Among those used for military purposes (and for some commercial purposes) are guncotton (nitrocellulose), nitroglycerine and dynamite, trinitrotoluene (TNT), Composition B, amatol, plastique, smokeless powder, and blasting oil. Some have been used as gun propellants while others have been used because of their sharp brisance as an explosive. Blasting oil has not generally been used in warfare but is strictly a development of the petroleum drilling industry, a combination of ammonium nitrate fertilizer and used lubricating oil which, when initiated by the brisance of a blasting cap, makes an excellent explosive. The Texas City disaster on 16 April 1947 is witness to the power of this simple explosive.

There is one important point about explosives that is relatively unknown to those working outside the field: in general, the more powerful an explosive, the more difficult it is to initiate it. Black powder in its finely divided meal or powder form can be initiated by the heat of friction. Comp B, amatol, and blasting oil are difficult to initiate, requiring in some cases the sharp concussion and attendant heat of a blasting cap. Comp B will withstand repeated impacts of .50-caliber ball ammunition. Some of the most energetic solid rocket propellants—which are also explosives with highly controlled burning rates—can withstand similar abuse and often require a complex series of chemical explosives to initiate or ignite them. Many modern explosives and solid propellant rockets must be initiated or ignited by first igniting a heat-producing squib made from black powder, which then ignites a more energetic explosive which then, perhaps, ignites or initiates the main explosive or propellant charge. The art of arming, fusing, and igniting modern explosives is a complex one.

This should be kept in mind with regard to nuclear explosives, as well, because it is even more apropos in that field.

One of the newest military explosives is the nuclear bomb. Maxwell W. Hunter II has estimated that a thermonuclear explosion produces more than 20 million times more energy release per unit weight than chemical energy release from conventional explosives. A nuclear bomb is not only exceedingly difficult and deadly to make, but extremely difficult to initiate. All nuclear explosives are based upon the energy released by the sudden attainment of critical mass of either 97 percent Uranium-235 (not 3 percent U-235 such as is used in nuclear reactors) or Plutonium-239 (the element most used in modern nuclear weaponry). The critical mass must be assembled or attained *rapidly* (within a few microseconds) else there is no force on Earth capable of bringing two subcritical masses together (they'll melt first). Once assembled or created by means of imploding a subcritical mass to increase its density and create a critical mass, the critical mass must be held together until sufficient fission energy is released to permit an effective explosion. Otherwise, the bomb comes apart in microseconds with only a fraction of its potential energy release and spreads the majority of its nuclear material within a kilometer of Ground Zero—and it's a dud.

Early nuclear weapons were heavy—5,000 kilograms or more—not because of the critical mass within them which was never much more than about 62.4 kilograms but because of the mass of the casing or "tamper" required to hold the bomb together long enough for the fissioning material inside to fission more or less completely. In most cases, nuclear weapons are initiated by chemical explosives, which currently operate by imploding subcritical masses to produce critical masses. Thus, the size of fission weapons has been steadily reduced through development of more efficient implosion schemes, more effective tampers, and better neutron reflecting materials. Although the smallest fission weapon has not been officially announced, the basic fission weapon along with all its arming, fusing, and initiation equipment has been reduced to the point where a 280-millimeter nuclear artillery shell was fired on 25 May 1953 and a 203-millimeter artillery shell was announced by the U.S. Army in 1957.

The largest fission explosion announced and documented to date was the Rushmore shot of Project Hardtack Phase II in Nevada, where a device was detonated under a balloon with a yield of 118 kilotons of TNT equivalent (the Hiroshima and Nagasaki bombs had yields of about 19 kilotons).

The first attempt at producing a bomb depending upon the energy of atomic fusion rather than fission was Shot Mike of the Ivy series at Eniwetok in the South Pacific on 31 October 1952. The yield, unannounced to date, was in the megaton range and the device was large, complex, and primitive. A far simpler method was used by the Soviet Union on 12 August 1953 when they detonated a simple fission-fusion weapon.

Today, it is known that a thermonuclear "device" consists of an initiator, a plutonium-implosion fission bomb that raises the local temperature to several million degrees, which is high enough to initiate a fusion reaction in the initiator housing. This is made of or contains lithium hydride, which in turn undergoes fusion at these elevated temperatures. This assembly is then surrounded by another casing made of Uranium-238, normally not capable of undergoing fission *except* at the very high temperatures created by thermonuclear fusion. Thus, modern high-yield thermonuclear devices operate on initiation by common explosives followed by fission-fusion-fission to produce yields up to the maximum admitted to have been fired by the Soviet Union: 50 megatons.

Nuclear and thermonuclear explosives produce blast and heat effects similar to those from chemical explosives but at a much higher level of energy release. Their primary function is performed by releasing a very large amount of energy very rapidly in a very small volume, thus producing radiant heat and, in the atmosphere, a compressive shock wave followed by other compression and rarification atmospheric pressure effects.

However, nuclear and thermonuclear explosives produce other effects that are not common to chemical explosives: (a) hard and intense radiation, including X rays and gamma rays, in the initial fireball of the detonation, (b) radioactivity from bomb and target debris that is lifted from the impact site by the updraft of the hot mushroom cloud and carried for hundreds or thousands of kilometers downwind of the detonation, and (c) an extremely strong pulse of electromagnetic energy at the instant of detonation as a result of the liberation of such great quantities of electromagnetic energy in such a limited volume of space.

Modern nuclear weaponry can be tailored to produce detonations that enhance one or more of the effects—blast wave, fireball heat pulse, electromagnetic pulse (EMP), fireball hard radiation, increased or minimized radioactive fallout (the dirty bomb or the clean bomb), or specific types of radiaiton from the detonation (the neutron bomb).

In spite of a policy of nuclear containment, a large number of nations are currently members of the Nuclear Club—the USA, the USSR, PRC, France, England, Australia, India, and possibly Israel and the Republic of South Africa. In the next twenty years, a new member can be expected to join the Club every five to seven years. Therefore, by the year 2000, there are likely to be between twelve and fourteen nations with nuclear weapon capabilities; by the year 2025, almost any nation who wants nuclear weapon capability will be able to obtain it because by that time, in spite of the tightest security classifications and restrictions, 1945–1950 A-bomb technology will have become *old* technology and enough disconnected pieces of data can be assembled to reveal all the techniques required to fabricate and detonate a primitive nuclear weapon.

The knowledge to *make* a simple nuclear weapon is currently readily available. For example, all the information given here and below came from unclassified sources in the public domain and available to anybody. Some of the information goes back thirty-five years to the original Smythe Report. Other bits and pieces have dribbled into the open literature from time to time.

Even though the knowledge concerning *how* to make a simple Hiroshima-type, or Little Boy, U-235 critical-mass atomic bomb is readily available to anybody, *making it* is not a basement activity. Almost anyone who is handy with tools and who can follow simple directions can make the trigger, the tamper, and all the rest of a Little Boy bomb. But obtaining bomb-grade U-235 is not only extremely difficult but very deadly. To obtain, say, 25 kilograms of bomb-grade 97 percent U-235, one cannot simply steal fuel rods from the local nuclear power plant and use them outright; fuel rods or elements for commercial nuclear reactors used to generate electricity contain only reactor-grade uranium which is perhaps 3 percent U-235 and 97 percent U-238. Uranium-238 will not undergo a self-sustaining chain reaction resulting in a nuclear explosion no matter how much is assembled. Only the isotope U-235 produces the slow neutrons necessary to create an explosive critical mass. A large amount of commercial nuclear-grade uranium will simply melt down, producing a messy radioactive puddle; it will not detonate.

To produce a nuclear explosion, bomb-grade uranium containing

97 percent U-235 is necessary. Enriching 3 percent U-235 reactor material to 97 percent bomb-grade material would require stealing on the order of 30 to 50 tons of fuel rods from a commercial nuclear reactor, a difficult task at best.

But an even more difficult task is faced by Little Boy U-235 nuclear bomb makers: setting up and operating a uranium enrichment activity (which requires special tools and materials) and finally arranging to cast and machine 97 percent U-235 subcritical masses which are very radioactive, very difficult to machine, and very deadly. Unless expensive and extensive safety precautions were taken, the enrichment operation would require a large operation using a large number of people, some of whom would be used to replace personnel who died from radiation poisoning during the theft, refinement, and final machining of the bomb material. It would be practically impossible to keep such a large operation on a clandestine level even if the radioactivity of the waste products, which have to be disposed of somewhere, didn't give it away. A visit to Oak Ridge, Tennessee, will give one some concept of the nature of the facility required for uranium enrichment.

The Little Boy U-235 nuclear bomb isn't the only type of fission weapon, however. But it is the simplest. It is possible to make a plutonium nuclear bomb of the Trinity-Nagasaki Fat Man implosion type. Plutonium-239 can be made in large quantities in nuclear reactors. However, a Fat Man implosion Pu-239 bomb is extremely difficult to make and extremely difficult to detonate, although the fissionable material is somewhat easier to obtain. The Pu-239 must be separated from the U-238 in the reactor elements and must be cast and machined with precision; this involves handling materials possessing high natural radioactivity and somewhat esoteric physical properties. Getting a Fat Man plutonium implosion bomb to implode properly, or getting a small subcritical plutonium bomb to go critical by implosion squeeze is extremely difficult and requires a large industrial effort. Since the plutonium implosion squeeze bomb is the easiest to obtain fissionable materials for, it is the type most nations who are recent members of the Nuclear Club have developed and tested, although it is the most difficult to detonate.

Although nuclear and thermonuclear weapons are highly effective area weapons for use on Earth, their utility in space warfare hinges on an entirely different component of their detonation.

As energy manipulators, both chemical and nuclear explosives will have definite utility in space warfare. However, because of the atmospheric interface and the radically different enviornmental characteristics on opposite sides of this interface, explosive energy manipulator weapons cannot be used in the same manner on either side of the interface.

An explosive—chemical or nuclear—operates by the sudden release of a large amount of energy in a small volume of space. Two primary effects result from the detonation of an explosive: (a) heat energy and (b) concussion or shock produced from the rapidly expanding gases or plasma produced by the change of state and energy release of the explosion.

On Earth surrounded by the atmosphere, the latter effect is usually predominant, because of the containment effects caused by the density of the atmosphere itself. The rapidly expanding pressure pulse of the explosion moves faster than the speed of sound in the atmosphere, thus producing a shock wave that contains most of the energy of the explosion. It is the nature of this explosive shock wave which produces most of the damage resulting from the explosion—an initial rapid, nearly instantaneous rise in pressure at the shock front followed by a rapid reversal of pressure as the shock front passes. This pressure "whiplash" creates most of the damage because of high overpressure followed by immediate reversal and underpressure. This is true with both chemical and nuclear explosions, although the effects are greatly magnified in a nuclear detonation by the higher energy density at the core.

In the vacuum of space above the atmospheric interface, an explosive behaves differently because the shock wave cannot be magnified and enhanced by the presence of the atmosphere. Any concussive effects desired by a space explosion must be achieved by the energy of the explosive's own expansion wave. This is much less in a vacuum than in air. To obtain a destructive effect by concussion in space, the explosive must be detonated in extremely close proximity to the object.

The reverse analogy to this is the antisubmarine depth charge. Because of the environment in which the explosion of a depth charge occurs—under water—the concussive effect is the primary effect. It is amplified by the presence of the water, which has higher density than the air. The shock wave of a depth-charge detonation is a water shock wave, which can create severe damage even though the center of the detonation is removed from the target.

The opposite holds true in the vacuum of space because of the *extremely* low (if even nonexistent) density of the traces of gas in orbital space.

The concussive effect of an explosive used in space warfare is secondary unless detonation takes place in extremely close proximity to fragile space facility structures. At that, only localized damage can be anticipated from concussive effects.

This does not rule out the use of shaped charges and other Monroe Effect explosive devices. Here again, however, direct contact between explosive and target is assumed. A shaped charge designed to concentrate the explosive's own expansion wave would be just as effective against any enclosure in space as in the Earth's atmosphere.

The detonation of a small amount of explosive *inside* a pressurized space facility is another matter.

Inside a pressurized container in space—say, a manned living or working module—invokes the atmospheric interface doctrine where the interface in this case is the actual wall of the pressurized vessel itself, a barrier with probably one atmosphere of pressure differential across it—life support air on one side, the vacuum of space on the other. At best it may possess a safety factor of two—i.e., ability to withstand twice its design load—although the airworthiness standards of the Federal Aviation Administration for pressure cabins of aircraft call for a safety factor of only 1.33 (one-third more pressure than designed for). In a small pressurized volume, a very small explosion could rupture the bulkhead, and the over-pressure would undoubtedly injure any person who happened to be in that enclosure at the time of the explosion. Even a small explosive charge placed in the vicinity of the outer wall of a pressurized space factory could easily blow a hole through it. Certainly, the application of a shaped-charge device would rupture the bulkhead. This is an area of research that will occupy the time and effort of many explosive and ordnance experts in the next quarter of a century: how much explosive of what sort of brisance placed how far from a bulkhead of given thickness and transbulkhead pressure differential will deform or rupture the bulkhead?

Because of the need to be in extremely close proximity to the target for either the heat or the blast from an explosive to create much damage, the major use of explosives—especially chemical explosives—in space warfare will be as dispersants of the masses of a fragmentation warhead.

Where direct and positive physical damage of a target is required, a fragmentation-type warhead will work equally well on either side of the atmospheric interface. In fact, it will probably work better in the vacuum of space because of the lack of atmosphere and viscous drag on the war-head fragments.

A very simple fragmentation warhead for use in space was dis-cussed earlier: the ASAT for use against LEO facilities, the simple rocket-sonde carrying a 100-kilogram payload of sixpenny common nails. A small explosive charge would be required to disperse the cloud of nails. Arming and fusing such a simple warhead is not difficult, a simple time fuse being sufficient to detonate the explosive charge at apogee, which will occur at a known time after launch. This is all 1981 state of the art ordnance technology, which could probably be used by almost any nation in the world today.

The technology of fragmentation warheads has become quite sophisticated in the past hundred years, progressing steadily from the classic "whiff of grape" alluding to the grapeshot cannon round. The equally classic "pineapple" fragmentation hand grenade first used during World War I—and still issued almost unchanged in design as the F1 grenade to Warsaw Pact infantry troops—is an excellent example of a fragmentation weapon. The continued development of guided missiles for antiaircraft applications (surface-to-air missiles or SAMs) has placed severe demands upon fragmentation warhead designers because of the need for warheads of very small size and light weight coupled with maximum damage radius. A SAM warhead must be able to damage an aircraft even though the SAM itself does not impact the target, an occurrence which is a rarity even with modern guidance and homing technology. Warheads have been designed and tested that will propel a ring of steel outward from the SAM in the desired direction to a distance of dozens of meters.

Since a fragmentation warhead is a combination weapon—a mass manipulator activated by an energy manipulator—it can be designed to make optimum use of the best characteristics of both weapon categories, depending upon the environment in which it is designed to work. Often, the velocity of the fragments is important, and such warheads use a larger proportion of explosive material. Other fragmentation warheads are designed for maximum penetration power of the fragments and use extremely dense fragment materials such as depleted uranium slugs that are waste from nuclear reactors or from uranium processing plants.

It is already obvious that a fragmentation warhead can be very effective in space warfare and is probably the only sort of chemical explosive warhead that can be effective in the space environment, given the rapid dispersal of the explosive blast wave itself in the low density space environment.

However, because most LEO space facilities will carry micro-meteoroid protection, frag warheads for use against these low-orbit facilities will require high fragment weights and densities. Warheads for use against the more heavily protected HEO facilities with manned solar flare storm cellars will require greater penetration capabilities similar to anti-armor ordnance.

Nuclear and thermonuclear warheads will also be utilized in space warfare, but for a totally different purpose than on Earth because of some unique characteristics of a nuclear explosion, especially in a vacuum or near-vacuum.

The United States has conducted five nuclear tests at very high altitudes—TEAK, ORANGE, and three ARGUS shots, all launched by rockets and with TEAK and ORANGE both in the megaton range.

In the absence of the Earth's sensible atmosphere, the fireball of a nuclear explosion expands quite rapidly and the thermal effects predominate over blast effects. However, there are two aspects of a space nuclear detonation that are of especial interest with regard to space warfare.

The first of these is the enhanced hard radiation from a space nuclear detonation with respect to the same detonation on the other side of the atmospheric interface. Because of the very low density of the environment surrounding the nuclear explosion in space, there is very little interaction between the X ray and gamma radiation from the fireball and the environment. Particle radiation from the explosion—primarily neutrons—is also increased because of the lack of interaction with a surrounding atmosphere. In the TEAK and ORANGE tests, there appeared to be enhanced radiation in the visible portion of the spectrum as well.

This effect of a nuclear explosion in space would have severe effects upon many materials used in connection with space facilities. The radiation would severely degrade the efficiency and output of silicon and gallium arsenide solar cell arrays used to provide electric power for space facilities.

Increased output of neutrons as well as X ray and gamma radiation could have detrimental effects upon the materials used in space structures. However, most of the information concerning the degraded properties of materials subjected to intense radiation remains under government security restriction. Be that as it may, it can be inferred that a nuclear detonation in space will undoubtedly have a deteriorating effect upon the materials of a space facility unless the facility is "hardened" against such effects by careful choice of materials or shielding.

However, the overwhelming military characteristic of a high-yield nuclear explosion in space is the effects caused by the electromagnetic pulse (EMP) produced by the explosion.

There has not been much discussion or publication of the nature and effects of the EMP. It is an electromagnetic effect created by the basic nature of the nuclear explosion itself and by the hard radiation produced. The EMP may be likened to a very strong electromagnetic field which, when it interacts with materials capable of conducting electricity (which is most materials, even some of the electrical insulators), creates very strong magnetic fields and very large electrical currents and voltages.

The EMP is exceedingly effective at extreme ranges outside the atmosphere.

A recent study of the military implications of a solar power satellite system conducted by Science Applications, Inc. for the Department of Energy and NASA estimated that the detonation of a 10-megaton thermonuclear device at an altitude of 200 kilometers would produce an EMP capable of completely disabling any solar power satellite—or other satellite with extensive solar arrays and large electric power handling capabilities—in GEO. It would, in fact, disable the entire SPS system in GEO around the world.

This sobering estimate has not been confirmed by other sources either because of lack of data or security classification.

The report of this study states that it is possible to "harden" a space facility against the EMP but does not go into details because of the obvious military security aspects of such "hardening" techniques.

Thus, a strong threat to military space facilities and activities exists from any nation with a tactical ballistic military rocket capable of lofting a multimegaton thermonuclear warhead above the atmospheric interface. An equally strong threat exists from any nation capable of orbiting even a single such thermonuclear weapon disguised as another type of satellite and capable of being detonated by remote command.

The 1963 Nuclear Test Ban Treaty specifically prohibits such things, but not all members of the Nuclear Club are signatories to that treaty. And, in time of general war, there are few treaties that the combatants tend to continue to observe save those whose abrogation would cause more harm than good.

However, the use of a thermonuclear detonation in space to create a disabling EMP would tend to be detrimental to the space facilities of the nation that did it as well as to the enemy's. Therefore, the use of such thermonuclear space detonations may be measures of last resort.

HIGH-ENERGY
LASER WEAPONS

Directed energy weapons (DEW) may be modern in terms of the technology necessary to bring them to reality, but they are certainly not new in concept.

There is an unconfirmed story by the satirist Lucian of Samosata that attributes the destruction of the Roman fleet attacking Syracuse in 214–212 B.C. to Archimedes, who supposedly designed huge concave mirrors to concentrate the light of the sun on the ships' sails, setting them afire.

But it is Herbert George Wells (1866–1946) to whom the laurels must go for first describing a modern DEW in Chapter The Fifth of *The War of the Worlds,* published in 1898:

Slowly a humped shape rose out of the pit, and the ghost of a beam of light seemed to flicker out from it. Forthwith flashes of actual flame, a bright glare leaping from one to another, sprang from the scattered group of men. It was as if some invisible jet impinged upon them and flashed into white flame. . . . An almost noiseless and blinding flash of light, and a man fell headlong and lay still; and as the unseen shaft of heat passed over them, pine-trees burst into fire and every dry furze-bush became with one dull thud a mass of flames. . . .

Wells could not have written a more accurate description of an infrared high-energy laser (HEL), even though the scientific theories to permit such a device had yet to be thought up and tested and the technology to accomplish it lay more than half a century in the future. Wells, a

99

biologist who graduated from London University in 1888, had to give up teaching because of ill health and was *forced* to make a living as a writer— and turned out to be one of the most prognostic writers who ever lived.

The laser itself rests upon the foundations of quantum mechanics, an intuitive theory based on the work of Max Planck, Niels Bohr, Max Born, Werner Heisenberg, Louis de Broglie, Erwin Schrödinger, Paul Dirac, and Pascual Jordan carried out between 1900 and 1930. There is no logical, rational basis for quantum mechanics in either Newtonian or Einsteinian physics; it just happens to work, and most of solid-state electronics exists because of it.

The word "laser" is an acronym for Light Amplification by Stimulated Emission of Radiation.

Depending upon its design, a laser produces radiation in the infrared, visible, and ultraviolet portions of the electromagnetic spectrum as its predecessor, the maser, produces radiation in the microwave radio frequency part of the same spectrum. Work is proceeding on gamma-ray and X-ray lasers.

The radiation from a laser is not the same as the light radiation from an incandescent bulb or the heat radiation from an infrared heater. Laser radiation is at one precise frequency with all cycles of the radiation precisely in step or phase with each other, a phenomenon called coherent radiation.

Coherent radiation is a great deal easier to collimate, refract, and focus. A beam of coherent laser radiation can be tightly focused into a pencil-thin beam that does not diffuse or spread out as distance from the laser increases. Because all the laser radiation is coherent and in phase, it does not easily diffuse, especially in a vacuum. In short, the laser radiation is *organized* like a troop of soldiers marching in step.

The concept of the laser was first proposed in 1958 by A. L Schawlow and C. H. Townes, and the first report of a working laser was made in 1960 by T. H. Maiman, over sixty years after H. G. Wells first described one.

To explain effectively how a laser works without presenting a background of quantum mechanics is difficult. Basically, energy in the form of light radiation or an intense electron current is introduced into either a gas, a semiconductor, or an ionized solid. This "pumping" action raises the energy of individual atoms in the material by exciting the electrons of the atoms, raising the electrons to a higher energy level. When these excited electrons release this energy by returning to a lower energy level in the atoms, it stimulates other electrons to make the same transition to the lower energy state. Furthermore, this stimulation causes all the electrons in all the atoms to release their energy together in precise phase. An intense beam of coherent radiation is produced, the frequency of which depends upon the material that is made to "lase."

Lasers can operate either in a pulsed manner or in a continuous mode. For the first decade or so of laser technology, pulsed lasers were capable of producing very concentrated, intense beams of radiation. Continuously operating or continuous wave (CW) lasers, on the other hand, had to operate at much lower energy outputs and were primarily used to produce radiation of great stability and purity. The first lasers used ruby crystals as the lasing medium and were pumped by xenon discharge lamps like those used in photographic flash units; they produced an intense red light of a single frequency.

The red spot of a ruby laser beam projected on a white wall exhibits the curious freckling or corruscating typical of the way human eyes see coherent light.

Initially, the laser was called an invention looking for a job. It did not take long for inventive souls to discover many ways to use the laser.

Combined with fiber optics, laser light provided an excellent new way to transmit information along "cables" made up of millions of hair-thin glass strands, each strand acting as a light wire for an individual laser which, in turn, was modulated by millions of separate voice or video channels.

Because of the ability of a laser to produce a tightly focused beam of energy, the energy density in a laser beam could be made to be very high indeed. One of the first demonstrations of the effects of concentrating so much energy on such a very small area was made with a ruby laser cutting a razor blade.

It does not take much imagination to proceed from this simple demonstration of a laboratory laser (of a type which can now be purchased in kit form from any number of scientific hobby supply mail-order firms) blasting its way through a thin steel razor blade to a more powerful laser cutting anything quickly, efficiently, and from a distance.

As the state of the art progressed over the years, lasers increased in power output, in frequencies available, and in categories. Lasers are used today in eye surgery and will probably find other surgical uses in the years to come. Lasers are used to cut steel. They are used to cut cloth in the garment district of New York City. They are used by the thousands by engineering surveying crews all over the world because it is possible to measure distance very accurately using a pulsed laser and measuring the time required for a laser light pulse to reach a mirror and be reflected back to the laser transmitter. (This sort of Laser Illuminated Detection And Ranging is also used in weapons systems and goes by the inevitable acronym "lidar.")

However, from a military viewpoint, if a simple lab laser can blast through a razor blade, there's no reason why a more powerful laser can't burn its way through armor plate—or anything else.

As a result, highly classified research and development on HELs has been going on in both the USA and the USSR for well over a decade. In the United States, a great deal of this work has taken place at Los Alamos Scientific Laboratories (LASL), the Lawrence Livermore Radiation Laboratories (LLRL), and at both Kirkland Air Force Base and White Sands Missile Range in New Mexico usually under contract by Zia Corporation, a military research and development firm that is a wholly owned subsidiary of Westinghouse.

The modern HEL doesn't look much like the first ruby lasers of the 1960 decade. In order to get higher energies in the beam, they must have more atoms that can be pumped and that can transition. A solid-state laser has limited atoms that can be energized. So nearly all HEL work has progressed with electric-discharge gas-dynamic lasers in which a supersonic flow of gas is the lasing medium, which is pumped by intense electric fields.

A closed-cycle laser of this type is shown in the photo insert. Its heart is the laser cavity where an optical resonator is used to extract energy from the pumping and population inversion of a fast-flowing gas. The beam control and projection system is a series of mirrors to focus and direct the resulting high-energy beam. A closed-cycle system is shown although this probably represents a highly advanced type of HEL. Nearly all chemical HELs at this time utilize an open-cycle system where the reactant gases are simply vented to the environment once they have passed through the optical cavity.

The type of gas used determines to a great extent the frequency of the HEL's output beam. The following provides an example of the gases and frequencies currently being employed in HELs:

Carbon dioxide (CO_2): 10.6 microns (infrared)
Cardon monoxide (CO): 4.8 to 5.2 microns (infrared)
Deuterium fluoride: 3.8 microns (high infrared)
Hydrogen fluoride: 2.7 microns (high infrared)
Iodine: 1.3 microns (high infrared)
Mercury chloride: 0.55 microns (visible green)
Krypton fluoride: 0.25 microns (ultraviolet)

There are many other candidates for lasing gases, especially in the visible and ultraviolet regions of the spectrum. However, some of these gases break down at higher energy levels and are not useful for HEL applications.

In general, the shorter the wavelength—i.e., the higher the frequency—the smaller, lighter, and more efficient a HEL becomes. The laws of optics also reveal that the dispersion of the HEL's beam can be reduced if higher frequencies and shorter wavelengths are used, because diffraction, which limits the performance of *any* optical device, is directly a function of wavelength and an inverse function of the diameter of the optics—the mirrors and lenses.

For use as a weapon, a HEL must be able to concentrate a very large amount of energy on a very small area in a very short period of time. This means high power output, among other things.

Maxwell W. Hunter, III, has worked out the equivalence between the application of energy from trinitrotoluene (TNT), which is a conventional explosive, and the energy of a HEL beam. Roughly, 5.5 million watt-seconds (5.5 megawatt-seconds) is equivalent to one kilogram of TNT. Thus, if one were able to impinge the beam of a 5.5-megawatt laser on a target for one second, it would be roughly equivalent to a kilogram of TNT applied directly to the target.

This does not sound like much of an advantage for a HEL over the energy release from conventional explosives until one begins to consider that a kilogram of TNT must be placed *directly against* the target. A 5-megawatt HEL using KrFl as a lasing gas could deliver the same energy per square centimeter on the surface of the target at a range of 36,000 kilometers.

The USA is currently developing a 5-megawatt hydrogen fluoride CW laser called Alpha.

Such a HEL operating in the pulsed mode could deliver significantly higher outputs.

The US Navy is testing a 2.2-megawatt deuterium fluoride laser, which is five times the power output of the 400-kilowatt laser they have already demonstrated as a weapon against a variety of military targets, including airborne drone aircraft.

HELs with power outputs up to 100 megawatts have been proposed.

Nuclear pumping has been proposed for space-based HEL systems. The detonation of a small nuclear explosive would provide enough energy to pump several HELs simultaneously, each HEL targeted separately. True, it is a one-shot unmanned system, but extremely high power outputs could theoretically be obtained.

There are technical limitations to the use of higher powers for HELs, but these are certain to be overcome because they are technical problems subject to engineering solutions through continual refinement of techniques.

For example, any mirror used in a HEL must have very low absorption—i.e., it must reflect as much of the incoming light energy as possible. A mirror with an absorptivity of only 0.1 percent of a 10-meter diameter beam from a 25 megawatt laser would absorb 320 watts per square meter or a total energy of more than 25 kilowatts. This is enough energy to distort, warp, or even melt any uncooled mirror.

The mirror's figure (surface roughness and accuracy of surface curve) must be many times better than the best mirrors used in the finest astronomical telescopes. Otherwise, the mirror will scatter and diffuse the beam of the HEL. The shorter the wavelength, the more important this factor becomes.

The beam of a HEL must leave the device through one or more apertures or windows, all of which must also have very, very low absorption of the energy lest they melt because of absorbed energy.

Many new optical techniques have been developed in the past decade. Segmented array mirrors and adaptive optics will be useful in the space HELs of the 1980 and 1990 decades.

Both manned and unmanned space-based laser battle stations may be deployed in LEO by 1985. As of this writing, the United States is engaged in planning for the deployment of space HEL battle stations and possibly later deployment of particle beam weapons. These early space DEW systems will probably be open-cycle gas dynamic HEL types with perhaps 10 megawatts of power with beam apertures up to 4.5 meters in diameter (the largest that would fit into the payload bay of a Space Shuttle Orbiter). The Soviet Union, on the other hand, may have available its TT-50 superbooster capable of orbiting up to 160,000 kilograms of payload. Since the exact size of the TT-50 is not known in unclassified circles, although the diameter of the upper stage and payload is estimated to be 8 meters by Charles P. Vick, one could anticipate a Soviet space laser battle station with an aperture diameter of at least 4 meters, this being compatible with the diameters of the Salyut and other space vehicles launched with the Soviet SL-13 Proton booster, or as large as 7 to 8 meters if boosted by the TT-50 launch vehicle. The Soviet space laser could be anticipated to have a power output of no less than 5 megawatts and probably more.

The military utility of these space battle stations would be as part of a combined ASAT and ABM system.

Even deep in the Earth's atmosphere, the U.S. Navy's deuterium fluoride 400-kilowatt HEL successfully targeted and destroyed four out of four TOW target missiles during tests at San Juan Capistrano, California, in 1978. The atmosphere attenuates a HEL beam in varying amounts. A HEL operating in the vacuum of space can therefore possess both extended range and more concentrated kill power due to the absence of an atmosphere that would disperse, diffuse, and attenuate the beam.

A 5-megawatt space-based HEL with irradiation wavelengths between 0.25 and 2.0 microns would therefore be effective as an ASAT, even for missions as simple as blinding the sensors of other satellites or disabling their solar power arrays. Sensors are especially vulnerable, particularly if they are not protected and "hardened" by prudent design employing a variety of passive and active countermeasures.

Solar cell arrays are also vulnerable because a HEL can heat up the components to their failure points. A typical solar cell consists of a protective front cover, the cell itself, the attachment of electrical conductors to the cell, and adhesives to bond these together. If the electrical connections are soldered, they are the most vulnerable element since typical solders melt at about 180 degrees C. If the connections are welded, the failure temperature would be higher. However, at 350 degrees C typical adhesives begin to loose their adhesiveness and transparency. Gallium arsenide solar cells experience contact metalization at this temperature. At 450 degrees C, both gallium arsenide and silicon solar cell types experience metallization and destruction of the cell material itself, although some research indicates this temperature could be raised to about 600 degrees C. Most HELs under consideration at this time could raise temperatures of solar cell arrays to 600 degrees C in about 2 seconds.

Whether a 5-megawatt space-based HEL would be an effective ABM is a question that isn't being discussed today in the open literature. However, an ICBM is by its very nature a thin-skinned vehicle; the Atlas ICBM had a skin thinner than the thickness of a dime. All of the Soviet ICBMs save the SS-16 are liquid-propellant rockets and therefore thin-skinned by technical necessity. The fiber-filament-reinforced plastic motor casings of solid-propellant ICBMs such as Minuteman and the Soviet SS-16, however, are thicker, but shrouds around such critical parts as the warheads and guidance systems must perforce be of extremely thin-gauge material to save weight. Thus, a modestly powered space-based HEL could project a beam at an ICBM during its launch phase as it leaves the atmosphere, and this beam could be moderately destructive to the missile's structure in critical areas and even to internal components such as guidance systems, autopilots, and even warhead systems.

There is no question that an Earth-based HEL is going to be an effective ABM device. The U.S. Navy's Sea Lite HEL has a power output of 2.2 megawatts. Even assuming that 50 percent of the Sea Lite's output is absorbed by the atmosphere, this HEL is quite capable of punching through to target an ICBM during midflight in space or even during reentry. Early plans, now shelved, called for basing Sea Lite types of ABM laser systems on a mountain near Albuquerque, New Mexico, and at China Lake, California.

The biggest problem with using HELs as ASAT or ABM systems is the detection, tracking, and pointing of these large-aperture devices. Once the beam is triggered, it proceeds to its target at the speed of light—

300,000 meters per second. But to aim a HEL and keep it pointed on target is at this time one of the biggest problems because of the very tight beam that is produced by a HEL. Ordinary radar is "too coarse." HEL weapons will be aimed by smaller low-powered tracking and pointing lasers, "flashlights" that will illuminate the target and tell the "rifle" where to shoot.

In the next two decades, HELs are going to be large devices, regardless of whether they are open-loop systems employing liquid propellants to generate their lasing medium or closed-loop systems employing either liquid propellants or solar energy. Earth-based HELs can grow to be very large. Space-based HELs will also be large and will be very difficult to hide because of their size; they will be among the largest satellites in orbit.

The critical technologies appear to lie in the field of optics, where polishing and figuring mirrors will be a major problem. However, technology projections indicate that by the year 2000 an increase in HEL power by at least two orders of magnitude can be expected with a major increase in primary mirror area through the use of the segmented mirror array concept.

HEL potential and effectiveness can be broken into three areas: space-to-Earth, Earth-to-space, and space-to-space. In the next two decades, the following HEL weapons can be forecast:

SPACE-TO-EARTH

Continuous-wave HELs will be deployed in LEO by the late 1980's but will probably not be deployed in GEO because the long range makes such deployment infeasible. A HEL could deliver on an Earth target as small as a single vehicle a beam with an energy density 100 times the normal solar intensity. To gain an appreciation of what this irradiance intensity will do, focus sunlight through a 3-inch-diameter magnifying glass into a spot 0.3 inches in diameter; this is not a difficult experiment and indicates the intensity of focused laser radiation of the level of this discussion. The beam width of the HEL would be one microradian (0.0000000174 degree). However, even though the laser frequency was carefully chosen, atmospheric effects of a beam with this energy density could reduce the ground intensity by as much as fifteen times.

Pulsed HELs will be deployed in LEO for this military application in the 1980 time period. Again, deployment in GEO is probably infeasible due to the increased range. By 1999, a space-based pulsed HEL using the output of a solar power satellite could deliver 20 megawatts of output with a beam width of 1.5 microradians (0.0000000261 degree).

EARTH-TO-SPACE

Continuous-wave HELs can be very effective ABM and antiaircraft weapons by the late 1980's and pose serious ASAT threats as well. A plausible HEL(CW) for 1999 is a chemical laser with a 10 megawatt output using a 4-meter aperture with a beam width of 1.5 microradians. This sort of HEL weapon is a serious threat to nearly any space facility at ranges from 200 to 10,000 kilometers (and nearer, of course) unless the target is shielded and hardened in advance against HEL irradiation.

HEL(P) ground weapons will undoubtedly be closed-cycle electrodynamic lasers with at least 10 megawatts output, a 4-meter aperture, and a pulse repetition or firing rate of several bolts per second with a beam spread no greater than 3.5 microradians (0.000000061 degree).

SPACE-TO-SPACE

In both CW and pulsed HEL categories, the level of capability increases with time.

HEL(CW) weapons for ASAT use will be deployed in the 1980 decade. Their 10-megawatt output and 1 microradian beam width would permit them to irradiate another space target at a range of 1,000 kilometers with a beam intensity of more than 3,000 watts per square centimeter. These are burner weapons and will be useful for ASAT and ABM applications, especially during the time ICBMs are above the Earth's atmosphere during their flight to target. Considering the fact that the US Navy has already destroyed TOW missiles in flight with 400-kilowatt lasers in the Earth's atmosphere with all the dispersion and absorption that implies, the 10-megawatt HEL(CW) space weapon is effective indeed, even at long ranges because of the very tight 1 microradian beam spread.

Pulsed HEL weapons become *really* effective once the outputs of solar power satellites can be directed to them for their use, even though such a power source would require very large space rectennas that would, in turn, make such very large HEL(P) weapons easily spotted and easily targeted. However, because of the potential of SPS power added to a potential 20 megawatt output coupled with a 1.5 microradian beam, such a HEL(P) could deliver a beam with 250 watts per square centimeter at a range of 100 kilometers, making it a prime GEO satellite defensive weapon against ASATs. And, if deployed in LEO with a power relay from GEO, the HEL(P) could become a prime ABM weapon as well.

The extremely large size of space-based HELs will demand that they be "hardened" against attacks from enemy HELs in space and on Earth. They will also have to provide for their own defense against ASAT weapons and thus be capable of detecting, tracking, pointing, and firing at close ranges—100 kilometers or less.

In a like manner, Earth-based HELs will be very large devices, but most of their equipment can be hidden or protected underground with only the final aperture being exposed. Unless provided with their own integral electrical or chemical power supplies, they will be vulnerable to attacks on any power sources coming into their installations. With internal power sources, they are necessarily limited by the energy storage capability of these internal systems.

Space-based or Earth-based HEL weapons are going to have a limited number of shots depending upon their power sources. Space HELs using the outputs of solar power satellites will have effectively unlimited shots because of a continuous supply of external power.

Because these HEL weapons in the next two decades are going to be very large systems, the speed and accuracy of their aiming and tracking will depend almost totally upon manipulation of the system optics. Otherwise, these large systems would be like battleships with fixed guns; the entire battleship would have to be turned to alter the firing azimuth of its fixed guns, just as it was in the days of Nelson and Jones aboard sailing ships with gun decks and without gun turrets.

There are engineering problems involved with making such large precision optics highly mobile while at the same time maintaining their optical integrity—the mirror figure, for example. Space-based HELs will not suffer these problems because there will be no stress on the optical parts caused by gravity; however, in space the movement of parts is accompanied by a reaction in which the rest of the system moves in the opposite direction. Stabilization of HEL battle stations to provide firm and steady firing platforms will require a considerable updating of naval fire control system and space vehicle attitude control system technologies.

Save for the nuclear-pumped laser, there is absolutely no international convention to prohibit the placement of such powerful HEL weapons in space. Because of the very narrow energy beams they are capable of projecting, they are not weapons of mass destruction but weapons of highly selective targeting.

The most vulnerable targets for HELs are the frail vehicles of modern military technology: aircraft and missiles. They would also be effective employed from LEO against fuel dumps, tank farms, liquid rocket propellant facilities, or electrical switching yards and distribution centers.

Space-based HELs, unless suitably protected and hardened against HEL attack themselves, would be vulnerable to such HEL attack. Earth-based HEL facilities would be assumed to be protected and hardened against HEL attack from orbit since it is much easier to place Earth-based systems underground. Space-based laser battle stations will be large, easily spotted, known in advance, and tracked by ASAT weapons for instant retaliation in case of HEL attack.

The big problem with HEL defense, especially in space, is the fact that the HEL beam arrives at the speed of light. There is no way for a target to know that a HEL has been fired against it until the beam arrives.

But both the space-based and the Earth-based HEL holds forth the promise of creating a highly effective ABM system. As few as six HEL battle stations located in LEO could offer total protection against an ICBM attack. Suitably located Earth-based HEL systems of high power could provide a point defense ABM capability.

One thing is certain: the high-energy laser—whether it is Earth-based or space-based—opens up a whole new area of strategic doctrine because the old MAD policy becomes completely obsolete once a single nation achieves an ABM capability with space-based HEL systems.

It is certain because both the USA and the USSR are now deep into development programs with high-energy lasers. It is only a matter of time before they become operational. By the end of the 1980 decade, HEL systems will be emplaced in low-Earth orbit.

And the whole global strategic balance is therefore changed.

PARTICLE BEAM WEAPONS AND NOTES ON SPACE DEW USES

Since at least 1977, United States' surveillance satellites have reported something going on near the Soviet city of Semipalatinsk located in Kazakhstan on the Irtysh River some 700 kilometers southeast of Omsk. A very large building was under construction there. In February 1978, US satellites detected high levels of thermal radiation and a large quantity of nuclear debris coming from Semipalatinsk.

By 1980, the Soviets had made at least eight successful experiments in the propagation of high-energy electron beams in the Earth's ionosphere (upper atmosphere) using Cosmos, Soyuz, and Salyut spacecraft.

There were reports of tests of beam weapons against targets in 1978 at a place near Gorkiy called Sarova (not on any maps, including 1969 strategic maps of the US Department of Defense).

Then in 1980 came reliable reports as well as reconnaissance photographs of a highly unusual device called Tora that was being assembled at a place called Saryshigan (or Sary-Shigan) in Kazakhstan on the western shore of Lake Balkhash. Partly designed by the Soviet physicist A. I. Pavlovski, Tora is a particle beam test weapon powered by explosively actuated magnetocumulative generators. This Pavlovski generator makes use of the conversion of the chemical energy of explosives into electromagnetic energy by compressing a magnetic field generated by conductors moving under the action of the explosive. Since the energy content of conventional high explosives is about 5 megajoules per kilogram, it is possible with the Pavlovski generator to create extremely high electrical currents in a very short time period on a one-shot basis. Basically, a Pavlovski generator replaces a huge bank of electrical capacitors.

Tora is a Soviet particle-beam weapon being tested at the USSR's equivalent of the United States' White Sands Missile range. It is apparently based on work already completed at Semipalatinsk.

A particle beam weapon (PBW) is another type of DEW, but differs considerably from the high-energy lasers discussed previously.

A PBW accelerates atomic particles—electrons, protons, or neutrons—at the speed of light in very large quantities, creating an energy beam with very high energy density. Its purpose is to destroy targets by concentrating large amounts of energy on a small area of their surface in critical locations, thereby creating thermal effects that are measured (in PBW terminology) in joules per gram.

The unit "joule" is named in honor of James Prescott Joule (1818–1889) who conducted a careful series of measurements with an ingenious variety of methods and established the equivalence among heat energy, mechanical energy, and electrical work. A joule is a measure of the mechanical equivalent of heat and is a constant: 4.185×10^7 ergs per calorie.

Thus, joules per gram indicates how much equivalent heat energy per unit weight is injected into a target by a PBW energy beam.

It does not take very much PBW energy to have military significance. An energy beam input of 125 joules per gram will cause destruction or slumping of nuclear materials in a warhead; an input of 210 joules per gram will melt Uranium-235.

Particle beam weapons have their roots in the experimental devices of nuclear physics where as long ago as 1930 physicists were working on devices to produce a high-energy beam of atomic particles in the laboratory in order to investigate atomic energy. E. O. Lawrence developed the basic linear accelerator in 1931 and went on to modify the principle into the cyclotron, which in turn was further developed into the synchrotron and the synchro-cyclotron. Dr. Luis Alvarez returned to the concept of the linear particle accelerator during the work on the atomic bomb in the US Army Corps of Engineers Manhattan District during World War II.

Certainly, none of these physicists had the slightest idea that their experimental laboratory devices would become the basic components of the most revolutionary weapons concepts in decades.

While a high-energy laser operates on the somewhat esoteric principles of quantum mechanics, a PBW is basically no more complex in its operation than the electron gun of a television picture tube. And, in fact, some types of PBW's operate much the same way as a huge TV picture tube.

The objective is to create a very thin beam with a very high density of atomic particles in it—the thinner the better, and the more particles in it the better. The faster the particles move along the beam, the more particles there will be in the beam over a given period of time—i.e., the higher the "beam particle current" and the faster this current flows, the more energy the beam will contain. The more energy in the beam, the more energy will be transferred to the target in a shorter period of time.

The way in which an atomic particle accelerator works is almost identical to the "gun" which produces and focuses the beam of electrons in a TV picture tube. However, for advanced PBWs, the methods used may differ somewhat because of the greater particle densities demanded.

First, a source of charged atomic particles is required. A TV tube generates electrons (e^-) by "boiling" them off an incandescent wire or filament like that in an ordinary light bulb. Electrons are the easiest charged particles to generate, and there are other techniques that are used to produce positively charged particles such as protons or nuclei of hydrogen atoms that have been "ionized" or stripped of their orbital electrons.

PBW concepts make use of highly advanced particle sources such as autoresonators, inertial homopolar generators, or Dudnikov surface plasma negative ion sources.

Once the charged particles have been created, they are accelerated to very high velocities. In nuclear physics research, the cyclotron invented by E. O. Lawrence in 1932 has been one of the most powerful tools for accelerating charged particles. But a cyclotron requires massive magnets which, at the power levels being considered for PBWs, must be cooled with liquid helium to attain superconducting conditions of extremely low electrical resistance. Therefore, most of the work in PBW development has concentrated on the linear accelerator which, again, is somewhat like the electron gun in a TV picture tube. Charged accelerating anodes essentially give the charged particles in the beam a kick which increases their velocity.

The beam must also be focused, and again this may be accomplished in the same manner as in a TV picture tube using electromagnetic coils or assemblies.

Finally, if the beam is to consist of neutral particles having no charge on them that would cause them to react with the outside environment, the beam passes through a neutralizer before it leaves the PBW.

The techniques used to create, accelerate, focus, and condition the particle beam in the high-energy PBWs under development are not as simple as described. The electron beam that makes a TV picture tube work is a "coarse" beam in PBW terms, is a slow beam, and has very low energy density because it amounts to less than an ampere of current. PBW beams have powers measured in gigawatts (billions of watts) with kiloamperes (thousands of amperes) of currents flowing in them. PBW beam generation requires powers of 10^{11} to 10^{12} watts over a period of 100 nanoseconds (10^{-10} seconds). Obviously, such beam powers require extensive electrical energy sources far beyond those required for a TV picture tube. New devices such as the compensated pulsed alternator to replace huge capacitor banks have been developed, along with homopolar generators. Furthermore, since present materials and techniques may not withstand such high energies continuously or for more than a fraction of a second, many PBW concepts work in the pulsed mode where all these energies are released in a matter of nanoseconds (10^{-9} seconds). Like the early World War II radar sets where the power required would burn out everything in the set if run continuously, the PBWs are pulsed at enormously high energies and then turned off before they have the chance to burn out.

Once the beam leaves the PBW in the Earth's atmosphere, the problems begin to occur, because the high-energy charged beam interacts with the atmosphere and with the magnetic field of the Earth. Although not much is being said these days, Dr. Edward Teller remarked in October 1978, "Striking new advances have recently been made in the [Navy's] Chair Heritage program in obtaining stability in propagating the beam needed for the advanced technology accelerator."

It appears that the Soviet Union has made some technical breakthroughs in the PBW field because the huge facility at Saryshagan appears to be a charged particle beam weapon powered by Pavlovski magneto-cumulative generators. It appears to be a pulsed air-core betatron, which would produce a high density electron beam of an estimated energy of several hundred MeV (million electron volts). Reports in the open literature indicate that more than a megajoule (a million joules) of energy has been applied to the Saryshagan betatron coils. If the Saryshagan beam is also neutralized, the device could operate effectively as a ground-based ABM PBW because only a few hundred MeV are required to kill an incoming ICBM.

From the standpoint of space warfare, however, the PBW appears to be far less effective as a space-to-Earth or Earth-to-space weapon.

Because of the wide difference in the propagation of particle beams in vacuum and in the Earth's atmosphere, it appears most unlikely that the

PBW in any of its forms will be useful across the atmospheric interface. Charged or partially charged PBW beams are not expected to propagate in near vacuum at the level of energies that would make them useful as weapons, at least not to any significant ranges because of the moderate-to-severe dispersion by the beam's own interal electric fields. The potential development of neutron or gamma ray PBWs can be anticipated, but they do not appear to be useful as weapons except at very close ranges because of the inherent divergence of beams that can be produced by any presently conceivable sources.

Thus, insofar as Earth-to-space deployment of a PBW as a weapon against spacecraft or space facilities, the current state of the art indicates that it is infeasible because of the interaction of the beam with the Earth's atmosphere, especially the upper atmosphere.

In the space-to-Earth operational mode, the PBW also appears to be an infeasible weapon against terrestrial structures and vehicles because of the effects of beam interaction with the Earth's atmosphere.

As a space-to-space weapon, however, the PBW appears to be more effective. However, the space PBW will require a neutral beam of lower intensity that must dwell on the target for a longer period of time than a HEL weapon to create damage. This will require highly sophisticated systems for target acquisition, tracking, beam positioning, fire control, beam steering, and damage assessment.

The size and power requirements for a space-based PBW can be determined because the levels of energy required to damage or kill a device in a space-to-space encounter can be calculated. Structural damage by melting can be accomplished at about 100 calories per gram. Slumping or melting of nuclear components occurs at somewhat higher energy inputs. And warhead damage might be accomplished at somewhat higher temperature rises by thermal initiation of high explosive contents. Damage to electronic components can be accomplished by melting solder or by the less-demanding method of simply heating semiconductor elements beyond their acceptable operating tolerances. Finally, in the case of large scale integrated circuits, lattice damage to semiconductor materials in the LSI chips can be caused by moderate heat energy inputs.

If a neutralized proton beam is used and if reasonably deep penetration of target structures is required, an energy input of at least 50 calories per gram would require a beam energy of 250 MeV and a dispersion of about one microradian. Such an accelerator is conceivable with the 1981 state of the art. Problems lie in the beam neutralizer and in the pointing/tracking/fire control system needed to get the beam on target and keep it there long enough to cause damage.

Even with the advent of heavy lift launch vehicles possible in the latter half of the 1980 decade, PBWs are going to remain massive and, because of their weapon performances vis-à-vis various HELs, will probably not be militarily useful until the 1990 decade or beyond. *This neglects any classified breakthroughs that have already occurred but are not reported in the open literature and neglects any potential future breakthroughs or developments that could solve the present problems or improve present performance.*

Linear accelerators capable of generating proton beams are favored for space use over circular accelerators because of the size of the magnets and the need for supercooling them in the circular units. A PBW program known as White Horse is currently being conducted by the US Army at Los Alamos Scientific Laboratories; it was formerly known as Sipapu, an Indian word for "sacred fire." Its accelerator, known as PIGMI, is designed to generate 600–700 MeV pi-meson beams for cancer therapy. PIGMI is 140 meters long with the accelerator occupying about 95 meters of this length. Based on this technology, a 200 MeV PBW accelerator would be about 40 meters long. Power requirements are given to be large—on the order of 400 megawatts in order to produce a PBW beam with 200 MeV energy. Although everything necessary to develop a space PBW now exists, some portions of the system have difficult technical problems to be solved before a PBW can become an effective directed energy weapon to compete with the HEL.

The best technical crystal ball forecasting in 1981 points toward these facts:

1. Proton or electron PBWs for space use are probably infeasible, because anything less than a fully neutralized beam does not appear to propagate well in space. Geomagnetic fields and anomalies in those fields can make both focus and aim extremely difficult because the magnetic fields tend to distort the beam. However, electron beams from PBWs at short range, even reasonably unfocused, may be able to create considerable damage from the electromagnetic pulse phenomenon discussed with respect to nuclear weapon detonations.

2. Neutron or gamma ray PBWs are probably infeasible because with any technology that can be foreseen at this time the beam divergence is far too great. The beam disperses far too much for any lethal effects to be generated at the ranges that a PBW must operate at in space.

3. Neutralized hydrogen PBWs appear to be feasible as space weapons in the 1990 decade and beyond. However, 50 to 100 megawatts of input power are required to deposit 100 calories per gram on a target at a range of 1,000 kilometers. Therefore, very large power sources will be required.

The deployment of PBWs as space weapons will therefore depend greatly on the massive availability of space power. The generation of this power through turbogenerators using liquid rocket propellants is inadequate to meet the needs of a PBW. Massive solar arrays on the PBW support facilities would be required, making it a highly visible and attractive target for HELs and ASATs.

However, should development and deployment of a commercial solar power satellite system proceed in the 1980 decade with construction and operation of the system commencing in the 1990 decade, beamed power from a solar power satellite (SPS) in GEO would make PBWs eminently feasible as space DEWs.

In the meantime, for space use, PBWs are likely to be overshadowed by HELs in the next twenty-year time period. Beyond that point, the continued development of both DEW types leads to the unassailable fact that the direct energy weapon is the primary tactical for use in space.

While any DEW that can be forecast today would be relatively useless against massive mass manipulator weapons such as catapulted lunar rocks or even a cloud of one kilogram rocks launched in rapid succession from a mass driver, the DEW—especially the HEL—promises a radical change in terrestrial military strategy, especially if the DEWs are space-based.

One industrial strategic dynamics study for the US Army in 1978 stated, "This is the only new strategic concept to present itself in a number of decades and the only one which merits the words 'potentially decisive.' "

In 1978, Maxwell W. Hunter III forecast the emergence of this new strategic posture:

The ability to concentrate beams of energy, moving at the velocity of light, so narrow that they overwhelmingly exceed nuclear bomb energy density delivery capability should be recognized as a weapons achievement with implications as shattering as the development of monstrous but uncontrolled energy releases of the nuclear bombs themselves. . . . When lasers are placed in space so that every location on this planet is placed continuously in the target area of a laser battle station, then one has the right to expect truly fundamental changes. It raises the distinct possibility that rapid delivery of nuclear explosives can be prevented by a weapon system that is itself not capable of mass destruction.

In November 1980, Hunter's words were echoed and reinforced by Senator Malcolm Wallop (R-Wyo) of the Senate Select Intelligence Committee:

It makes a great deal of sense to escape from our predicament by doing things which make obsolete the Soviet Union's huge investment in offensive missiles—an investment measured in years of privation for a poor economy. Laser ABM defenses have the twin virtues of making the current Soviet missile force obsolete and doing so in a way that protects the American public and does not threaten Soviet lives.

The Soviet Union's leaders obviously understand this fact as well, for they are working hard on DEW devices of various sorts. The laser threat against orbiting satellites may already be a reality for there are reports that the USSR has positioned at Troitsky (Krasnaya Pahkra) 15 kilometers south of Vnukovo aerodrome near Moscow a HEL capable of destroying US reconnaissance and surveillance satellites in LEO. This is reported to be a carbon-dioxide gas dynamic, electron-beam-pumped laser with a multikilojoule output and a pulse width of between 10 and 100 microseconds.

The United States is concentrating on space-based HEL for the simple reason, as has been presented above, that PBWs appear to be at least ten years behind HELs in terms of technical progress and capability to deploy them as effective space weapons. Since PBWs appear to be ineffective across the atmospheric interface, further development of PBWs would appear to be justified until there is a greater military presence in space to defend space facilities against.

The primary objective of a space-based HEL system would be as an ABM system capable of highly selective targeting. Such a system offers no *direct* threat against any terrestrial military force but does pose the threat of obsolescence to every current ICBM and sea-launched ballistic missile system.

The technology to achieve this ABM system is difficult but apparently attainable in the 1980 decade with the Space Shuttle for the USA and with the SL-4 and SL-9 launch vehicles of the USSR.

The technical problems lie not in the HELs themselves, but in the systems that must be developed to utilize them properly.

For example, the requirements for a space-based ABM system utilizing HELs requires that the ICBM be detected at or shortly after launch, tracked to determine its trajectory, and targeted within 50 seconds of its emergence from its launcher, silo, or submarine. The ICBM should be targeted within this time period while it is still within the Earth's atmosphere, in order to destroy it so that its pieces fall in an ocean short of its target or, hopefully, on the territory of the launching nation. Targeting and destruction of an ICBM after it has reached burnout and is coasting through space to its target will result only in the debris landing around the target; this is a second-best choice to targeting during launch phase and certainly a far superior choice to letting the ICBM and its warheads get through to its targets unhampered.

To do this, the space-based HEL system will have to detect the launching within 50 seconds after ignition, then acquire and track the ICBM within 1 to 5 seconds after detection. The HEL itself will require an output of 5 megawatts with an aperture of 4 meters. The beam width must be 1 microradian or less with beam jitter stabilized to 0.05 to 0.5 microradians. It will require more than a single shot, although a single shot should be designed to destroy an ICBM. This is because current MAD doctrine and emplaced ICBM forces would result in an anticipated salvo of more than 1,000 ICBMs within the span of a few minutes.

The targeting of additional ICBMs is, however, a much simpler problem once the initial ICBM launch is detected and targeted. This is because the Soviet ICBM force is deployed in three major missile fields and because the initial launch salvo will undoubtedly be targeted against the three major USA missile fields in the Dakotas, Arizona, and Arkansas. This means that 1,000 ICBMs must pass through three distinct "windows" or "keyholes" in space. In short, the gross trajectories of the salvo will be known in advance, and it will be easier for the HEL ABM system to target missiles launched after the initial firing.

Assuming a 10 percent efficiency (which is conservative), and assuming that the initial space laser battle station obtains its power from onboard combustion of liquid propellants as a chemical electrodynamic laser, it would require an estimated 5,000 kilograms of propellant to be expended to kill an ICBM. To handle the kill of 1,000 ICBMs would require 5 million kilograms of propellant in orbit.

Obviously, more than one battle station will be required because the range limitation will dictate the use of a low-Earth orbit. To keep enough laser stations in view of the launch fields at all times, a minimum of thirty stations would be required. Each station would require the capability to kill a minimum of fifty ICBMs, allowing for the fact that some stations would be on the other side of the Earth at launch time. This puts the propellant mass per HEL station at 250,000 kilograms, giving a gross weight in the neighborhood of 500,000 kilograms.

This can be carried out with the US Space Shuttle but would require an almost total commitment of all four Space Shuttle Orbiters to the program of deploying the HEL space battle stations in the 1980 decade. Obviously, this ABM system will require vehicles similar to those necessary to deploy the solar power satellite system discussed in Chapters 3 and 4.

The Soviet Union will be in a better position to deploy such a system if and when the big TT-50 vehicle becomes operational with its expected orbital payload of 159,000 kilograms per launch.

However, if a lower ICBM kill number per battle station can be tolerated, the size and mass of the battle station can be reduced. System trade-off studies have probably been made concerning this matter and are probably classified. Smaller laser battle stations may be acceptable if there are more of them, if they can be more efficient, and if they are emplaced in Molniya-type orbits over the USSR.

However, any HEL battle station deployed in LEO must also be considered as a prime target for ASAT weapons. A smaller HEL battle station may therefore be preferable because, if targeted and put out of action, its loss represents a lesser percentage of force loss.

Part of any space-based HEL system must therefore also be dedicated to satellite defense with a mission to take out any enemy ASAT stations or to intercept any ASAT missiles. This is really two separate missions: ASAT and satellite defense.

Once a HEL system acquires the power capabilities for ABM use, the power requirements for ASAT are a minor addition. ASAT capabilities for a HEL demand a power of only 200 kilowatts with a 2.8 meter aperture and a beam jitter of 1 microradian. These requirements can be met by any ABM laser battle station. To defend itself against ASAT missiles, the laser battle station needs the same capabilities as for ABM work: 2 to 5 megawatts power in a beam aperture 4 to 8 meters in diameter with a beam jitter of 0.2 microradians.

A start can be made on laser space battle stations in the 1980 decade. The United States will have to begin such a deployment because of the threat of a Soviet HEL space deployment, or even a Soviet breakthrough in PBW systems which, combined with the TT-50 launch vehicle, would permit a massive Soviet DEW presence and threat in space, if not to Earth targets then to the military satellite systems upon which so much of the USA and NATO military operation depends today and in the future.

With both the USA and the USSR possessing DEW space capability—a forecast that may become reality in 1990 and after—the entire MAD doctrine and all strategic thinking that accompanies the present situation will become obsolete and will have to be replaced with the doctrines of space warfare: the gravity well and atmospheric interface doctrines based ever more firmly on Cole's Panama Theory.

The stage is set, and the forecasts herein are as solid as can be made without engaging in outright prediction. The only factors that might prevent the deployment of DEW systems in space in the next twenty years would be the total political or economic collapse of either the USA or the USSR or a general war involving massive exchanges of thermonuclear warheads between the USSR and the USA or, more probably, between the USSR and the PRC. However, once DEW systems are deployed in space, the general war with thermonuclear exchange becomes nearly impossible.

SPEED, SURPRISE, AND SHOCK: THE SPACE CRUISER

A large space transportation system will probably be developed or evolved in the 1980 and 1990 decades by either the USA or the USSR. Other space-faring nations such as Japan, China, or the Western European Common Market group of nations will undoubtedly participate in one way or another. There is even a potential scenario in which OPEC might provide the capital base for the large space transportation system needed to support an SPS program for the simple reason that an SPS system may be perceived as a natural extension of OPEC's role as a world energy supplier—or as a means to meet competition in the energy area.

This transportation system may be utilized in either of two programs or both. It is required for the construction and operation of a solar power satellite (SPS) system for the production of commercial terrestrial electrical power. Or the transportation system may be developed and placed in operation for military purposes that may involve placing large DEW systems in space and constructing a military SPS system to provide the required power supply.

Regardless of which route is followed in the development of the necessary lift capability to carry out the big space projects that can be accomplished before the end of the twentieth century, the space transportation state of the art as it will develop over the next twenty years contains within it some spin-offs that relate directly to manned military operations in space.

Some of these spin-offs from space-transportation technology will provide new manned military space vehicles capable of carrying out a number of varied missions on either side of or across the atmospheric interface.

Naturally, the development of HLLVs by any nation or by commercial interests serves to improve the capability of national military departments to deploy space military devices of increasing size, power, complexity, and capabilities such as very large and powerful HELs as well as early versions of PBWs. A HLLV capable of delivering 500,000 kilograms of payload to LEO amounts to an important military space logistics vehicle as well as a commercial carrier. Since the same type of vehicle can be used for both military and commercial purposes, it becomes exceedingly difficult for a potential enemy to keep track of the type and ultimate uses of payloads being lofted into LEO. Intelligence operations in the USA now face this identical problem with the ubiquitous Soviet Cosmos satellites since the USSR does not openly differentiate between its military and "peaceful scientific" space operations. In a socialist nation such as the USSR, there is no such division, and in a militant country with an announced long-term goal of world control there can be but one utility for all scientific and technical knowledge: military utility.

The military application of space transportation technology also bears directly upon a series of vehicles which, for want of a better term, can be grouped in the classification of "space cruiser."

The term "space cruiser" was selected in spite of its obvious comic book and science fiction connotations because it describes most accurately the most obvious consequence of the military application of space transportation technology: an armed, manned vehicle capable of cruising and maneuvering at will in space and capable of multirole mission operations on either side of the atmospheric interface.

Some space cruiser types may, however, be strictly deep-space vehicles capable of operating only in the vacuum of space and carrying out extensive forays and sorties anywhere in LEO, HEO, CLS, LSO, and TLS (see Chapter 5).

However, the initial application of space transportation technology will undoubtedly come about in the development of the hypersonic space cruiser capable of both endoatmospheric and exoatmospheric flight. It is possible to forecast this military space vehicle with some accuracy, because it can be based upon NASA Space Shuttle technology and other aerospace technology available in 1981.

In fact, if it is to be operational in the late 1980 decade or even in the early years of the 1990 decade, its design will have to begin soon and be frozen with 1981–1982 technology.

For the past fifty years, every airplane or space vehicle that has been built and operated has been based on technology that was state of the art five to ten years before the initial flight took place. In actuality, every aerospace device in the past half-century has been technically obsolete the instant it first flew, and there is not very much that can be done about the situation because of the amount of time required to design and build a new aerospace vehicle. A new vehicle must always be based on known and proved technology that existed and was available to its designers at the beginning of the design process.

Often, however, state of the art technology improvements can be incorporated into a design as it progresses toward initial flight, and some outstanding designs have been created with considerable technological "stretch" in them—i.e., it has been reasonably easy to incorporate new engines, new equipment, and new technology into the design to improve its performance and/or efficiency. There are outstanding examples of this: the Boeing B-52 bomber (which has been technically stretched out of sheer budgetary necessity), the McDonnell-Douglas F-4 Phantom II fighter-bomber, the Soviet Mikoyan MiG-21 fighter, the Boeing 707 and 727 designs, the Douglas DC-8, the Piper PA-28 and PA-32 Cherokee tribe, the McDonnell-Douglas Thor IRBM booster, which is the core of the Delta launch vehicle, the Korolev R-7 Semyorka ICBM and its SL-4 space booster version, and the Cessna 120/140/150/152 series of training aircraft. These are but a few that come immediately to mind and serve to illustrate the principle of technology stretch that will also be applicable to space vehicles, especially the ones that grow out of Space Shuttle technology.

Some of the theoretical roots of Space Shuttle technology go back to the days of the German work at Peenemünde during World War II and, unknown to most people, the extensive Soviet work on rocket-propelled aircraft dating from the early 1930 decade.

However, the most complete theoretical consideration of the winged hypersonic aerospace vehicle operating across the atmospheric interface was carried out by the Austrian scientists, Dr. Eugen Sänger and Dr. Irene Sänger-Bredt, during World War II. Their work for the Luftwaffe between 1937 and 1944 resulted in the first true space cruiser design, which was far beyond the state of the art of the time in the fields of rocket propulsion, hypersonic aerodynamics, and aerothermodynamics. But the Sänger-Bredt rocket bomber was the true ancestor of the Space Shuttle and the future manned military space cruiser.

The Sänger rocket bomber design was a manned, winged, rocket-propelled bomber with a length of 28 meters and a wing span of 15 meters, small in comparison to the NASA Space Shuttle, which is 37.24 meters long with a wing span of 23.79 meters. Empty weight was calculated at 7,000 kilograms and lift-off weight with maximum propellant and bomb loads would have been in the neighborhood of 100 tons. It was to be launched horizontally from a rocket-propelled sled, capable of flying around the world, delivering a bomb load up to 50 tons (depending upon attack range), and gliding to a horizontal landing on an airfield. The concept was so intriguing to Joseph Stalin in 1945 that the Soviets expended considerable effort trying to locate the Sänger team and proselyte them to the USSR; however, the Sängers were safely ensconced in France following the collapse of the Third Reich.

Why wasn't the Sänger rocket bomber work followed up? First of all, the technology base was not up to the accomplishment of the project and did not reach that point until about 1960; there are some aspects of the program such as the large subsonic rocket sled launcher that may still be beyond the state of art today simply because no effort has been put into solving the problems of such a large and heavy rocket sled. The same can be said for the rocket bomber itself; once the small fission-fusion-fission thermonuclear warhead became a reality, its intercontinental delivery by ICBM resulted in a concentration of research, development, test, and evaluation (RDT&E) in vertical takeoff boosters and nonlifting ballistic warheads.

While the Sänger rocket bomber project was not followed up by either the USA or the USSR following World War II, the USSR concentrated its efforts on ballistic missiles while the USA dithered between ballistic missiles and high-speed manned aircraft. The Sänger rocket bomber was too big a piece of technical pie to swallow.

The United States amassed a great deal of know-how in hypersonic technology with the USAF/NACA X-series of research aircraft, particularly the North American X-15. This found utilization in the Century Series of fighter aircraft—the F-100 through the F-106—and culminated in the Lockheed A-11 (SR-71 or YF-12) Mach-3 aircraft.

The closest the USA came to developing the Sänger rocket bomber was the USAF/Boeing X-20 Dyna-Soar project. This involved a small one-man winged recoverable space vehicle boosted by the Titan ICBM vehicle. Development began in November 1957. The Dyna-Soar had a wing span of about 6 meters and a length of 10.6 meters with an orbital weight of about 6,800 kilograms. A full-scale X-20 Dyna-Soar vehicle was under construction when the USAF canceled the program in 1963. The Dyna-Soar had become a dinosaur with growing complexity and escalating costs. The X-20 Dyna-Soar, built with the technology of 1955, was more than twice the weight of a ballistic space capsule with the same payload capability.

But all of this work laid the foundations for the NASA/USAF Space Shuttle of today. Its own unique development history tends to reinforce the forecast that its technology will follow the trend and serve as the basis for military space vehicles of the next two decades. The basic NASA Space Shuttle space truck concept came originally from the NASA Manned Mars Landing Program studies of the late 1960 decade. The Space Shuttle was designed and its payload sized on the basis of the requirement to establish a manned space station in LEO to launch and support a manned Mars landing mission for 1990. As the whirling knives of politics whittled away at this planned mission during the decade of space disenchantment that followed the Apollo-11 manned lunar landing, the manned Mars landing mission evaporated. The large manned terrestrial space station then disappeared into the limbo created by budgetary reductions for space activities, leaving only the Space Shuttle looking for a job to do.

By the time the first Space Shuttle Orbiter *Columbia* was launched several years behind schedule because of marginal funding that depended upon total technical success, aerospace technology.had progressed to the point where the Space Shuttle's design was obsolete. In short, it could have been done with 1975 technology cheaper and better. In all fairness, it must be said that such a delayed decision probably would have meant a delay in operational readiness of a reusable space shuttle system until 1985.

However, obsolete as the NASA/USAF Space Shuttle is and must be because of the way technology is applied, it is laying the groundwork for the space transportation state of the art of 1980 and 1990 because there is only just so much theoretical study and evaluation that can be done in wind tunnels and with computer simulations. There is only so much work that can be carried out in laboratories under laboratory conditions. There always comes a time when the project manager must gird for battle with the theorists and manage to freeze the design. In the parlance of the early days of White Sands Proving Ground, when scientists would tweak and tune and adjust their scientific rocket payloads and devices, always looking for that extra fractional bit of performance, oblivious to range schedules and the frustrations of engineers and technicians trying to keep a balky rocket ready to launch when conditions were just right, "Get them scientists away from that rocket and *shoot it!*" Theory must be tested in the real world, and new technology must be proved by actual use.

The NASA Space Shuttle is the largest rocket-propelled winged airframe ever to fly; it uses the largest solid propellant rocket engines ever made; and it is the fastest winged vehicle ever flown, more than ten times faster than trisonic SR-11 Blackbird or the bisonic Concorde SST. Space Shuttle technology is proving the concepts of recoverability of very large vehicle elements such as the Solid Rocket Boosters. It is proving the feasibility of hypersonic aerodynamic winged entry into the Earth's atmosphere. It is proving out the technology for protecting a fragile aluminum airframe against the searing 3,000 degrees C. of atmospheric entry. It is proving the new technology of reusable high-performance liquid propellant rocket engines. It is proving the technology of horizontal landing of very large spacecraft. It is proving the unknown technology of total reusability of a major component of a space vehicle: the Orbiter itself.

The Space Shuttle is not a one-of-a-kind experimental research vehicle. Its first seventy-eight flights through calendar year 1986 are booked and scheduled. It is a truck, a hauler, a load lifter, a carrier of goods and equipment. It can haul to and from LEO across the atmospheric interface. This is the most difficult task faced by space transportation technology, because all operations take place across the atmospheric interface and deep within the Earth's gravity well, where large amounts of energy are required to accomplish any change of position.

Out of Space Shuttle technology comes the technology to create the hypersonic space cruiser, strike bomber, and reconnaissance craft.

The aerospace technology of 1980 makes feasible at last the concept of the Sänger rocket bomber and the X-20 Dyna-Soar.

There is a definite military utility in both a LEO space cruiser and a deep-space cruiser, in spite of extensive progress in automation and the outstanding successes of unmanned space vehicles. Again, a quick look at military aerospace history will confirm this contention. In the 1950 decade following the Korean War cease-fire, early work on guided missiles appeared so exciting that general officers of the United States Air Force were seriously speaking of the demise of the human pilot and talking about the new Century Series of fighter aircraft as "manned missiles," guided missiles with a pilot aboard whose only job was to monitor the performance of the automatic equipment. The E-6 fire control system and the early Falcon air-to-air missiles deployed with the Convair F-102 Delta Dagger interceptor did indeed appear to confirm this prediction. But the human being in the "loop" continued to snatch victory from the jaws of random failure of automatic equipment. A quarter of a century later, the pendulum has swung the other way, and the pilot is again the master of the machine in such aircraft as the F-15 Eagle, the F-16, and the A-10 Thunderbolt-II.

The manned-versus-unmanned controversy has racked astronautics since the very beginning as well. The "black box" advocates claimed—and still claim—that unmanned spacecraft can do anything a manned spacecraft can do and many things a manned spacecraft cannot do. The "man in space" advocates continue to point toward the huge success of the manned Skylab program, which would have been a disaster from the start without the human fix-it mechanic in space. The Soviets have no such disabusement; they know that people can do things that machines cannot, and the history of their space program has been one of carefully replacing automatic machines with people.

The place for man in space for military purposes should be as inarguable as the place for man in any terrestrial military situation. War is a human activity; it is not conducted by machines that have no consciousness and hence no concept of the use to which they are put. Machines do what they are designed or programmed to do—and nothing more. An automatic machine left to itself long enough will eventually malfunction and, in spite of safety circuits, tear itself to pieces. It may take hours, or it may take decades, but it will happen, and it has happened even with the highly reliable automatic machines of space. In an activity as varied and nonprogrammable as war or any prelude to war, the automatic responses of a machine can be as disastrous as the fictional triggering of the fully automatic Doomsday Device in the classic film *Doctor Strangelove,* which was not an antiwar film but a tragedy based on the complete human trust of machinery to do what humans had previously done.

General George Smith Patton, Jr., put it:

Weapons are only weapons after all. Wars may be fought with weapons, but they are won by men. It is the spirit of the men who follow and of the man who leads that gains the victory. In biblical times this spirit was ascribed, and probably with some justice, to the Lord. It was the spirit of the Lord, courage, *that came mightily upon Samson at Lehi which gained the victory—not the jawbone of an ass.*

The military purpose of the hypersonic space cruiser is to be able to place a piloted vehicle in any portion of the Earth's atmosphere at any altitude over any territory at will and, insofar as an enemy or potential enemy is concerned, apparently at random times, places, and directions. The capability to do this creates an incredibly complex defensive posture that becomes more complex as the potential enemy becomes bigger in terms of territory. A large volume of airspace must be kept under constant surveillance with rapid reaction time required for identification of any target, tracking the target, attempting to determine the intent of the target, activating defensive systems, aiming, firing, and assessing the result. In time, perhaps advanced technology will be able to take over some of these chores, but the decisions will have to remain with human beings—and making such decisions always requires time. It is possible to penetrate the most intense air defense zones in the world and carry through a mission, as the USAF learned at Hanoi-Haiphong and as the Egyptians and Israelis have learned several times. The Soviets know that it is possible to penetrate the airspace over the so-called Iron Curtain in Europe because refugees flying a variety of aircraft have done it repeatedly. It is possible to penetrate the border airspace of the United States at will because drug smuggling airplane pilots do it every day along the Mexican border and even across the reaches of the Caribbean Sea.

The hypersonic space cruiser can be brought to operational status during the 1980 decade in a crude and early form as an updated X-20 Dyna-Soar, so to speak, utilizing current technology to reduce the vehicle weight and make possible a broad operational envelope by means of modern rocket propulsion. This early space cruiser would use a vertical takeoff rocket boost using recoverable boosters. Launching could take place from any one of a number of reasonably simple launch sites, including silos or horizontal underground enclosures. The vehicle would have the capability to launch at will into any orbit with any orbital altitude, eccentricity, or inclination. It would thus have the capability to appear in enemy airspace at any time from any direction at any velocity and at any altitude with a wide variety of maneuvering capabilities. Velocities could be as high as Mach 20 or more over the target areas at altitudes in excess of 30,000 meters. Modern hypersonic aerodynamics will permit considerable maneuverability even at these high Mach numbers. The vehicle itself would be a small version of the Space Shuttle with delta-shaped wings and would look much like the early X-20 glider except for the refinements permitted by current know-how.

As the technology of space transportation systems progresses and the Mark-1 version of the hypersonic space cruiser gains operational experience, the technology of the horizontal takeoff, horizontal landing space shuttle can be applied to it in the 1990 decade. Thus, the Mark-2 version becomes operational with the ability to take off and land at any airfield. During takeoff and climb-out to semiorbital altitudes up to 150 kilometers, it is totally indistinguishable from a peaceful single-stage-to-orbit (SSTO) launch of a passenger or cargo shuttle—and there will be several of those launches per day in the 1990 decade. It will require an outstanding space surveillance capability to detect, identify, and track these Mark-2 space cruisers because, while operating in the airspace of the launching nation, they will resemble aircraft and spacecraft on everyday peaceful missions of commerce.

The existence of DEW systems as ABM defense in space would appear to negate the utility of such a space cruiser. Indeed, such a space-based ABM defense would seem to offer such a defense. But since the right of passage of spacecraft over national territory was abrogated by all nations of the world with the launch of the Soviet Sputnik-I satellite on

4 October 1957, the question arises regarding the rules of engagement for such a space vehicle. It could be on a mission involving only reconnaissance, and such reconnaissance missions are tacitly accepted today when carried out by unmanned satellites.

Thus, the manned space cruiser in time of peace is invulnerable to ABM systems, because it cannot be determined in advance by a potential enemy whether or not the space cruiser's mission is peaceful. The space cruiser *does* become vulnerable and probably expendable in a war situation once it has performed a strike or ASAT mission. In essence, the manned space cruiser becomes the aerospace analogue of the naval vessel on the high seas in time of peace. In time of war, of course, any vessel of an adversary and even those of neutral nations become legitimate targets.

A hypersonic aerospace craft will certainly provide an excellent infrared signature, however, since it will be dissipating considerable kinetic energy of velocity in terms of aerothermodynamic drag. Like a reentering spacecraft or ICBM warhead, it will be surrounded by a distinctive hot plasma sheath and trailing an obvious ionized tail. Even its launch will be detectable, at least in the rocket-boosted Mark-1 version, by the same systems now emplaced in orbit for detecting ICBM launches. If, however, there is extensive space traffic devoted to commercial purposes, it will be difficult to single out these military space cruiser launches. The Mark-2 HTOHL SSTO version is a separate case, since it will literally fly into space with a different launch signature but still share the same aerothermodynamic characteristics of the plasma sheath and ionized trail during entry into the upper atmosphere. The extent to which military requirements for stealth in hiding or reducing the plasma sheath and ionized trail demand, military technology may develop means for handling this blantant series of signals from the hypersonic space cruiser operating low in the atmosphere.

Techniques exist for greatly reducing both the radar and infrared signatures of aircraft—and therefore also of future spacecraft—by means of stealth measures, the existence of which were leaked from classified sources in 1980 but which could be and were anticipated to some degree by technological forecasters.

In spite of modern radar technology, it is *not* easy to detect and lock onto small airborne targets. Any FAA Air Traffic Controller and most general aviation pilots will confirm that a small aircraft produces a primary radar return that is increasingly difficult to detect as the slant range increases. Modern air traffic control regulations require radar transponders in aircraft flown in tightly controlled airspace, where aircraft detection, identification, and tracking is mandatory for separation purposes. Although almost any material will produce a radar return—the intensity of the return is a function of the difference in dielectric constant between the object and the surrounding environment—some materials obviously produce a stronger return than others. Target shape also has a great deal to do with the strength of the radar return. A corner reflector that directly bounces the signal back to the radar is an example of an optimum shape while a smooth sphere that returns a specular reflection is an example of a nonoptimum shape.

Thus, there will be shapes for the hypersonic space cruiser that will be best for stealth purposes, giving low signal levels to both radar and infrared sensors. Balanced against the requirement for stealth are the aerothermodynamic requirements dictated by performance demands and material characteristics. The hypersonic space cruiser may be a compromise between these requirements, particularly if the requirements are conflicting. On the other hand, military analysis may determine that stealth is of little consequence when compared to the ability of the hypersonic space cruiser to perform with speed and surprise.

Space cruisers need not be launched or operated from the surface of the Earth. Undoubtedly, the first versions will be. However, Mark-3 or later versions of the advanced Mark-2 may be based at or near orbiting military facilities and capable of sorties across the atmospheric interface at any time.

Deep-space cruisers operating totally in space are outgrowths of late twentieth-century space transportation technology, and such military space vehicles would not be anticipated before 1995. Whereas the hypersonic space cruiser working across the atmospheric interface would carry a crew of one or two people, the deep-space cruisers will probably have larger crews along with some passenger and cargo capability as well. While only three types of hypersonic space cruisers have been discussed—Mark-I using VTOHL and recoverable rocket boosters, the Mark-2 using HTOHL and working in the single-stage-to-orbit mode, and the Mark-3 having the capability of being either Earth-launched in the SSTO mode or space based—deep-space cruisers may have as many forms, functions, and sizes as naval vessels today.

In the face of rapid developments in DEW and especially in the technologies required to detect and identify targets, aim and fire the DEWs, and assess damage or effectiveness, the manned hypersonic space cruiser described herein may indeed be an obsolete concept, leaving the basic Sänger rocket bomber as an idea whose time never came at all because technology proceeded in a different direction. It may be considered to be too vulnerable. However, very few weapons have turned out to be totally vulnerable even in the face of highly effective countermeasures. The space cruiser is both a psychological weapon and a strike weapon; both weapons have historically been difficult to defend against. It may be considered to be a cost-ineffective system because existing unmanned devices—surveillance satellites, reconnaissance satellites, DEWs, or even the space catapult—could carry out its tasks at less cost, reduced vulnerability, greater accuracy, and so on.

While this may well be true, neither battles nor wars are decided on the basis of cost effectiveness studies prior to the conflict. In most cases, notably South Viet Nam, studies and analyses turned out to be dead wrong. While it is true that modern infantry tactics demand a light assault rifle capable of automatic fire with high-velocity, small-caliber rounds, the ancient Mauser-type bolt-action rifle is *still* an effective sniper weapon in most tactical situations, although it would probably come out on the losing side of any cost effectiveness study against an M-16 or AK-47. Recent US Army and Marine maneuvers in Egypt have shown the need for a more powerful infantry rifle than the M-16 in desert warfare.

In the case of the space cruiser, the presence of a human being in control of the craft may be the deciding factor as it always has been with any military vehicle or weapon in the past. The manned space cruiser will provide something that has *always* been of value in military operations: mobility for a human warrior capable of using his eyes and brain. No unmanned system, even one with remote visual transmission capabilities, can equal the human being on the spot.

If that were not true, neither the USA nor the USSR would continue to build tactical assault aircraft in the 1981 arena of electronic, automated warfare.

The space cruiser will certainly be a reality of military activity across the atmospheric interface. In 1981, the USSR is probably closer to having the capability with their smaller "shuttle" than the USA with its space truck. In fact, the USSR shuttle may not really be a space station personnel and resupply vehicle at all; it may be a hypersonic space cruiser because, during the 1980 decade, there will be few defense systems capable of countering it as a weapon.

RULES OF ACTION AND ENGAGEMENT

What response should be invoked for various perceived military actions in space?

And what would be considered to be "military action" against a facility in space?

Should the launch of any space vehicle from the Earth be challenged, or should the vehicle be challenged only upon an approach to a space facility? If the object is approaching, what are appropriate measures to take to insure it is not an attack?

Questions such as these and others arise in connection with space warfare because they have come up in the past in military confrontations on Earth—on the land, on the sea, and in the air.

This has led to the development of "rules of engagement," which are planned and usually announced responses to military threats or military actions that suggest to the potential adversary a methodical and upward escalation of possible responses. Rules of action and engagement also serve to provide a unit commander with guidelines for action, response, and reprisal, if any.

Although an uninformed person might believe that "all's fair in love and war," this is certainly not true in the case of war (and usually in love as well) where, for centuries, basic rules have been worked out and codified until today they are part of that large body of carefully structured relationships known as international law. Over the years, conferences on various aspects of war have been held at Geneva, Vienna, and the Hague, which have resulted in a highly structured series of definitions and rules of behavior for periods of transition to war, during war, and following cessation of hostilities. Although in most cases there is no international enforcement action possible against a nation that violates a convention of international law, most nations assiduously conform to international principles—or try to—because it is easier to do so than to flaunt them. It is also usually to the benefit of a nation to adhere to the principles and codes of international law. There have been some obvious exceptions to this, including some that are still fresh in many people's minds. But even the biggest and most barbaric general war ever fought, World War II, was conducted within the bounds of international law *in most cases*; propagandists at the time and some historians since then have emphasized the exceptions for reasons having to do with morale during the conflict and ideology afterward.

Rules of action and engagement in space activities can be drawn up based on what has been learned thus far regarding rules of the road at sea, the rules of war, and the generally accepted rules of action during peace and war here on Earth where, contrary to the belief of many people, real progress *has* been made over the past two hundred years. Space rules of action and engagement can also be worked out by keeping firmly in mind the principles of celestial mechanics—how objects move in space—along with the gravity well and atmospheric interface doctrines.

Rules of action and engagement can be formulated for three potential categories of activity: (a) that which takes place in a time or period of peace, (b) that which occurs during a perceived transition from peace to war, and (c) that which occurs during war.

It is possible, even in these days of the MAD doctrine and the threat of instant general warfare that is announced by the mass launching of a nuclear missile strike, to consider these three phases because no war to date has commenced without a transition period during which a significant number of definite signals was generated and transmitted indicating escalation to a wartime situation. Only when one adversary ignored the signals, misinterpreted the signals, or attempted to bluff through in spite of the signals has a war occurred. With 20/20 hindsight, students of war and the causes of war know that every war has been preceded by a transition to war.

This is true even in the infamous case of Pearl Harbor had anyone (a) bothered to analyze Japanese military publications prior to 1941, (b) given credence to Japanese communications which had been decoded and were available to the military commanders from the highest level to the theater level, and (c) believed the defense surveillance reports of the incoming first wave of Japanese aircraft detected in ample time by American radar on Oahu.

Even the Seven Days War in the Middle East had its escalating prelude, which the Egyptians chose to ignore in 1967.

Any surprise attack is preceded with numerous overtures, which can be recognized by most diplomats and easily detected by any astute military intelligence and command staff. It is usually the political or military leaders who choose to ignore or degrade the importance of the escalation because of wishful thinking, preoccupation with other matters, the Ostrich Syndrome, or misplaced belief in their military invulnerability. Time after time after time in history, wars and battles have started and gone to their ultimate conclusions not only because of lack of adequate C^3I (command, control, communications, and intelligence) but also failure or refusal of leaders to believe the data obtained by C^3I activities.

It is only fair to observe that the political and military leaders are not alone in this sort of behavior. It also happens in the field as well because of the "haze of battle," which field commanders know only too intimately. It results in failure of C^3I there because of confusion, hesitation, poor leadership, or assignment of low priority to the information. For example, the failure of Confederate General R. S. Ewell to follow the orders of General Robert E. Lee at Gettysburg on 1 July 1863 and to occupy Cemetery Hill "if possible" probably cost the Confederate forces the battle and, ultimately, the war itself. There was a failure of command on the part of Lee by including the phrase "if possible" in the order, there was a failure of nerve or will on the part of Ewell, who elected not to take the risk in spite of the fact that Union forces had been routed, sustaining more than 50 percent casualties, and had not rallied on Cemetery Hill.

Military failure in the field cannot always be blamed on the field commanders, either, for often the troops themselves, whether they are green or seasoned, have time after time in history panicked, broken, and run. Most Americans who were involved would just as soon forget Kasserine Pass. There have been other routs since that time, but to some extent those that took place in South Viet Nam, for example, are not discussed. (They should be; that is the only way to prevent some of them from happening in the future—and there will always be similar military incidents in the future.)

This is only one reason why discipline and morale are of such great importance in military operations of *any* sort—and the same will be true of space as well.

Insofar as space rules of action and engagement are concerned, many aspects of the current law of the sea, law of the air, and law of war will have to be observed. Initially—during the 1980 decade, for example—many of the rules of action and engagement in space will be unwritten but tacitly observed. However, as nations and corporations begin to assemble and operate space systems and facilities that involve huge capital investments, they will be forced to reduce the risk of these facilities becoming military targets because of perceived threat, and they will have to adopt rules of the road in space to protect themselves.

The development of these rules will require time, considerable effort, and the work of people who are experts and professionals in international law. However, it is not presumptuous here to suggest basic rules of action and engagement based upon the discussion thus far, some knowledge of celestial mechanics, and a consideration of the question "What can be tolerated and what can be done if it cannot be tolerated?"

The proposition can be applied equally well to the three potential categories of activity: peacetime, transition to war, and war. Suggested rules can be worked out for all three and also for general utility in each category as well as for Earth-to-space, space-to-space, and space-to-Earth actions. Then, once rudimentary rules have been stated, it is possible to look at the requirements for their implementation: the weapons or other systems needed to make them workable. No attempt can be made at this time relating to the time-phasing of the systems needed for implementation, but it can be assumed that the 1990 decade will see the deployment of weapons and systems discussed thus far.

In the peacetime mode, one is concerned with the protection of one's national space facilities and vehicles primarily against unconventional warfare techniques such as terrorism, about which more will be said later. One is also concerned that activities in space will not be viewed or construed by another nation as being hostile and a prelude to a sneak attack. Careful steps must also be taken to preserve those elements of national sovereignty as well as personal property that will exist in space.

The peacetime mode in space is analogous to a social affair to which everyone, including those who may not like one another very well, are invited and interact. Protocols, etiquette, and formalities amount to a structured code in which everyone knows what is expected of him and what response to make to anything. They amount to social lubricants that reduce friction and permit the activity to proceed with a minimum of frictional social heat being generated and with no hostilities involved. Any reader who has been to any international meeting or social affair will recognize this immediately. Anyone who has watched the highly structured conduct of the Olympic Games will sense that there is a great deal to be said for the rules, conventions, protocols, and formalities behind the activities.

It is obvious that, in the peacetime mode, a standard rule that is derived from today's air transport scene will be implemented for the Earth-to-space area at launch sites: physical security measures and careful screening of all passengers and cargo at the launch site prior to lift. This might be nothing more elaborate than a cyclone fence around the area and inspection of passengers and cargo by X ray, metal detection, and other security techniques. The rationale for such security measures will undoubtedly be an extension of the current rationale: to protect facilities, vehicles, and people against acts of terrorism, hijacking, or psychotic behavior.

Another rule will also have to be adopted, and it will require at last a definition of "airspace." Current international convention requires permission in order to transit national airspace. It is quite possible that some Earth-to-orbit space vehicles, shuttles, HLLVs, and the like may climb into space or descend from LEO while passing through the national airspace of another nation. As such, according to the current definitions used by the International Congress of Aviation Organizations (ICAO), by which all international air commerce is conducted, an ascending or descending space vehicle passing through national airspace will require permission to do so. But *nothing* is said about where "airspace" ends. This matter has lain unresolved for a quarter of a century since the Soviet Sputnik-I satellite technically violated the airspace of most nations on the Earth possessing territory in a band between 65.1 degrees north and south latitudes over which Sputnik-I passed in its orbit. All nations thus involved have therefore tacitly agreed to the passage of spacecraft over their territory. But at what altitude does this tacit consent take effect?

A firm number for the upper limit of national airspace cannot depend upon such intangibles as the limit of altitude above which military action cannot be taken against a nation; we have seen that a space-to-Earth offensive military action can be initiated from the Moon using a lunar surface catapult to launch lunar rock. Suggestions have been made that the upper limit of "airspace" is that altitude at which a vehicle can no longer sustain itself against gravity by means of aerodynamic lift. This is technically meaningless since it depends totally upon the design of the vehicle, upon possible new aerodynamic technology yet to be discovered and developed, and upon the dynamics of the atmosphere itself—the upper atmosphere moves up or down depending upon season, time of day, latitude, and solar activity. In drafting any sort of national or international code, one must *always* put firm numbers on limits if possible, even if they are somewhat arbitrary, with the idea of updating the code later as more data becomes available. Since the military vulnerability rationale and the aerodynamic lift rationale are both almost meaningless in light of current and forecastable technology, a firm number *with tolerances* must be adopted.

An altitude of 100 kilometers above mean sea level (100 kilometers MSL) plus-or-minus 2 kilometers is suggested as an upper limit to national airspace. Environmental conditions above this altitude are almost 100 percent space equivalent in terms of aerodynamics. The United States currently awards "astronaut" ratings to persons who have piloted craft above 50 miles (80.6 kilometers) altitude. 100 kilometers is considered herein to be the upper limit of the EA zone and the lower limit of the LEO zone. It is a number that can be preprogrammed into the computers of surveillance and tracking radars both on the ground and in space. The tolerance of 2 kilometers takes into account that there are errors in altitude reporting systems, radar systems, and human systems. It could be expanded to a greater tolerance of, say, 5 kilometers without undue concern because it is *not* a firm interface.

Therefore, a rule of action in the peacetime mode could be adopted, stating that ICAO rules of airspace apply to all space vehicles when operating below an altitude of 100 kilometers.

In the space-to-space category, one is concerned about two things: (a) identification of objects, and (b) closing rates and minimum approach ranges.

UN conventions now require the registration of all objects launched into space, but not identification of these objects. There are already more than 100 satellites in various locations in geosynchronous Earth orbit and thousands more in other, lower Earth orbits. By the year 2000, the space traffic in the Earth-Moon system will increase dramatically—if not for commercial reasons, then certainly for military purposes. Identification of the object by means of a radio beacon, radar beacon transponder, or voice response in the case of manned vehicles will be absolutely necessary to reduce the level of threat. Currently, all aircraft entering the airspace of the United States—and most other nations as well—must have prior permission, operate according to a prefiled flight plan, identify themselves in flight, and respond to voice challenges on predetermined radiotelephone frequencies. If not, unidentified aircraft are intercepted by military aircraft and face the possibility of being attacked. Positive identification of the thousands of aircraft currently in the air has not been a problem either to operators of the aircraft or to air traffic and defense personnel on the ground.

(True, a large number get through the US Air Defense Identification Zone or ADIZ, carrying drugs or other contraband. But no military aircraft carrying a bomb has made it through. The ADIZ requirements of the United States in 1956 were *extremely* tight, but the threat of attack by bombers did not materialize, and the restrictions were partially lifted.)

Positive identification of space vehicles by radar beacon transponder and, in the case of manned vehicles, also by voice communication should prove no insoluble problem *technically*. On the political front, it should be well accepted by all since it benefits every nation or organization having facilities in space or desiring security against terrorists.

The commander or manager of a space facility, whether it is manned or unmanned and whether he is stationed in the facility or at a remote site, will not want *any* object, identified or not, to approach his facility within a specified distance *or* with a closing velocity that would cause severe destruction if the object impacted the facility.

This is analogous to the limits of territorial jurisdiction regarding ocean frontiers, which is exercised and enforced by all ocean-fronting nations of the world. The basis for the early territorial jurisdiction limit of 3 miles (4.84 kilometers) was precisely the same as the basis for considering such a concept for space facilities: military security. The 3-mile limit was set on the basis of the range of the cannon of the day. The same rationale holds true for space facilities. However, a firm range limit and closing rate cannot be established for all space facilities because of the gravity well doctrine.

Space facilities in LEO are deeper in the Earth's gravity well and are more susceptible to ASAT assault than facilities in HEO or CLS. They will also have less time to deal with an approaching threat. Depending upon the value—military or commercial—of the facility, the nation, or the organization responsible for it may establish approach limits of tens of kilometers; any object on a potential rendezvous or collision course would have to identify itself prior to entering the zone of vulnerability. In LEO space, closure rates may be high at the range limit, but there would be a preannounced requirement that, say, within 5 kilometers the closing rate should not be more than 500 meters per second and, at 1 kilometer, closing rates higher than 20 meters per second would not be permitted without retaliation.

The higher on the gravity well the facility is, the closer its range limit could be, because sensors would be able to detect any potential approach or collision at a greater range. However, closure rates might have to be the same since the reason for closure rate limits is to allow the station to react to defend itself against being struck by the approaching object.

Basically, range limits are going to depend upon many factors, the least of them being the distance at which an approaching object could be effectively reached by station defensive systems.

Closure rate limits will depend upon both the reaction time of the defensive systems and the closing velocity/distance relationship. Rendezvous—which means a closure rate of zero at a range of 1 kilometer or less—and docking—which is direct linking of two space objects at near-zero closure rate and zero range—will have definite upper limits on range/rate, probably at different ranges, depending upon the station and its location in the Earth-Moon system.

The space-to-Earth category is considerably simpler *if* the upper limit of ICAO national airspace can be set. The major space-to-Earth threat is space-launch ballistic weapon attack—rocks or warheads—because ICBM attack is an Earth-to-Earth threat with different rules of engagement. Therefore, a nation has the right under international law to defend itself against any unknown threat in its airspace. The rule of action in this regard is that the entry time and trajectory of any space vehicle should be announced in advance if it would violate the national airspace of another country and permission should be received for the flight of a space vehicle through national airspace. The exception to this rule would be an announced emergency or "Mayday" radio transmission.

There are some general rules of action that will apply to all three categories. One of these should be the general principle of freedom of movement in space subject to the existing rules of action and engagement discussed above: identify, observe approach ranges and rates, and do not violate airspace without prior permission unless an emergency exists.

And, in peacetime, facility commanders and managers along with space vehicle captains should be permitted retaliation with utmost discretion against any hostile activity directed against them. They will have to deal with criminals, hijackers, and terrorists according to the laws of their respective nations in accordance with the 1976 UN registration convention, which established the principle that national laws have jurisdiction over any space object or activity within it if the object is enrolled on that nation's space register.

Similar operational rules are implemented today in air and sea commerce by means of national traffic control centers backed up by radar and other detection and tracking systems and by manned cutters or interceptors for inspection of suspects or unidentifieds. There are also defensive weapons to provide protection in the final analysis, although these are normally not on alert during peacetime.

These rules of action and engagement will require the eventual

establishment of Space Traffic Control (STC) Centers by national governments with military and/or commercial activities in space. This, in turn,
will require either an expansion of ICAO into the space area (considered
unlikely in light of the past history of aeronautical organizations extending jurisdiction into space) or the establishment of an international
body charged with the development of international rules for astronautics. Nationally, the same pathway will undoubtedly be followed in
light of the history of aeronautics in the United States.

In 1926, the United States government officially recognized aviation as a national activity, and Congress passed the Air Commerce Act,
signed into law by President Coolidge on 20 May 1926, a year before Lind-
bergh took off for Paris. The act created a new function for the Department of Commerce to license aircraft and airmen, to establish and enforce
air traffic rules, and to collect and disseminate aeronautical information.
Over the years, the Aeronautics Branch of the Department of Commerce
evolved into the Federal Aviation Administration of the Department of
Transportation. Part of this evolution was the development of air traffic
control centers. These were initially set up and operated by the individual
commercial airlines in the United States, but they were taken over by what
was then known as the Civil Aeronautics Administration, predecessor of
today's Federal Aviation Administration, in the 1930's. Today, there are
twenty-two FAA Air Route Traffic Control Centers in the contiguous forty-
eight states, four hundred airport control towers, and more than three
hundred Flight Service Stations, which provide information on weather
and route conditions to more than 94 million individual flights per year
(1979) of which only about 5 million were commercial airliners. With
108 long-range radar stations, the air traffic control centers keep track of
more than 250,000 flights per day.

By the beginning of the twenty-first century, space traffic will be
nowhere near that level of activity, but will have reached an activity level
where the interests of both safety and defense will demand that each
spacefaring nation establish its own STC centers for its own airspace,
space facilities, and traffic control. As with the air traffic control centers
of 1981, these STC centers will be in constant communication with one
another by voice, teletype, video, and computer data exchange. They
will know where space vehicles under their national registry are at all times
and will therefore be able to insure that their national responsibility for
liability is under control.

It is as unthinkable to consider future space activity without such
STC centers as it is to consider aviation without similar control and reporting functions or of seaborne traffic without the Coast Guard and its
counterparts in other countries.

In the transition-to-war or alert mode, the rules of action and engagement are changed somewhat, because of the heightened interest in military security.

In the Earth-to-space category, it is likely that the nation on alert will require that all vehicles launched and expected to exit the Earth's atmosphere at 100 kilometers identify themselves and reveal their flight intentions either prior to lift-off or immediately thereafter and prior to reaching 100 kilometers altitude. Action in this case would involve an escalating series of moves beginning with an intercept of obvious spacecraft for identification, rendezvous, and boarding if manned, or attack and destruction if the identity is established as an ASAT or potentially hostile spacecraft. This, of course, could escalate toward war itself since either the unannounced launch of the unidentified spacecraft would be considered as an act of war and so announced in advance or the launching nation would retaliate in an escalatory fashion following the possible destruction of its spacecraft.

In the space-to-space category, the alert mode is an especially tense one since attack can, under these conditions, be expected. The nation on alert would announce in advance the minimum approach distance for all its facilities, the maximum approach rate permitted, the absolute requirement for advance positive identification, and permission to approach. It would be announced that violators would be subject to intercept, boarding, and/or attack and destruction. In fact, the nation on alert would announce that *all* unknown or suspect space objects would be subject to intercept and/or destruction.

Since the rules of action and engagement are, by nature, escalatory as full wartime mode is approached, the nation on alert could also insist that all vehicles approaching a space facility must carry an approach pilot licensed and identified by that nation before the vehicle approached within a given distance. The pilot, operating much like the pilot of an oceangoing vessel making port, would either accompany the vehicle from its point of origin or be put aboard by an inspection cutter outside the zone of sensitivity of the facility.

A similar escalation of rules of action and engagement would be required for any space-to-Earth operations as well. The nation on alert could announce that all space objects approaching Earth and/or on an atmospheric entry trajectory must broadcast identification and intended entry corridor subject to engagement by ABM systems.

There is an additional general rule of engagement in the alert mode: the nation on alert should make it publicly known that any space object engaged in electronic countermeasure (ECM) activity would be presumed hostile and intercepted and/or destroyed. In an alert situation,

ECM activity could be considered as action preparatory to a strike.

The rules of action for space-vehicle captains and facility commanders and managers would be escalated into permission not only to retaliate but to take counteraction as well. There is a subtle difference between retaliation and counteraction. Retaliation is technically a response with force no greater than that received, while counteraction is response with as much force as necessary to insure the continued safety and security of the command.

In the actual war mode, there are two operational submodes for rules of action and engagement: defensive and offensive.

In the defense submode, all rules of action and engagement are predicated on the defense and protection of facilities and vehicles. Different responses are called for in the face of different enemy actions.

The defensive war submode requires preclearance prior to the movement of any vehicle, friendly or neutral, along with assignment and use of special identification and radio codes—encrypted and coded in the case of friendly vehicles and perhaps subtly encoded in the case of neutrals. While the general rule is that all traffic is subject to control—a factor which contravenes the accepted terrestrial practice of freedom of the high seas for neutrals even during wartime—the extreme vulnerability and great capital investment of space facilities, especially in LEO, would require that the concept of freedom of movement in space be abrogated in time of war.

In general, all nonessential friendly commercial and scientific traffic would be curtailed or prohibited, and all C^3I facilities commandeered. Under the right of angary, all commercial vehicles and/or facilities would also be commandeered.

In the offensive submode of open and declared war, the rules of engagement are also simple: Any and all vehicles, facilities, and/or objects in space would be (a) attacked to disable them or to render them useless to the enemy, (b) seized for use or to deny enemy use, and/or (c) destroyed if it is not practical to disable or seize them. It would have to be an announced policy that all noncleared, unidentified traffic launched from Earth or moving in space would be considered hostile and would be fired upon and destroyed or intercepted and seized. This would apply to Earth-to-space, space-to-space, and space-to-Earth traffic. It would also apply to the vehicles, facilities, and objects of a neutral nation considered to be benevolent to the enemy. (By definition, a benevolent neutral nation is one not technically or legally at war but supplying matériel to the enemy; the United States was a benevolent neutral in both World Wars before entering the conflict.)

Whether or not this is a complete and thorough listing or consideration of the rules of action and engagement for space activities ranging from the peacetime mode to full wartime status remains to be seen. Its consideration was made within the strictures of the Earth-Moon theater of operations and probably will not serve when applied to larger theaters such as the Solar System.

But it is a start.

IMPLEMENTING THE RULES OF ACTION

Working out the rules of action and engagement for space military activities is one activity; establishing means to ensure that they are capable of being observed and enforced is something else.

In any area of human endeavor, it is impractical to adopt and announce laws, rules, and regulations unless there are also capabilities to observe and enforce compliance with them by some form of coercion. The imperatives "Thou shalt" and "Thou shalt not" become merely advisory in nature unless some authority coerces compliance and has the means to do so.

Moral measures to insure compliance are perhaps the most powerful and are the easiest to police, but they are difficult to establish. They require an enormous effort over a period of years to bring to an acceptable level of effectiveness by educational means that may include propaganda. Moral measures are highly effective, as history has shown. However, on the international scene, moral pressures for compliance to international law are often unreliable, because they may be subject to counterpressures from national self-interest or cultural factors.

This is particularly true in the case of civilizations, cultures, and nations that are in a descendancy and are therefore the underdogs at any given historical moment, as C. Northcote Parkinson has pointed out in his book *East and West.* He goes on to observe that the habits engendered by a feeling of inferiority to an alien but dominant civilization included untruthfulness, cunning, dignity, corruption, patience, and mute obedience to authority. Parkinson—who is an outstanding historian although most people know him only for his humorous work, *Parkinson's Law*—goes on to say that these traits were much the same as those found in medieval Europe. European people in that historical period were habitually untruthful, hence the practice of making witnesses give testimony under oath. The point here is that total dependence upon moral measures to ensure compliance to laws, rules, and regulations is risky, especially when dealing with people having an inferiority complex, which may lead them into a war which they believe will make them the superior people. It is also true when dealing with a semiparanoid culture such as the Russians have lived in for a millennia, a factor which is reflected not only in their overt actions but also in the very language they speak.

Since all men may be created equal but may not have the opportunities to develop equally because of cultural, economic, ideological, and other social differences, military and paramilitary (police) forces exist to enforce compliance by physical coercion when all other measures have failed.

Thus, even in the peacetime mode, military and paramilitary measures and weapons will be necessary to insure compliance with the rules of behavior and action upon which the general security and safety of both the terrestrial and the space segments of future activities depend.

In the peacetime mode, these measures and weapons need not be onerous, oppressive, or overly threatening to the general peace any more than the presence of a corporate security guard or the local policeman on patrol is in the United States. (Visitors from other nations and cultures are often astounded by internal American police activities. Some are amazed at both the lack of visibility of the American military and the polite behavior of most of the American police officers. Some are equally amazed at the sight of armed American police officers. Most cannot understand the American policy of police and military subservience to civilian political authority.)

Structuring the organizations and weapons for implementation of the space rules of action and engagement will necessarily be widely different in various spacefaring nations such as the United States, the USSR, the PRC, Japan, and Western Europe. Regardless of the organizational arrangements, however, certain basic weapons and other systems will be required regardless of the nation or culture involved.

In the peacetime mode of activity, these are relatively simple.

Launch site, in-flight, and space facility physical security against such unconventional warfare threats as sabotage, terrorism, and hijacking (basically peacetime threats) can largely be maintained by systems as simple as strong chain-link fences around the launch sites, restricted access to critical areas, prior clearance for admission to sensitive locations, positive identification of workers on the site or in the facility, physical inspection of cargo and passengers, and random patrolling of facilities. The techniques for doing these are well-developed today and can easily be extended to cover space activities on Earth. While it is true that an occasional person slips through the screening, such failures of physical security measures have been largely the fault of the people involved in making the system work and not the fault of the system itself.

Other areas involved with physical security measures have been developed to a high level by the USAF Strategic Air Command. One of these is the concept of "no lone zone"—i.e., no person is allowed to be alone in critical areas and is always accompanied by another person. USAF has also perfected the techniques involved in carrying out critical activities in the "no lone zones" so that any critical function is performed simultaneously by more than one person. Additional progress has been made by the Department of Defense in its human reliability programs, which are testing and psychological profiles and evaluation methods developed over the past quarter of a century to continually screen and monitor those personnel involved in military command and control activities and those which have access to or can control nuclear weapons.

Such screening of personnel in addition to physical security measures must also be brought into play for the security of the various STC centers, in addition to the considerable amount of training given to individual controllers in the centers.

It has been emphasized that STC centers will be an absolute requirement for future space operations not only for general safety but also to reduce perceived military threats and improve security. The embryonic beginnings of the STC centers of the future now exist in the US Mission Control Centers at Johnson Space Center in Houston, Texas; in the North American Air Defense Command (NORAD) operation beneath Cheyenne Mountain in Colorado, in the Strategic Air Command operations center under Offutt Air Force Base near Omaha, Nebraska, and even in the Soviet mission control center in Kaliningrad. Many of these C^3 facilities, especially those already involved with space flight, will undoubtedly evolve into the initial STC centers later in the 1980 decade.

It is almost imperative for international security that the various STC centers be in constant communication with one another via hot-line communications link if necessary. Obviously, there will be a greater volume of communications between some STC centers than others, and one would not suspect at this time that the Soviet STC center would engage in open continuous communication since they have not opted to do so in the past except during the Apollo-Soyuz Test Mission in 1975.

Allied to the complex of STC centers will be the requirements for both Earth-based and space-based systems for detection, identification, and tracking (DIT) applied to space vehicles. Although an international convention will undoubtedly be required to implement standards for frequencies of voice communication and radar transponder beacons, identification codes for both voice and beacon use, and the other operational rules elaborated in the previous chapter, and although such an international agreement may not be forthcoming before the 1990 decade, there will be joint international agreements of an informal nature in this regard long before the international rules are formulated and incorporated into accords that are binding on all spacefaring nations and organizations. This is to be expected, because international concordances have historically followed the development and implementation of national standards and bilateral agreements, expanding the expertise and experience gained in these early activities into the final international conventions.

However, the technical means to implement the DIT systems already exist, and no great technical breakthroughs or developments are needed to make a space DIT system a reality. In the USA alone, the USAF SpaceTrak and SPADAT systems are currently tracking thousands of primary targets in space without identification beacons. Some of these objects, whose orbits and radar return signatures are computer recognized and filed for future identification, are as small as metal interstage clamps 1 meter or so long and 2 centimeters wide. NORAD keeps track of thousands of space objects and even debris, so that these signals can be separated from any possible ICBM warheads or the warheads of the Soviet Fractional Orbit Bombardment System (FOBS), if and when it is deployed.

Even in the peacetime mode, however, military systems will be required in space activities to ensure compliance with the rules of action and engagement as well as the international rules of the road.

No nation will be willing to risk expensive and complex space facilities in the face of the existence of ASAT systems that include ASAT missiles as well as DEW units whose range and power will increase with time. Therefore, existing C^3I facilities in space will not only be continued in use but also upgraded and "hardened" against potential attacks.

There is no question that space-based satellite defense (SATDEF) systems will be deployed on or near critical facilities to protect them against threats arising from unconventional warfare activities as well as surprise attacks and mistakes. (Mistakes do happen. Murphy's Law is still valid. A malfunction of a critical system in a friendly approaching space vehicle could cause a damaging impact with a space facility, for example.)

The SATDEF system would include not only short-range missile defenses and defensive DEW devices, but also the defensive version of the manned space cruiser, the space cutter that is analogous to today's Coast Guard cutter.

The space cutter would be a lightly armed manned space vehicle capable of making rendezvous with a space object for purposes of external inspection and, in the case of manned vehicles in trouble, of docking and boarding as well. There may be several versions of the space cutter. For operations deep in the Earth's gravity well, the cutter will require the capability for large velocity changes (delta-vee) and extreme maneuverability. Higher on the gravity well, much less delta-vee capability will be required, but, on the other hand, longer sortie times may be required with life support consumable masses offsetting the LEO cutter's large propellant mass for large delta-vee capabilities required in LEO operations.

How will it be possible to know that a space cutter is not an offensive space cruiser? The analogy between the seagoing cutter and naval destroyer/frigate holds true here as well. While one can mount torpedoes or even antiship missiles on a Coast Guard cutter, it is difficult to equip it with long-range strike aircraft or a large-caliber naval gun capable of long-range bombardment because of the small size of the cutter. The space cutter will be a smaller space vehicle than a space cruiser. Its radar signature will indicate its size, and to some extent, its shape by means of radar signature analysis. While it might be capable of carrying long-range offensive missiles in a concealed manner, the space cutter could not mount a long-range offensive HEL because of the size of the optical elements, beam generator, heat rejection apparatus, and power supplies required by a HEL large enough and powerful enough to reach targets at ranges of more than a few kilometers with any degree of damaging irradiance.

The same rationale holds true of SATDEF for space facilities. In possessing a capability to defend itself against space vehicles, ASAT, and other objects that breach its announced minimum range zone or that approach faster than the announced maximum permissible closure rate, a space facility will sport short-range defensive weapons in the form of missiles and HELs.

But how can it be proved that these weapons are defensive and not intended to attack other space facilities or the space vehicles of other nations?

Missiles, which are basically "hard kill" weapons, are almost last-resort devices and are launched to make a positive kill of an oncoming target. As such, they will probably be high-acceleration rocket-propelled guided missiles with reasonably high final velocities. They could be viewed by others as potential offensive weapons because their velocities might be high enough to permit them to reach other orbits or to deorbit for an Earth entry and surface strike. However, several design features would limit the effective range of high-velocity, hard-kill defense missiles. One of these would be an automatic self-destruct if a target had not been intercepted within a given period of time, and the other would be the lack of design features that would permit atmospheric entry. In any case, the size of a defensive missile capable of reaching out to as much as 10 kilometers from its space facility would be quite small. The size as well as the velocities and trajectories of SATDEF missiles would be almost immediately evident to the DIT and SATDEF systems of other nations. If a SATDEF missile or salvo did not intercept the target and did not self-destruct outside the facilities sphere of sensitivity, then the SATDEF systems of other facilities, perhaps those under the control of other nations, would be justified in either intercepting the wild-running missiles with their own missiles or by targeting them with their DEW weapons.

However, to truly protect itself, a space facility should not rely entirely on missiles for SATDEF because missiles are like ammunition; in any type of saturation attack, sooner or later the ammo runs out in the defending facility. Therefore, space facilities will also mount short-range defensive HELs for added protection.

Although offensive high-energy lasers were discussed at length earlier, it is quite feasible to build a less-powerful HEL with restricted range that would be used solely for space facility defense purposes. Such a HEL would obviously be a defensive HEL because of its size and because of the size of the power supplies available to it.

The laser performance equations are very simple because they are based on the well-known and totally unclassified principles of optics. It is no great problem to determine the basic characteristics of a defensive HEL. Short-range defensive space HELs could be built and deployed with 1980-decade technology.

A defensive HEL mounted on or near a space facility between now and the year 2000 will have an aperture of 4 meters or less and a power of 10 megawatts or less.

An early SATDEF HEL would probably have an aperture of 4 meters, the same diameter as the NASA Space Telescope scheduled to be launched by Space Shuttle Flight STS-16 on 12 January 1984. A 4-meter HEL operating at a power level of 2 megawatts as a gas-dynamic laser using mercury-fluoride would emit radiation with a wavelength of 0.55 micrometers in the visible portion of the spectrum. Taking into account quite conservative numbers for optical performance, beam jitter, beam turbulence, and diffraction effects, and considering that an irradiance of 40 watts per square centimeter will melt aluminum, this 1980 decade defensive space HEL will provide this level of irradiance out to a range of 2 kilometers. If an object is targeted earlier during its approach and irradiated at a greater range as the range closes, the HEL will probably be effective out to approximately 5 kilometers. Based on unclassified data concerning HELs in 1981 and with modest projections of development during the 1980 decade, the weight of this HEL defensive laser, including beam generator, optical train, heat rejection subsystem, and fire control system, would be approximately 40,000 kilograms. This would be well within the lift capabilities of an uprated Space Shuttle or two flights of a standard Space Shuttle. It is certainly well within the capabilities of any HLLV envisioned to be in service in the late 1980 decade, including the Soviet TT-50 booster.

By the 1990 decade, progress in both space-lift capability, optics technology, and HEL technology would indicate that a defensive HEL could be built and deployed with greater effective range. Utilizing a series of small mirrors with adaptive optics techniques capable of providing an equivalent HEL aperture of 10 meters, and with a modest increase of HEL power to 10 megawatts, the effective defense range could be extended to between 20 and 50 kilometers.

These defensive HELs are obviously quite modest in size and power in comparison to the big HELs that will be feasible during the late 1980 and the 1990 decades for utilization as ABM weapons and long-range space weapons.

Again, verification of the intended use of these SATDEF HELs as defensive measures can be made by visual or electronic inspection. High energy lasers must obey the same physical laws of optics and radiative energy as anything else in the Universe, and it is a proved fact that radiation intensity decreases as a function of the inverse square of the distance and directly as the size of the optical system or source because of optical diffraction and other phenomena. The defensive HEL apertures would necessarily be limited and their power supplies small in comparison to the 50-megawatt and 100-megawatt long-range "burner" HELs with apertures of 30 meters or more. Furthermore, because of interactions with the Earth's atmosphere that would degrade the laser beam power by one-half or more, depending upon the wavelength and the atmospheric path length, a defensive HEL mounted on a space facility would have no possibility of irradiating a target on the Earth's surface at any level of power that could cause damage. Therefore, a defensive space HEL with its restricted aperture and power poses no space-to-Earth offensive threat.

Thus, a space facility can mount defensive weapons such as ASAT missiles and HELs without creating the threat of their use as offensive weapons at greater ranges against other space facilities or, because of the atmospheric interface, against Earth targets. Here is one instance where *distance* in space is a definite factor operating in favor of a concept, and distances in space, even in the Earth-Moon system, are greater than those with which people are used to working on Earth.

When it comes to the transition to war or alert mode rules of action and engagement, a number of new weapons and systems are required to implement the requirements.

In addition to all the weapons and security systems required and in use during the peacetime mode, SATDEF systems should be increased in range and power for the alert mode, anticipating the possible escalation to the wartime mode. This will mean installation of larger hard-kill missiles with longer ranges or supplementing the existing short-range missile forces with additional launch facilities nearby in space. The extreme vulnerability of LEO facilities to attack with the short warning and defense times involved because of their position deep in the gravity well will probably require the speed of targeting of long-range HELs in preference to hard-kill missile systems for these LEO facilities. HELs can, once the target is detected and tracked, project their energy beams at the speed of light (about 300,000 kilometers per second) whereas defensive missiles, even at high boost, might be able to achieve velocities of 10 kilometers per second.

The effective irradiant range and kill power of defensive HELs can be increased by ganging them in the equivalent of an instantaneous phased salvo, concentrating their combined output on the same target and thus being effective at an increased range.

However, since there may be time available in the alert mode to increase defensive measures, it may be possible to deploy previously prepared long-range defensive HELs in orbit for protection of space facilities.

The alert mode will also require activation of space-based antiballistic missile (ABM) systems to protect space systems against Earth-launched ASAT weapons by rocket-powered ASAT interceptors (anti-ASAT). These defensive anti-ASATs should attempt to intercept incoming ASATs during the attacking ASATs' boost phases or before they have reached their terminal velocity and are therefore on a collision course with a space facility. These anti-ASAT systems may not be utilized during the alert mode, but they must be on hand, deployed, and ready for use to protect facilities should the alert mode escalate into the wartime mode.

Similar protective measures during the alert mode must be afforded to Earth-based launch sites by means of deployed antiaircraft (SAM) and ABM weapons. Otherwise, a simple Earth-to-Earth air or ballistic missile strike of modest proportions could, in the event of escalation to wartime status, take out of action one or all of the launch sites providing logistics services to space facilities.

Space cutters for inspection, boarding, and attack will not only carry heavier armament during an alert mode but would be supplemented with the full fleet of space cruisers as backup.

The space cutters and space cruisers would be responsible for transportation of the necessary approach-phase space pilots if these human safeguards were not already aboard an approaching vehicle from the time of its departure.

Electronic countermeasures equipment would be deployed at the ready for potential use.

On Earth, ABM and space missile defense systems would have to be brought to alert status to handle any possible attack by enemy space cruisers, ballistic missiles, or mass driver/catapult strikes.

All of these alert mode measures will require additional energy for implementation, for operation, and on standby for possible war action. Therefore, power beams from solar power satellites may be redirected to military installations and facilities in space, especially to provide the necessary standby energy for offensive HEL and PBW devices as well as electronic warfare activities.

Basically, in the alert mode everything possible in the way of weapons, C^3I, transportation, DIT systems, energy facilities, and personnel in space become ready for instant battle. Fingers are on triggers, but the triggers are not pulled. The longer the alert mode lasts, the more systems, devices, facilities, and personnel can be transitioned to a wartime status.

Once escalation to full wartime status takes place, all systems activated and required for the alert mode go into full operation. Space cutters become armed space cruisers. As many vehicles as possible are armed with missiles and DEW to the extent they are capable of supporting such systems.

In the wartime defensive mode, one additional factor would be quite helpful in permitting tenacity—holding on and outlasting the enemy. This one factor is an extraterrestrial logistic source to permit continued operation of the space forces even in the event of destruction or seizure of terrestrial launch sites.

In a like manner, STC centers that will transition to military C^3 centers during wartime should be prelocated in the most defensible position possible atop the gravity wells: the Earth-Moon Lagrangian points. Because of the capability to burrow within the Moon, a contingency C^3 center might probably be wisely located on the far side of the Moon, where it can be buried deep beneath the lunar surface and therefore become a target that is hard to hit and kill with Earth-launched vehicles and missiles. The L-4/L-5 Lagrangian points are preferable locations because of their high view of the entire theater, but they suffer the vulnerability of being in line of sight of DEW weapons emplaced in GEO and capable of utilizing the outputs of solar power satellites with their 10-gigawatt outputs.

The longer that a space war in the Earth-Moon system can be delayed by diplomatic maneuvering or by stretching out the alert mode, the greater the opportunity for one or both of the adversaries to deploy the big killer weapons of space warfare: lunar catapults and mass drivers.

It is unlikely that these mass-manipulator devices will be available for use as weapons before the turn of the century. However, once they are in place and being utilized for commercial purposes, the more dangerous a space war becomes for people on Earth and the more difficult it becomes to mount an adequate defense against the awesome potential of these rock throwers unless the threat potential is recognized well in advance and suitable defenses prepared.

Offensive wartime activities in space *may not be extensive* during the remainder of the twentieth century in spite of the potential of DEW systems. It has been historically true that new military theaters of operation such as space and the new doctrines, methodologies, techniques, weapons, and military systems that are made possible by the characteristics of the new military theater are normally utilized initially in the passive mode (C^3) as at present. Their first actual wartime utilization commonly comes in the defensive mode. It usually requires another war before the theater and its military systems are utilized as the main center of activity. This has been true in the development of military aviation. However, military aviation may be an exception.

Regardless of whether that concept is valid or not, it is reasonably certain that the weapons and systems to implement the rules of action and engagement in space will be available within the next quarter of a century even considering that there are no unforeseeable breakthroughs in technology—which there usually are.

UNCONVENTIONAL WARFARE IN SPACE

Thus far, the discussion has centered on what might be termed conventional warfare in the space environment. Basically, this has concerned itself with the use of and defense against the two most common categories of weapons in wars that have been fought to date: mass manipulators and energy manipulators.

However, chemical and biological warfare (CBW) and psychological warfare (psychwar) also have historic backgrounds and could conceivably be grouped in the conventional warfare category. Most military students and civilian observers would categorize CBW and psychwar as unconventional forms of warfare. Therefore, CBW and psychwar will be so categorized here along with other elements of unconventional warfare.

In light of the almost constant conflict that appears to have taken place in the twentieth century thus far, many people would tend to believe that most of the forms of unconventional warfare are new. They are not. They are as old as military history itself, and they will therefore undoubtedly follow the general forecasting concept of this work: that all forms of human conflict will find means of expression and operation in the new space theater of war.

These other unconventional warfare categories include sabotage, mutiny, espionage, and terrorism (SMET) and should be discussed separately in terms of their application to, utilization in, and operations in conjunction with space warfare.

Chemical and biological warfare (CBW) has been widely used in military history. Probably the most recent widespread use of CBW was in the Viet Nam War in Southeast Asia during the 1960 and early 1970 decade. CBW was used by *all* sides in that conflict and was used in a surprisingly broad spectrum of military applications ranging from defoliation of vegetation to consciousness-altering drugs, an area that overlaps CBW and psychwar to some extent.

Often, CBW has been implemented without knowledge of the enemy and without a conventional state of war existing at the time. This implementation is also true of other forms of unconventional warfare and may be the factor which differentiates unconventional from conventional warfare.

CBW has been implemented also unknowingly on the part of the aggressor. This was probably the case in biological warfare before the studies of Lister and Pasteur resulted in the development of the germ theory of disease. Typhus, plague, typhoid fever, cholera, tuberculosis, smallpox, malaria, yellow fever, and even venereal disease have been traditional biological enemies of all armies and navies throughout history. In some instances, these CBW agents have been deliberately used to decimate an enemy or potential enemy. Perhaps the most flagrant deliberate use of biological warfare in our recent American history occurred when Indian agents under instructions of the US Army generously provided blankets to the Sioux and Comanche tribes that had been recently interned on their reservations; the blankets were loaded with smallpox and German measles viruses. The "Indian menace" of the Wild West was only partly put down by military action, massacres such as Wounded Knee, and decimation of the bison herds by white hunters; a large portion of the conflict was won with primitive but effective CBW conducted by people whose ancestors had survived the filthy cities of London, Brussels, and Frankfurt.

The use of heavy smoke screens in chemical warfare on land and sea may not have been exclusively for the purposes of concealment of movements and positions from the enemy, but also for irritating and partially disabling enemy personnel. Some forms of smoke were probably recognized as being severe irritants to human respiratory systems and may have been used as such, although the record is not necessarily clear on this point. Certainly a soldier or sailor who is coughing, wheezing, gasping for breath, and partially blinded by tears from an irritant smoke is not in top fighting condition. However, one of the problems of successfully utilizing CBW is revealed by this example: conditions for the use of CBW weapons are often opportunistic in nature, depending upon vectoring factors such as wind direction and speed to carry the CBW agent or weapon into enemy positions while at the same time keeping it away from friendly troops.

CBW weapons are notoriously egalitarian; they will attack friendly troops as readily as enemy troops. Since CBW is normally considered an anti-personnel measure, it can backfire and has done so. Commanders are usually hesitant to utilize CBW because of this, and this may be one reason why the use of most forms of antipersonnel CBW has not become widespread in wars to date.

Burning pitch and sulfur were used in the Peloponnesian War (431–404 B.C.) to produce suffocating gases. But it was the advance of industrial chemistry that led to the wide use of chemical agents in warfare. Even though CBW was foreseen and the Hague International Peace Conference of 1899 produced a resolution that nations "abstain from the use of all projectiles, the object of which is the diffusion of asphyxiating or deleterious gases"—the United States did not support the resolution—CBW was widely used in World War I by the Germans because of the high level of technology achieved by their chemical industry, which had developed a number of debilitating and lethal chemical gas agents. The first use of gas by the Germans was against the Russians in Poland on 31 January 1915. At 5:00 P.M. on 22 April 1915, the Germans released a cloud of chlorine gas in the Ypres (Ieper) region of the Western Front in Belgium, marking the first effective use of gas in warfare. French, British, and Canadian soldiers would have been saved if the Allies had listened to their intelligence sources, but no one in the Allied command believed that such an inhumane weapon as gas would be used. Within a year after Ypres, the Germans had phosgene and mustard gases, many times more effective than chlorine, which was desperately needed for other products by the German chemical industry.

Modern chemical warfare agents are primarily gases with various levels of debilitation and persistence. They range from tear gas (chloracetophenone) with immediate action but short persistence as a lachrymator to choking gases such as phosgene, blister agents such as mustard gas and lewisite, nerve gases such as tabun, sarin, and sobin with varying persistencies but immediate action, to vomiting gases such as adamsite. Some are colorless and odorless. Some have actions that are delayed as much as two hours to eleven days.

Chemical warfare as conducted in Viet Nam also involved the use of defoliating chemicals such as Agent Orange, whose purpose was to kill the lush vegetation under which the Viet Cong and North Vietnamese soldiers could maneuver.

This information about CBW comes from totally unclassified sources available to anybody having access to a public or school library where considerable data can be found on this and other military subjects. Most of this information may be "old" because the newer chemical agents that have been developed under military security classification are, of course, unknown to all but those with a need to know. Obviously, both the United States and the USSR—as well as other nations with well-established industrial chemical industries—possess military chemical agents that are far more effective than the unclassified information would indicate. Some of these classified agents may have very long action times, may be effective in extremely low concentrations in air, food, or liquids, may debilitate for a limited time period only, or may have limited or extended persistence. It is also possible that they may be delivered or vectored in new and unusual ways other than by the classical gas-filled artillery shell, aircraft bomb, grenade, and so on.

All CBW agents of the chemical type are not necessarily designed to be effective against human beings. One of the biggest problems with electronic equipment in the South Pacific during World War II was the existence of various species of fungi that fed upon materials used in electronic components or that grew upon the components and rendered them electronically useless. The enormous progress in genetic engineering may already have produced artificially bred fungi or other organisms that can selectively attack and disable critical elements and components such as the plastics or even the composite materials of electronic systems, life support systems, and even structures.

The primary difference between a chemical agent and a biological agent is that the latter can reproduce itself under proper conditions. Thus, the effectiveness and persistence of a biological warfare agent need not diminish over a period of time as it spreads and its volume of effectiveness increases. There has been much speculation about biological warfare agents, but very little information has been released. The advent of genetic engineering has certainly not gone unnoticed in biological warfare laboratories. One may therefore suppose that a plethora of biological warfare agents will be added to those already in existence with the number and effectiveness of these new agents increasing as time goes on.

Like chemical warfare agents, biological warfare agents must be transported or vectored to where they are to be applied. Vectoring has been one of the biggest problems to date in CBW since a positive means of vectoring is required lest the CBW weapon backfire on friendly personnel through back-vectoring or by means of extended persistence in the target area until occupation forces arrive, thereby permitting the CBW agent to act on friendly forces.

Space appears to offer unique and highly effective means for utilizing CBW. A space facility is, by its very nature, a highly isolated location that is for all intents and purposes a closed ecological system chemically and biologically isolated from Earth and other space facilities by the vacuum of space. Each manned space facility will have one or more life support systems whose functions will include maintaining the composition and flow of a breathable atmosphere and provisions for the recycling of water and the preparation of foods. These space-isolated conditions provide an excellent opportunity to vector any CBW agent throughout the facility in a very short period of time once the agent is introduced into the facility.

Many CBW agents, especially biological agents, require an extremely small amount of material in order to be strongly effective. It may prove to be quite easy to introduce such agents into space facility life support systems. The chances of vectoring the CBW agent to other facilities or back-vectoring the agent will depend entirely upon the frequency of visits by space vehicles whose crews and life support systems would be the *only* means for cross-vectoring, back-vectoring, or spreading the agent to other facilities.

Protection against CBW is difficult since the amount of agent required can be extremely small and possibly very difficult to detect. The most thorough inspections would not prevent an immune carrier from vectoring a CBW agent into a facility and subsequently departing, particularly if the agent was not immediately effective and thus allowed the carrier to escape unsuspected.

The careful use of CBW would permit an aggressor to disable the personnel in a facility without harming the facility itself. An option would then exist permitting the aggressor to leave the facility unoccupied and its use therefore denied to the enemy or to occupy and utilize the facility in safety himself once the CBW agent had exceeded its known effective life span, chemical or biological.

Counteragents would be effective only as a result of outstanding C^3I activities that would permit foreknowledge of what a potential enemy possessed in the way of CBW agents and how such agents might be vectored into a facility. Counteragents might be prepared in advance and stored in a facility to provide CBW defense once the agent was vectored in and detected.

As the years go by and bioengineering of all sorts becomes more highly advanced, CBW warfare may well turn out to be far more effective than any other form of warfare. This is likely to be true in the twenty-first century. However, CBW can be highly effective in the remaining years of this century and should not be dismissed because of wishful thinking concerning the difficulties of vectoring, effectiveness, life span, and back-vectoring. The nation that makes that mistake, suffering from the Ostrich Syndrome, invites a nonviolent conflict with CBW in this new space environment, where the environmental characteristics appear to be highly favorable to CBW use.

Space facilities do not offer themselves solely as targets for CBW, however. Because of the extreme biological isolation possible with space facilities, they become strong candidates for clandestine CBW laboratories and factories involved in the highly controlled production and storage of CBW agents. As such, it is feasible that they could operate under the guise of laboratories conducting recombinant DNA research or as space pharmaceutical labs and factories producing high-purity biologicals requiring extreme isolation to insure quality.

Because of the discovery of mood-altering and consciousness-altering drugs such as the meprobamates and LSD, there is now a hazy zone of differentiation between CBW and psychwar. As defined earlier, a psychological weapon is one that will permit one to impress his will upon the adversary by means of altering the beliefs, values, or actual mental processes of the adversary. One of the means to do this is with mood-altering and consciousness-altering drugs, which might also be considered to be part of CBW.

The United States was confronted with psychwar in the Viet Nam War in Southeast Asia and, to some extent, is still battling a psychwar with no clear indication of the adversary. It has not yet been widely admitted that the United States Army and, to a perhaps lesser degree, the United States Air Force were the targets of intense psychwar in South Viet Nam. The will to fight of the American troops in Southeast Asia was profoundly affected not only by powerful and persuasive propaganda—some of which was conducted openly by American citizens—but also by the massive infusion of psychological drugs into the fighting forces there. Tetrahydro-cannabinol was perhaps the most ubiquitous drug—and still is—in the form of marijuana and hashish. But LSD, Angel Dust, opium, morphine, cocaine, and even methadone were introduced into the theater of war and resulted in the disablement of thousands of soldiers, the sapping of the willingness to follow orders, the decline of discipline, and the deaths from both drugs and battle wounds of thousands of others, some of whom were "stoned out of their minds" when they went into battle and therefore made their last fatal mistake while under the influence of psych drugs.

There is no proof that this drug infusion was deliberately conducted by the adversary in South Viet Nam. However, in future analyses of that conflict, the use of drugs by United States forces will undoubtedly be pegged as one reason among many for the failure of the United States to conduct a decisive campaign in Southeast Asia. The interface between the American culture and the oriental culture was certain to result in a broad range of cultural interchanges. The cultural milieu of Indochina has always included opium and its derivatives, while the North American culture and the European civilization from which its roots spring accepts the widespread use of mild, nonhabituating psych drugs such as nicotine and ethyl alcohol. Although American troops had fought in the region twice before during this century alone, the Viet Nam experience was the first one in which the drug factor in the oriental culture was a definite factor in the conduct of the war. This leads to a strong suspicion of psychwar with the use of mind-altering drugs as weapons. And it apparently succeeded.

The Southeast Asia psychwar had somewhat less effect upon the USAF and even less upon the US Navy because both of those services require a high level of mental activity and alertness on a constant day-to-day basis, utilizing weapons based on high technology. An airplane pilot may often be able to fly with a modicum of ethyl alcohol in his blood, but more often than not the operation of modern tactical jet aircraft will not tolerate much. Certainly, these complex and fast devices will not tolerate a pilot whose mind is muddled by more powerful drugs. Nor will mechanics and technicians responsible for maintenance and repair of the aircraft on the ground be able to function well under the influence of today's psych drugs.

The US Navy is even more sensitive to psychwar with drug weapons, has a somewhat more isolated situation at sea with somewhat tighter controls over shipboard living, and simply cannot tolerate any sort of reduced level of mental activity and acuity that might be accepted in the Army. (As a naval officer once remarked wryly, "The Army has never had to face the possibility of having a battlefield sink.")

Psychwar with drugs against space military activities can therefore be approached with somewhat mixed feelings. The mind-altering drugs are so new and medical and psychological experience even with the ancient and classical mind-altering drugs is yet so limited that one cannot firmly forecast at this time whether or not military personnel in space would be vulnerable to the sort of infusion of psychwar drugs that occurred in Southeast Asia. It is quite probable that they would not, given the high level of technology with which all of them will have to live every day and the extremely hostile environment in which they will exist.

This does not necessarily mean that an enemy may not develop some new and potent psych drug that could be vectored into a space facility as a CBW agent might. However, psych drugs introduced into the military theater of space in this fashion are rightfully considered in the same category as CBW.

On the other hand, psychwar can be easily waged in space, and it has been in the past. Few people in the United States who had any knowledge whatsoever of rocketry, ICBMs, or strategic doctrines can forget the strange feeling of both dread and helplessness that came from watching the huge Soviet satellite Sputnik-2 and its booster winking through the night sky during the winter of 1957–1958. It was bright, and it was unmistakable evidence that the Soviets at that time possessed the capability for mounting a rudimentary ballistic missile nuclear strike against the United States. Actually, the Soviet Union did not at that time have such a capability, but Sputnik-2 was a typical psychwar demonstration. It helped shape the politics of the 1960 presidential campaign with the "missile gap" issue.

The Apollo manned lunar landing program of the United States was, in a sense, a psychwar program.

The deployment in space of *any* system that is visible from the ground and which projects the image, correct or not, of a military threat from space is an element of psychwar in the space war of the future. In point of fact, a great deal of preliminary effort has been mounted by the United States already in blunting the psychwar issue of the military threats of a solar power satellite system, an issue that is founded on baseless claims and that can be used in a propaganda campaign against the SPS system.

In due course of time, however, space psychwar against most nations of the world will diminish in effectiveness. There will remain for some time yet to come primitive peoples in the world who will be vulnerable to lights in the sky, reentry fireworks displays, and other technological space pyrotechnics that show "the gods are angry." As Arthur C. Clarke has pointed out, a sufficiently advanced technology is indistinguishable from magic. And Robert A. Heinlein observed, "One man's magic is another man's engineering." This is psychwar in its essence.

When it comes to elements of SMET (sabotage, mutiny, espionage, and terrorism), one is truly in the realm of unconventional warfare.

Sabotage can be as effective in space as it is in naval and air warfare. High technology is involved in all in these areas and is usually highly vulnerable to sabotage. C^3I facilities, DIT systems, and space transportation systems are vulnerable because there exists in all advanced and complex systems and devices a number of highly vulnerable and sensitive critical elements whose malfunction or destruction results in the malfunction or destruction of the entire larger system or device. The introduction of a small amount of contaminant into life support systems, corrosive gases into areas containing microelectronic circuitry, or simply sand in the gears is extremely difficult to prevent, even with the most advanced and sophisticated physical security measures, inspection procedures, and human reliability tests and techniques. Sabotage of high technology systems, relatively simple as it may be to carry out, usually requires an intimate knowledge of the technology involved and of the system elements themselves. The one serious shortcoming to sabotage in space is that a saboteur is faced with the problem of doing it without becoming the victim of it. The situation is rather like a paratrooper sabotaging the anchor point for all the parachute static lines in the jump aircraft.

One would not anticipate having to deal with mutiny in space warfare. In the first place, space crews will be carefully selected, thoroughly trained, and highly motivated. Existing techniques of human reliability measurement and testing will be used. In a sense, military space personnel will be analogous to today's military and naval personnel in the Strategic Air Command and in the Blue and Gold Crews of ballistic missile submarines. Outright mutiny involving rebellion of a crew against legally constituted authority and the forcible replacement of a commanding officer has not occurred in modern military and naval forces of the superpowers for several decades and *never* in the United States Navy or the United States Air Force. While it is possible in space, it may be improbable as well due to modern knowledge of human psychology and leadership.

Espionage, on the other hand, goes on all the time and can be anticipated in space. Critical military data and information is always vulnerable to espionage, both overt and covert. This is more than mere intelligence activities, because espionage involves clandestine personnel operating within the adversary's organization to obtain critical data directly. Of greatest military importance in space during alert and wartime modes of operation will be the DIT codes and schedules, approach pilot IDs and codes, operational lift and orbital transfer schedules, and so on. One can anticipate the enemy making active attempts to obtain such critical information by any possible means, and military staffs and commanders will do their best to obtain similar data about the adversary's operations. Space military espionage activities in the future will certainly have their Mata Haris and James Bonds. Space espionage will differ in kind, not in degree, from classical espionage, because it may take place in the new and unique environment of space.

Terrorism, like sabotage, is an element of unconventional war that can be anticipated in space in spite of safeguards similar to those deployed to prevent sabotage. While a launch site is likely to be a poor target for terrorist activities and be reasonably invulnerable in most cases to acts of terrorism, space facilities could be nakedly vulnerable to the sort of actions carried out by terrorists because it is infeasible to expect 100 percent effective screening at launch sites. There is nothing that would prevent a suicidal or kamikaze attack on any space facility, especially those in LEO, by terrorists who had somehow managed to obtain a suitable space vehicle. In fact, it is likely that most terrorist activities in the space environment are probably suicidal and would destroy the terrorist in the act of committing terrorism. Security experts must plan on handling the sort of fanatical, suicidal personality with whom there may be little opportunity or chance for negotiation. By and large, however, terrorism, along with mutiny, *appears* to be among the less likely threats to space facilities. The rationale to justify that contention is that a person who has the sort of education and training to enable him to operate in the space environment usually has a personality profile without terrorist characteristics. But the rationale may be wrong; it has been wrong in the past in isolated cases.

Guerrilla warfare in space must also be considered in the same unlikely category but should not be considered as unconventional warfare. This form of warfare is carried on by independent, quasi-military groups usually in connection with a conventional war and generally in the rear of the enemy. The terms "partisan" and "irregular" are synonymous with "guerrilla," which serves to indicate the nature of this type of warfare: irregular. While the general principles of regular warfare involve destroying enemy will and capability to fight, seizure of enemy territory, or denial of territory to enemy use, guerrilla warfare usually involves attempts to prevent or avoid exploitation of terrain by an enemy. Basically, guerrilla units are loosely organized and rarely conduct operations in coordination with regular military units; the exception to this was the French maquis during the Normandy invasion in 1944. Guerrilla tactics are the tactics of hit-and-run, nibbling at enemy operations, and keeping large enemy forces occupied in defense of themselves and their facilities. Legally, guerrilla personnel can be considered as legitimate soldiers and treated as prisoners of war only if they meet the qualifications set forth in the Hague conventions of 1899 and 1907: (a) they must be commanded by a person responsible for his subordinates, (b) they must wear a fixed distinctive sign or uniform recognizable at a distance, (c) they must carry arms openly, and (d) they must conduct their operations in accordance with the laws and customs of war. Although guerrilla war has been useful to the operations of a regular army on Earth in the past, military commanders know that the irregular nature of guerrilla warfare means that not a great deal can be counted on or expected from guerrillas, who are, by their very nature, loosely knit and poorly disciplined. Because of this, guerrillas have never won a war but, under the direction of a wise leader who understands them, they can count in regular warfare.

Guerrillas should not be confused with the multitude of revolutionary armies that now operate in many countries of the world. The Continental Army under the command of General Washington was not a guerrilla army, but an insurgent army comparable in many ways to most of the so-called guerrilla armies of revolution today.

Space *may* see the return of one form of irregular and unconventional warfare that is specifically permitted under Article 1, Section 8 of the Constitution of the United States of America. This clause gives Congress the power to grant letters of marque and reprisal. Few people know what that means. When the Constitution was drawn up and adopted in 1788, governments had the right to hire "privateers" or armed vessels belonging to private owners and commissioned by the government to carry on operations of war or reprisal, the government not paying the owners or crew and the privateers therefore cruising for their own profit, taking enemy vessels as prizes. A letter of marque and reprisal is a commission to operate as a privateer, and the early Congresses of the USA believed that this was an excellent way to maintain naval forces at little expense to the taxpayer.

But it is unlikely that privateering a la *Buck Rogers* or *Star Wars* will be seen in the Earth-Moon theater of operations. Privateering was abolished by the Declaration of Paris in 1856, although the United States refused to ratify that convention for the same reason that Congress was given the constitutional power to issue letters of marque and reprisal. The development of the US Navy in the latter part of the nineteenth century finally led to US acceptance of the principles abolishing privateering, which was finally legally abolished under international law at the Second Hague Conference in 1907. All armed private vessels must now be registered as warships for which the state of registry assumes all responsibility, although the right of self-defense of armed private vessels was tacitly admitted during both World Wars. This does not mean, however, that a nation could not commission space privateers or mercenaries. Indeed, some Third World nations might well do so to provide themselves with some space warfare capability, in order, for example, to back up territorial claims for geosynchronous equatorial orbital slots and other Panama Points in space.

Space privateering would be permissible under the terms of the 1972 UN International Liability Convention.

Although many aspects of unconventional warfare appear to be unlikely in space, it is highly possible that the future will see totally new and unsuspected forms of warfare developed because of the uniqueness of the space environment, just as modern technology has seen the birth of other new forms of warfare based on technological development.

WIZARD WAR IN SPACE

Although a great deal of modern technology has come from military needs—an engineer was originally a person who designed and built military fortifications and equipment—it was not until World War II that the intellectual forces of scientific research and development were deliberately and intensively applied to the conduct of war. This led Sir Winston S. Churchill to coin the term "wizard war." He was one of the first political leaders with no admitted background in science to draw scientists into the ranks of his advisers, to listen to them, and to utilize his political power to translate their scientific knowledge into practical wartime technology.

In today's world of advanced science and applied technology in military affairs exemplified by secret government laboratories and classified "think tanks," most people cannot recall the times prior to World War II when wizard war was not an everyday matter and military planning and operations were conducted by techniques that would now seem to be highly empirical—by rule of thumb, by "guess and by gosh," and by trial and error in developing, proving, deploying, using, and evaluating military devices.

Space warfare is very much a wizard war even today when, as this is written, activity is basically in the peacetime mode. Political and military leaders who are well aware of this are likely to prevail in *any* war in the future. Those who do not will likely suffer the same fate as mounted warriors made obsolete by technology and actually defeated before the fighting begins.

The military development and use of high technology has become so persuasive today that modern fighting forces simply cannot hope to accomplish their assigned missions not only without high technology in general, but without electronic systems in particular.

Complex electronic systems are required today for military activities at all levels of command and action. They include radars, lidars, laser target designators, identification equipment, image enhancement devices such as infrared snooper scopes, and high-speed general purpose electronic computers. A wide variety of electronic equipment is necessary to establish and maintain secure command, control, and communications on a worldwide basis down to the level of the unit field commander. If denied the use of most electronic military systems, a military commander, staff, and operational force conducting any sort of a mission is at a severe disadvantage that usually leads to mission failure. One needs only study the openly published reports of the US Joint Chiefs of Staff to the Congress concerning the abortive Iranian hostage rescue mission in 1980 to realize this.

Because of the unique nature of space and military operations that can be conducted in the Earth-Moon system under the doctrines discussed herein, electronic systems and electronic warfare are not only important elements in space war, they are critical.

For this reason, electronic countermeasures (ECM) become of vital importance if EW systems are to carry out this critical operation.

EW has its primary objective of preventing effective ECM operations by the enemy and of maintaining the operation, integrity, and security of one's own C³I systems. Space EW now includes and will include in the next twenty years the military EW functions of surveillance, reconnaissance, warning, survivable command/control/communication/intelligence (C³I), detection, targeting, weapons control, weapons delivery, and target damage assessment.

Initially, EW utilizing space technology will primarily be used to support military operations on Earth as it is doing today. However, the increasing development and improvement of the military space EW capabilities is being accompanied by an equally increasing emphasis and amount of effort on the development of methods of ECW to prevent the use of EW by a potential adversary. This obviously leads to a justifiable forecast of increasing EW activity in space.

An indication of the increasing level of activity in this regard can be gleaned from a study of the NASA Space Shuttle flight assignment schedule which, as of September 1980, shows seventy-nine Shuttle flights booked with payloads through 1986. Of those flights, twenty-one are booked for Department of Defense payloads, and absolutely no details are given concerning them—no payload weights and no orbital elements. The schedule of Shuttle DOD flights in each calendar year shows the increasing tempo:

1982: 1 DOD flight scheduled.
1983: 3 DOD flights scheduled.
1984: 2 DOD flights scheduled.
1985: 7 DOD flights scheduled.
1986: 8 DOD flights scheduled.

The Department of Defense also has available the Titan-III launch system and the various modifications of the small Thor IRBM vehicle—known in its various forms as Delta, Thor-Agena, TAT-Agena, and so on—which has been in use as a basic space booster since 1958 and is capable of placing almost 1,800 kilograms in LEO and 500 kilograms in GEO. The launch schedules for these military space missions are not openly published and usually never announced except to report that a launch has been accomplished. DOD depends heavily on its current stable of these expendable boosters and, even in the face of the Space Shuttle usage directive from the White House, is extremely reluctant to phase out these highly reliable, if expensive, launch vehicles.

Because of its ubiquitous presence in modern military operations, electronic warfare will pose a significant threat to military space activities and will probably be extensively used for mutual and self-protection of military space vehicles and facilities, both manned and unmanned.

Electronic warfare consists of two elements: electronic intelligence (ELINT) and electronic countermeasures (ECM).

Just as surveillance and reconnaissance have been vital to the acquisition of intelligence on the adversary's movements, strengths, concentrations, and likely intentions, intelligence regarding the characteristics, operations, location, function, and possible operational use of the electronic systems of the adversary is essential to military operations on Earth and in space. ELINT depends primarily upon the *detection* of enemy electronic radiations followed by their identification as to other military characteristics.

Perhaps the first ELINT activities were conducted by the Germans. On at least two occasions in late May and early August 1939, the 776-foot LZ-127 *Graf Zeppelin*— thought to have been laid up with its hydrogen gas cells deflated in a hangar at Rhein-Main, Frankfurt—cruised off the coasts of England with the assignment to determine covertly the nature and disposition of suspected new British radar stations. The British naturally detected this huge airship, the largest blip they had ever seen on their radar scopes, especially when the LZ-127's navigator made a mistake and the airship positioned itself in a cloud well inland over the city of Hull.

Flight Lieutenant (later Air Marshal) W. P. C. Pretty recalled, "We were sorely tempted to radio a correction message to the airship, but this would have revealed we were actually seeing her position on radar, so we kept silent." This historic example indicates that the tactics of EW have not changed since the very beginning of the activity.

The ability of ELINT to provide information depends upon the signal power density of the adversary's transmitter, upon the ELINT receiver's system sensitivity, and upon the line-of-sight (LOS) geometry. The latter poses the greatest constraints upon ELINT operations on the Earth's surface and in aircraft operating in the atmosphere; it is especially critical with respect to the high frequencies (VHF, UHF, L-band, S-band, C-band, X-band, and K-band) normally associated with military electronic activity. The ability to deploy ELINT receivers in orbit, thus gaining all the classic advantages of the high ground, has been a very attractive proposition to the military of all nations capable of orbital space operations. The distances in the Earth-Moon system and the atmospheric absorption of some wavelengths work to the disadvantage of orbital ELINT facilities to some degree. However, distance and transmitter antenna characteristics— i.e., the degree to which a given signal is directionally transmitted by the antenna—are the only negative operational considerations of space-to-space ELINT. For example, if the hostile satellite is in orbit on the other side of the Earth, although still in LOS, its distance may be too great for the ELINT receiver's sensitivity and selectivity to be able to discriminate the signal out of the cosmic radio noise level. Or the enemy signal could be tightly beamed, forcing the ELINT receiver to depend upon detection of the antenna's transmitted side lobe radiation or back radiation, if any.

Space ELINT operations may be conducted to satisfy a variety of requirements. It can locate hostile elements, update hostile force electronic order of battle information, obtain information on specific transmitters and emissions, test hostile force ECM capabilities, evaluate hostile force command and control procedures, and a host of other intelligence functions. ELINT operational and system requirements to accomplish these missions are determined by specific ELINT equipment characteristics such as frequency coverage and resolution, signal and signature analysis capabilities, degree of system integration and automation for rejecting noise and known signals, type of displays, and ability to select specific signals for observation, recording, and study.

On a firm foundation of accurate ELINT data, effective EW can be waged with ECM. Again, electronic countermeasure has a history that dates back to World War II, the first wizard war. The British were not the only ones to possess highly effective radar systems. The German Würzburg radar equipment covered most of the airspace on the approaches to the European continent, and the Luftwaffe therefore had ample advance warning of bombing raids forming up over England for attack on the continent. The first British method of retaliation against Würzburg was an attempt to bomb out the stations, an effort that failed. What did succeed was a classic example of ECM: turning the Germans' own equipment against them through the use of an ECM weapon known as window and now called chaff. It had been first suggested in 1937 by Professor Frederick Lindemann, Churchill's science adviser, who proposed lengths of metal foil cut to match the wavelength of a radar transmission. When scattered in a cloud from a bomber, the chaff strips would each send back very strong radar echoes to the radar station, echoes that appeared on the radar scopes as large formations of bombers. On 24 July 1943, radar chaff was first used as an ECM over Hamburg. The Luftwaffe scrambled interceptor aircraft only to find clouds of fluttering silver tinfoil and no British aircraft anywhere in sight. RAF Bomber Command losses to Luftwaffe fighters were halved thereafter.

Since this first ECM encounter, countermeasures against counter-measures against countermeasures have been developed in a continuing race to outguess and outperform the adversary's equipment and ECM. Chaff is only one ECM device. There are uncountable others today.

A continual stream of ELINT activity goes on around the world, a great deal of it using orbital ELINT equipment. Soviet Tu-20 Bear and other long-range aircraft continually probe NATO and North American airspace to identify radar capabilities and determine critical radio frequencies and techniques. With U-2, SR-71, and other aircraft, the United States and other Western powers do the same. The Soviets continually probe and play with the sensitive over-the-horizon ABM and air defense radars on the North American continent. *Nothing* is ever revealed publicly about this activity, which takes place on both sides of the atmospheric interface.

EW has been fiercely waged over Viet Nam, Korea, and the Middle East.

EW and ECM techniques have now become so highly sophisti-cated that electronic warfare personnel must utilize the most modern computer equipment to assist them. Radar and other signals can be jammed by powerful transmitters operating on the same frequencies. To counter this, transmitters and receivers have been built to operate on skip frequency techniques, where the transmitter and receiver change frequencies apparently at random but actually according to a prearranged sequence and lately according to coded instructions sent along with the main signal. Multiple frequencies are also used. Critical radars no longer transmit a continuous series of pulses or even a continuous carrier wave;

they operate as monopulse units capable of transmitting a single burst of radiation and obtaining needed radar signature and tracking data from the characteristics of the single returning pulse. Radars shift frequencies on an apparent random schedule. Lasers are rapidly coming into use for lidar (Laser Illuminated Detection And Ranging, the laser analogue to radar). High speed computers are used to analyze both echoes and signals that appear to be random noise, and the required information is extracted from the "noisy" signal by analysis methods operating billions of times faster than the human mind.

Because of the tight security surrounding all EW activities and also because of the explosive nature of development in the fields of electronics and computers, it is practically impossible to make a rational forecast of EW capabilities and their operational utilization in space even in the next decade, let alone over the next quarter of a century. It is possible to look only in a superficial manner at a few of the conceptual (and possibly sophomoric) applications and consequences of EW in space warfare.

For example, the simple ECM example of chaff, albeit still effective against unsophisticated radars, can be a two-edged sword in space warfare. Chaff strips or dipoles can be fabricated of random-length aluminum-coated glass fibers to provide a broad-band frequency response. Chaff can be used to deploy as a signal attenuator between space facilities. It could even be used to cause severe attenuation of the radio-frequency power beam from a solar power satellite belonging to the enemy. A little bit of chaff goes a long way. For example, current pod-type chaff dispensers used on military aircraft of the United States can carry more than a billion aluminized glass-fiber dipoles. In the atmosphere, they can be deployed into a cloud in less than three minutes. In space, they will have to be forcibly deployed by explosive or pressurized gas systems. The chaff cloud will indeed attenuate radio transmissions and provide abundant target echoes to unsophisticated radars. But the cloud will either continue in orbit—if it is in orbit when deployment takes place—or with the same velocity as its carrier possessed when deployment occurred. It will not fall as atmospheric chaff does. It will remain in space, perhaps as a continually expanding cloud with decreasing ECM properties, and probably will have to be swept up at some future date, if possible. It may even pose a severe man-made micrometeorite threat if closing velocities between a vehicle or facility and the chaff needles is high enough.

Because of the very narrow beams and coherent radiation of lasers, it is probably infeasible to consider LCM (laser countermeasure) techniques at this time.

Except for those facilities in the vulnerable LEO zone, the distances in the Earth-Moon system provide the valuable asset of *time* in order to react to most EW threats and activate appropriate ECM as well as retaliatory EW methods. LEO positions are indeed vulnerable to EW and ECM techniques intended to disable any defensive equipment in those facilities; ranges are short in comparison to the rest of the Earth-Moon system; time available to react and counter is short because a strong EW or ECM attack will probably be a precursor to the immediate follow-up of an ASAT or DEW attack.

It is *quite* unlikely that an adversary would utilize the damaging or even destroying EW technique of the electromagnetic pulse from a thermonuclear device detonated about 100 kilometers altitude, although the EMP effects of such an event could be expected to affect unprotected and unhardened electronic equipment as far out as GEO. It is unlikely *unless* the enemy has suitably protected and hardened his own electronic equipment against the EMP and is willing to tolerate the extreme degradation of his own radar and C^3I electronic transmissions for periods of hours or even days. However, such a ploy could be anticipated from any nonspace nation with the thermonuclear and missile capability to do it, perhaps if for no other reason than to disable or destroy the electronic space capabilities of an enemy with spacefaring capabilities and facilities.

Defenses against the EMP cannot be discussed because little can be learned of whatever techniques have been developed to date. Such critical information would obviously be a high state military secret. Therefore, whether or not the USA could protect or harden its space facilities against an EMP threat of this brief scenario cannot be a matter for discussion because there is nothing upon which to base a discussion.

The very nature of EW and the fact that it will undoubtedly play a major role in any alert situation—or even in a peacetime situation—involving space military facilities means that military space activities *cannot* be totally automated. People are going to have to be in space with the equipment if for no other reason than to handle judgment calls and make creative decisions on new techniques that will be forced upon them by the use of EW by an adversary. Not even computers will be able to call the shots, so to speak, in a complex milieu that includes EW, although computers will certainly assist people because of computer speeds.

Although today's technology—let alone that of twenty years' hence—would permit a great deal of space EW and ECM to be conducted automatically, there is a strong requirement for people "in the loop," for manned activity supervising the EW and ECM.

The need for man in the loop has been discussed earlier, but nowhere is it more important than in the conduct of this wizard war in space. Military men of today and the future need heed the prophetic words of Fleet Admiral Ernest J. King, who spoke in part as follows to the graduating class of the US Naval Academy on 19 June 1942:

We hear very much indeed, in this day and age, of machines and of war waged with machines. We hear so much that we do not, all of us, stop to think that war is not different, in principle, from what it has been since before the dawn of recorded history. Mechanized warfare is no more than evolution. . . . We must not fail to realize that machines are as nothing without the men who man them and give them life. War is force—force to the utmost—force to make the enemy yield to our will. . . . War is men against men—mechanized war is still men against men. Machines are mere masses of inert metal without the men who man them.

King's words are true even when contemplating space war. This is because warriors—men *and* women who wage war—have not changed over the years. They are *Homo sapiens*, Mark-1, Mod 0, and they will continue to be *Homo sapiens*, Mark-1, Mod 0 for a long time to come.

The mental image of the warrior in the minds of those with no military background, knowledge, training, or understanding is usually quite false to fact. For example, a warrior is considered by nonmilitary people to be an automatic piece who, because of military discipline, blindly carries out the orders of higher command. It is also believed that military discipline and training leaves no room for individual volition, that soldiers instantly obey without question the orders they are given, and that military commanders would prefer subordinates who behaved according to this bit of wishful thinking. It is partially the rationale behind the belief that electronic devices, automatic machines, robots, and computers can replace people and especially warriors.

As Admiral King implied, this mental image of a warrior is quite incorrect. Any military policy or doctrine that relies upon that false image is more dangerous than any actual adversary.

War is a gigantic gamble based on warriors using weapons according to an overall strategic plan based on sound doctrinal foundations and with maximum possible flexibility allowed to unit commands and individual warriors to act in a tactical fashion with individual volition in a way that will best accomplish the goal: *decisively* winning the battle *and* the war.

The United States has (hopefully) learned to its detriment that technology, hardware, and even superior numbers of warriors do not guarantee a decisive victory. To conduct a *decisive* war, whose outcome leaves no recourse to the enemy except to yield to the victor, requires human action. A machine does not care and will turn on its operators as readily as it will act against the enemy. It cannot surrender but must be destroyed. Any nation relying to a large degree upon automated warfare probably will be unable to surrender as well and therefore faces destruction.

Reliance upon computers and automatic equipment to take the place of warriors does not win decisive wars, but such reliance may decisively lose a war.

However, there is a role for automation and computers in future warfare, particularly in space. Defining this role requires an assessment of both human warriors and computers as two totally different types of systems that, properly interfaced, can complement one another. These two systems are (a) the human being who can be considered to be a colloidal system, and (b) the computer/robot which is a crystalline system. The characteristics of both systems are different and because of these differences, the two systems can act in a synergistic manner. (Synergism is the action of two distinct systems in combination, whose effect is greater than the simple sum of the capabilities of the two.)

A colloid is a suspension of fine particles of atomic or molecular dimensions. A colloidal system can operate only within very limited pressure and temperature ranges. Transfer of energy or information within a colloidal system occurs chemically or by means of ion exchange mechanisms. Therefore, a colloidal system has very slow response and reaction times measured in milliseconds (thousandths of a second). Colloidal systems appear to be complex because they are not yet well understood; biochemistry is a young and emerging science. But colloidal systems such as human beings compensate for their slow operational or switching times by operating in a multichannel mode of extreme complexity and high redundancy. Because of this characteristic, colloidal systems can be highly adaptive and can carry out a surprisingly large number of simultaneous operations with a very large amount of feedback, effectively shortening the system operation times. The most highly evolved colloidal systems are human beings.

A human being using his colloidal computer system has a very large memory and occasionally exhibits the ability to make novel correlations between memory matrices. In short, a human being can be creative.

It is not certain at this time whether or not crystalline systems are creative or even if they are self-aware as advanced colloidal systems appear to be. There are serious attempts under way to investigate these questions at such places as the Artificial Intelligence Laboratory at the Massachusetts Institute of Technology under Dr. Marvin Minski. But the answers may not be available until it has been determined what "intelligence" (as applied to thinking processes instead of to militarily important information) really is. However, intelligent or not, crystalline systems are causing a major revolution in the everyday actions of colloidal systems such as human beings.

Crystalline systems utilize components locked into geometrical arrangements of atoms, in contrast to the random arrangement of atoms and molecules in a colloid. Crystalline systems also must operate within similar limited ranges of pressure and temperature as colloidal systems. But their mode of operation is on the atomic level with an exchange of electrons within a crystalline lattice. The state of the art in crystalline computer technology is now at the point where the movement of a single electron within a crystalline lattice constitutes a signal. Crystalline computer systems are very fast with operation or switching times in picoseconds (10^{-12} seconds or a trillionth of a second). The difference in switching times between colloidal and crystalline systems is a result of their different operating modes and the relaxation times of molecular versus atomic mechanisms. Crystalline systems are capable of performing many operations in an extremely short period of time using linear, single-channel logic. They appear to be able to do this much better than colloidal systems only because of their extremely fast switching rates.

Crystalline systems can reproduce only on a low level of complexity—at this time. Colloidal systems are capable of self-reproduction on a very high level of complexity. Furthermore, colloidal systems can be rapidly produced by relatively unskilled labor.

Since there are such major differences between colloidal and crystalline systems, a discussion of one system replacing the other becomes moot. Given the advantages and shortcomings of both systems, the military planner and commander would logically prefer to use the colloidal systems with which he and his predecessors have been working since prehistoric times and utilize the new crystalline systems to supplement the advantages and overcome the shortcomings of the colloidal systems. In short, in a military operation, one would like to obtain the optimum human-computer interface.

Such a matching/pairing activity appears to be the trend, in contrast to total dependence upon either human warriors or their computer counterparts. Computers have been used in warfare for centuries to assist the warrior. The first military computer may have been the gunner's quadrant used by a cannoneer to determine the elevation angle of his cannon.

The trend toward total automation and taking the warrior out of the loop peaked in the 1950 decade when it was fashionable in military circles to speak of "manned missiles" instead of "interceptor aircraft," for example. Any industrial engineer could have explained to a military engineer that one does not automate any system until one understands it fully, can measure and control all the variables involved, and can anticipate and program for all possible future contingencies. One automates an industrial process by evolutionary steps, always keeping the human operator in charge. As experience increases and the process or system becomes better understood, the human being is moved to higher and higher positions of authority and control in the system, turning over the repetitive and understood operations to the automatic device or computer but never relinquishing overall command or authority.

In spite of the "total automation" fad, military planners and designers are attempting now to combine the human colloidal system with the computer's crystalline system to create an effective supersystem with as many of the advantages and as few of the disadvantages of both systems as possible. It will take some time to develop an optimum relationship, because a major problem is created by attempting to link the two systems: the human colloidal system is at best a billion times slower than the computer crystalline system.

Nine orders of magnitude of difference currently exist between the speeds of the two systems—the human colloidal system operating in milliseconds and the computer crystalline system operating in pico-seconds. From the human point of view, a computer seems to function instantaneously. From the computer's point of view, if it has one, com-municating with a human being involves sending a message and waiting a computer-equivalent length of time of six human years for a reply. Keyboard inputs are slow for a computer, and so are voice-actuated inputs. Even the fastest computer outputs and displays require the com-puter equivalent of years to operate.

Two possible approaches to the solution appear to suggest them-selves: (a) speed up the human colloidal system, or (b) slow down the computer crystalline system.

Because of the multichannel operating mode of human colloidal systems, it may be possible to achieve perhaps two orders of magnitude of speedup of mental processes by means of training. The real promise in psychedelic drugs may lie in providing the key to understanding human thought processes and the wide apparent discrepancies often noted be-tween physical time and psychological time.

Slowing down the computer appears to be more feasible at this time with the data in hand. Engineers have spent several decades in-creasing computer switching times. That portion of the computer which now communicates with humans is the slowpoke or idiot portion of the crystalline system and, by means of proper programming, need only communicate to the human system the data that the human desires and not all of the internal operations taking place within the computer.

The most significant advance in this area may have already taken place and be classified information. However, the concept has occurred independently to a number of people, including the author. Computers can and eventually will be linked directly to the human nervous system. Data has been transmitted directly from the human colloidal system to the computer system and vice versa. Direct-system linkage removes the need for display systems, printouts, key pads, and other input devices, replacing peripherals and input-output devices with direct linkage between the circuits of both systems.

Computers have "read" human minds by means of deciphering the outputs of electroencephalographs (EEGs). Early work in this area was reported by the Defense Advanced Research Projects Agency (DARPA) in 1978. EEGs are now known to be crude sensors of neural activity in the human brain, depending as they do upon induced electrical currents in the skin. Magnetoencephalographs (MEG) have since been developed using highly sensitive electromagnetic sensors that can directly map brain neural activity even through the bones of the skull. The responses of the visual area of the brain have now been mapped by Kaufman and others at Vanderbilt University. Work may already be under way in mapping the neural activity of other portions of the human brain using the new MEG techniques. It does not require a great deal of prognostication to forecast that the neural electromagnetic activity of the human brain will be totally mapped within a decade or so and that crystalline computers can be programmed to decipher the electromagnetic neural signals.

It is also possible to input directly the human nervous system with electronic signals, bypassing normal sensors such as the eyes and ears. Work is currently under way at the Institute of Medical Studies near San Francisco, evaluating an invention that has been both neglected by medical science and suppressed by government intelligence agencies, the Flanagan "neurophone," which appears capable of injecting audio information directly into the human nervous system at any location on the human body. Considerable work has also been carried out on the sensitivity of the skin to light by an increasing number of researchers in the Soviet Academy of Sciences.

Early work in the infant science of biocybernetics is already being done. Human colloidal nervous systems and computer colloidal electronic circuits will undoubtedly be communicating directly with one another within the next twenty-five years. This work may culminate in the intelligence amplifier or merely in a better way to allow humans to utilize the advantages of computers. A novel entitled *Firefox* by Craig Thomas was published in 1977 with a theme that is based upon this potential advance.

Thus, space warfare in the next twenty-five years may see a totally new and unsuspected turn of events: the human-computer direct link with the human in control. This is a totally different forecast from those which foresaw the cyborg or bionic man—a human being with parts replaced by mechanical components or a human brain in vitro controlling a specially designed robotic body. It is different from the forecasts of robots themselves, humanoid machines that would perhaps resemble human beings but would be based upon crystalline-system technology. And different as well from the classic robot forecast of Karel Capek's *R.U.R.* ("Rossum's Universal Robots").

The wizard war is now space oriented, and it appears that some of the developments of this will seem to be as fantastic as radar, computers, and lasers were at the time of their development in the past. Electronics, cybernetics, biocybernetics, and artificial intelligence would seem to be the direction the developments of the wizard war is now taking. Its impacts upon space war may be profound.

SPACE WAR: A NEW ERA AND A NEW HOPE

It should be obvious that space warfare is not exceedingly different in principle from any other form of warfare once it is rationally considered and proper strategic doctrines have been developed based upon an understanding of the space environment.

Analogues from the doctrines and principles of sea power, land warfare, and air power are applicable in some degree to space war and, in fact, indicate that the space war will be a combination of evolution of the warfare practices of the past and unique adaptations of them because of the characteristics of the space environment and the new types of weapons that can be deployed there.

However, analogues rarely bear a one-to-one relationship to the real world. There are always different circumstances that create significant differences, and it is difficult, if not impossible, to take all the variables into account. One big hazard in the consideration of space war is that conventional military thinkers may directly transfer too many doctrines and principles of terrestrial warfare in all its forms directly to space where the analogues may not work. Those who do this unknowingly or even willingly and who are wrong will cause the loss of lives, equipment, and even defeat in the space wars of the future. Those who do it properly will probably win, all else being equal.

The prize of space war may not be merely political and military control over people on the entire Planet Earth, but control over the Earth-Moon system in space, whose characteristics and utilization are critically essential to the future welfare of people on Earth in terms of communications, education, energy, new and improved pharmaceuticals, and even within fifty years a number of extraterrestrial sources for raw materials. Without this open-system future, the human race on Planet Earth may well be facing the limits-to-growth scenario so bleakly painted by many futurists unaware of the potential of space exploitation.

However, if going into space to provide an open-system future also means space war as discussed herein, the question legitimately arises: Is the basic concept of space exploitation itself self-defeating because of its military implications? The answer must be rationalized by pointing out that the social potentials and military implications are not as important as the way in which these factors are handled by the people themselves who do the job. Badly handled by wishful thinking, self-righteous policies, ideological fervor, irresponsible greed, or the unbridled lust for power, the ultimate outcome may be as bad or worse than the consequences of the limits-to-growth scenarios. If they are carried out with careful, thoughtful, long-range policies, the result can be a future that permits the evolutionary maturation of the entire human race over the coming centuries.

With these thoughts in mind, it is possible to confront what may be the biggest hurdle in the careful consideration of the implications of space war: the perception, based upon decades of living with the terror of nuclear weapons, that space warfare is total, massively destructive, and impossible to mount a defense against.

However, it should be clear by this time that space war is more like classical warfare of the eighteenth and nineteenth centuries than the mass general warfare of the twentieth century. Because of the doctrines of the gravity well and especially the atmospheric interface, space warfare probably has its closest analogy in naval warfare. There are conceptual approaches to both offensive and defensive space warfare. Space war returns the art of war to the classic offensive-defensive duel because there are effective defenses that can be mounted against most space war weapons.

In the discussion of weapons that would be useful in space warfare or weapons that could be developed in the next two decades for space use, only perfunctory remarks were made concerning potential defenses against their use or countermeasures that could be taken to protect a target against their particular form of attack.

The first principle of defense against any offensive weapon is, of course, to "be where it ain't"—i.e., avoid it. Or in the immortal words of the first sergeant (any first sergeant in any war), "Keep your butt down, and it won't get shot off."

The second-best principle of defense is camouflage: Do not appear to be a target, to be vulnerable, to be worth the time and effort to attack. Do not appear to be a threat. "Maintain a low profile."

Defending facilities in space from attack and defending terrestrial territory and equipment from attack by space weapons obviously fall into two separate categories because of the basic space warfare doctrines, the gravity well and the atmospheric interface.

It is often advantageous when discussing complex issues such as the space defense matter to be able to divide the subject into categories. This was done in the consideration of space weapons themselves. The same categorization of use will also serve in the discussion of defenses— i.e., Earth-to-space, space-to-Earth, and space-to-space. In the first two categories, both the gravity well and the atmospheric interface doctrines rule, while only the gravity well doctrine impacts space-to-space military actions.

Weapons that are likely to be used against space facilities in the Earth-to-space and in the space-to-space category include ASAT and DEW in their various forms. The best ASAT defense, especially for LEO facilities, would be defensive HELs as previously described. Defense against the very powerful Earth-based HELs and, later on, HELs and PBWs utilizing the energy available from powersats remains to be developed and tested, but could include reflective coatings derived from the same research required to produce HEL optics of low absorption.

Space facilities may be designed to possess a defensive mechanism probably unavailable to Earth-based installations: maneuverability. Even though a DEW beam travels at the speed of light, it requires *time* to move the optics to direct the beam at the target, time to arm the system, and time to fire it. Targeting a DEW may involve more than pointing it visually. There may be enough time delay in the overall DEW system—milliseconds— and enough time of beam propagation even at the velocity of light— microseconds—for a space target moving at several kilometers per second to maneuver *away* from where the beam will be directed. A delay in targeting and firing that amounts to a tenth of a second (100 milliseconds) would permit a space vehicle moving at a relative transverse speed of a mere 1 kilometer per second to move 100 meters in that time delay period. A DEW tracking system would have to perform on the basis of extrapolating the target's movement on the basis of immediate past movement data just as predictive weapon direction systems of today operate. Therefore, a space vehicle with excellent maneuverability, probably under control of a human pilot, could outmaneuver a DEW beam. Thus, it is not much different from classic confrontations between adversaries shooting at each other with slower-moving weapons at shorter ranges. The speeds and distances are greater in space, and these may be somewhat equalized by the light-velocity propagation of DEW beams.

Space battles, if fought, will be highly dependent upon the nanosecond response time of computer control with respect to both the weapon and the defense of the target. Space war encounters between meneuverable vehicles and DEWs will be a contest between maneuvering capabilities and tracking/fire control systems.

Thus, with the distances of the Earth-Moon theater involved, DEW weapon engagements are *not* one-sided affairs.

But ground-based DEW *and* ASAT facilities either on Earth or on the Moon offer the decided historic defensive advantage of fortification: burrowing beneath the surface for protection.

Both ASAT and DEW weapons offer defense against bombardment warheads, but aside from hardening with robust mass shielding, there appears to be little in the way of defense for a LEO facility against the simplest ASAT weapon: an Earth-launched rocketsonde carrying a payload of nails that was discussed earlier. Only a planetwide surveillance, detection, and identification system would be able to provide any degree of warning of the launch of such a weapon, and only a counter-ASAT weapon such as another ASAT or a long-range HEL could possibly react in time to intercept the simple ASAT during ascent and before the payload is deployed.

As the years go by and large mass projector weapons such as the lunar catapult or the space-based mass driver become available as weapons of conversion from commercial applications, one might be led to believe that there would be no effective defense against the simplest of all space weapons: catapult-launched rocks. It might well be true that DEWs in the early years of space development before the turn of the century might not be able to irradiate a large lunar rock with enough energy to deflect its trajectory or break it up. But by the time the lunar catapults and space mass drivers become available for military applications, directed energy weapons themselves will have undergone continuing development to the point where they may indeed be able to irradiate such a large mass with sufficient energy density to insure either a deflection of its trajectory or its breakup into smaller pieces that would not survive atmospheric entry or penetrate the micrometeoroid shields of space facilities.

The very existence of lunar catapults and space mass drivers will make them highly vulnerable military targets that will probably be under constant surveillance against possible military use and continually tracked by DEWs powerful enough to incapacitate them if used for military purposes. Thus, these catapults and mass drivers would require the deployment of extensive military systems to defend them, systems which may be far too expensive. Commercial interests owning or operating these catapults and mass drivers would not want their huge capital investments to have the extreme military vulnerability associated with potential weapons systems having the capabilities these catapults and mass drivers might possess. Therefore, commercial interests may act to reduce this vulnerability by design features that would make the devices less attractive for conversion to military applications.

When all space weapons and the defenses that could be mounted against them are considered, it becomes obvious that the basic weapon of space warfare in the future is not a mass projector weapon such as an ASAT, but the directed energy weapon such as the HEL and PBW. As the tracking, targeting, fire control, and damage assessment problems are solved, perhaps through the application of the human-computer direct linkage that offers the adaptability of the human operator married to the speed of the computer, mass projector weapons such as ASAT and even energy-projector weapons such as high explosives and even nuclear explosives become increasingly less effective, easier to defend against, and obsolete as a result.

And this offers a high degree of hope for a future without the MAD doctrine and the continual threat of thermonuclear mass destruction on Earth.

This may appear to be an astounding statement in a work concerning the ultimate form of human conflict, war. It may seem to be incongruous when the discussion has centered on new weapons and devices concerned with the extension of warfare into space. But it is these very weapons, devices, systems, concepts, and doctrines that can form the basis for the demise of the MAD doctrine and the potential obsolescence of nuclear war.

If thermonuclear war with ballistic missiles can be prevented long enough to permit the development by the United States of advanced and efficient space transportation, solar power satellite systems, and high power directed energy weapons stationed both on Earth *and* in space, the resulting space war capabilities render ICBM thermonuclear strikes difficult, if not impossible, and thereby obsolete.

The only effective ballistic missile defense system is the deployment of high energy laser weapons in orbital battle stations. Laser space battle stations will be the primary military development of the decade ahead. Once deployed in orbit, these HEL battle stations will have the capability to destroy ICBMs within minutes of being launched so that their debris, including the nuclear warheads, fall either on the territory of the launching nation or in the oceans.

A HEL battle station has the capability to defend itself with its own primary weapon against ASAT or against an enemy HEL space battle station by the very technology that permits the construction of its low-absorption optical train. Therefore, space HEL battle stations may be defensible against their enemy counterparts, offering no threat to these counterparts or to the people of the nation on Earth below that built and deployed them.

The Earth-to-space threat against space HEL battle stations is strongly affected by the atmospheric interface doctrine. Destroying a space HEL battle station from the Earth's surface requires an extremely large and powerful ground-based HEL because of atmospheric absorption.

Directed energy weapons—HELs on Earth or in space, and PBWs in space further in the future—are *not* weapons of mass destruction. They are selective targeting weapons, rifles with energy beams for bullets, not shotguns with wide dispersion patterns.

DEWs do not pose the awesome threat of mass destruction with megaton energy releases and radioactive exposure and fallout.

Yet a DEW in space can stop the delivery of a thermonuclear warhead by an ICBM or submarine-launched ballistic missile.

An interesting concept emerges at this point: The nuclear explosive weapon came about with unexpected suddenness when compared to the development of other weapons in history. It has been used only twice to date in warfare, and that use came at the end of the war in which it was developed, the last general war to be fought to this time in this century. Its existence has created an almost unreasoning fear among most of the people of the world. Almost extreme diplomatic and political actions have been used to prevent further nuclear warfare and to attempt to control nuclear weapons. The nuclear weapon has created the first and only international balance of terror in history to date.

The nuclear weapon may therefore be an anomaly in military history, and the end of its reign of terror may now be coming with the advent of the directed energy weapon based in space.

Nuclear disarmament may occur within the next twenty-five years not because of disarmament agreements, which have never been successful previously, nor because of the intangible "pressure of world opinion," nor because of the protesting activities of the scientists who developed nuclear explosives, nor (hopefully, if space activity proceeds quickly enough) because of forced disarmament resulting from losing a nuclear war.

Nuclear disarmament will come about because of continued

weapon development, which makes nuclear warfare impossible and there-fore obsolete.

This concept also offers the optimistic characteristic of historic integrity. Disarmament has never taken place in history. Disuse of a weapon *has* taken place because continued weapon development rendered its continued use ineffective.

There are still spears in the world. They are obsolete weapons. Today, they are used in the sporting competition of javelin throwing in the Olympic Games.

There are still bows and arrows in the world. They are obsolete weapons. They are used today in the sport of archery.

There are still cavalry troops. They are obsolete military organi-zations because of the machine gun. Today, dressage and cavalry drills are carried on for recreation and for parade exhibitions.

ICBM silos exist. By the end of this century, they may be extremely useful for the long-term storage of nuclear waste from nuclear power plants because their design makes them perfect for such use. They are hardened against a direct hit from a thermonuclear weapon that would create a strong local earthquake and severe atmospheric overpressure. So the contents of these silos cannot easily be disturbed.

ICBMs exist. By the end of this century, the rocket technology that makes them possible may be useful only for travel to and in space, including deploying and maintaining the weapon systems that made rocket-propelled ICBMs obsolete.

The bright satellites sweeping across the twilight skies of the coming decades may not create the stab of fear that came from viewing the winking star of Sputnik-2. They may be the bright man-made and manned space HEL battle stations capable of only selective use against individual targets on Earth and in space, a use that would be triggered only by aggression and war if they are those of the United States.

Wars will still be fought because people fight people. The space laser battle stations will not be like the impersonal, automatic, unmanned ballistic missiles which, once launched, cannot be recalled from their programmed, automatic mass destruction. They will exist to prevent the launch of ICBMs and the start of the general thermonuclear war that is the basic foundation of the MAD doctrine.

And the human race will have worked its way out of a very difficult position: a closed-system planetary existence whose stability depends upon a suicidal policy of mutual destruction.

At this point, a legitimate question of jingoism may be voiced. It has been tacitly assumed that it would be the United States of America or the consortium of Western nations in NATO and other military-diplomatic alliances that would best serve the interests of the peaceful deployment of the space HEL battle stations and other space weapons discussed herein. There is a general disaffection among certain groups of people that the United States of America may not be as benevolent as many Americans would like to believe and may be, in the words of one young person to the author, "the most dangerous nation in the world."

The USA may well be the most dangerous nation in the world *if* it does not live up to the legacy and to the principles it loosed upon the world in 1776 as the *first* political group to conduct the *first* of the popular political revolutions based upon principles of individual human dignity, rights, and freedom to choose. The thirteen American colonies started something more than two hundred years ago, and the job is not finished as long as a single human being is denied what that first revolution was fought for. It may be a generality to state that most Americans do not like to fail to finish a job. It remains to be seen if Americans will finish what they started more than two hundred years ago. If they do not, the USA probably is the most dangerous nation in the world for raising the hopes of more than ten generations of humanity only to opt out at what appears to be the climax of what they started.

The United States may well be the most dangerous nation in the world if it permits others to gain the upper hand in space warfare capabilities instead.

Considerable criticism has already been leveled at the United States of America for failing in this regard and for failing to live up to the high principles upon which it was founded. There are probably some justifications for these charges because Americans have realized from the time of the founding fathers that human beings are not perfect and therefore human institutions cannot be perfect, that human institutions must therefore be permitted to evolve, to change, and to solve their inherent problems in the process in a sort of dynamic stability, which is the characteristic of any system that makes it appear to exist always on the teetering edge of disruption. Any engineer will confirm that it is extremely difficult to design and maintain the dynamic stability of any system. However, dynamic stability is preferable to static stability. Many human political institutions have possessed static stability; they were eventually overcome by dynamic new institutions usually brought in by invading conquerors.

The United States may not have the perfect system and may not totally live up to its high principles. *But it tries.* And among nations with competing ideologies today, it certainly does not suffer in the comparison and certainly has a system that is greatly envied elsewhere in the world.

The question must be asked: What is the alternative to the United States of America trying to break the deadlock of a MAD closed-system Earth? Is it a preferable alternative? Is it a realistic alternative?

Uncountable numbers of human beings have already answered that question. Few people have abandoned all their physical property and risked their lives to make an eastbound crossing of the Iron Curtain in Europe, to sail in leaky boats from Florida southward, to drift on anything that would float in order to return to Viet Nam, or to flee across the border from Thailand to Cambodia. They may not have understood or known much philosophy, and they might not even know about space weapons, but they understood the reality of the world.

The tasks of freedom must be completed by those who sparked the world to revolt. These tasks are not yet finished. The ultimate consequences are not yet clear. Historian Will Durant, quoted earlier with his wife, once was asked what he believed the consequences of the American and French revolutions were; he replied, "It is too early yet to tell."

Since the reality of human life is that people fight people, it follows that there must be some things worth fighting for, even in the sophisticated high-technology cultures of the world.

Perhaps the goal of planetwide human freedom is, after all, only a *short-term* goal.

Since we do not know *why* human beings fight—only that they do in spite of cultural restraints and political inventions—and since it appears that the human race is indeed leaving behind its childhood and the comfort of Mother Earth for a journey of indeterminate length and partially understood destiny in the universe, perhaps there is a bigger reason why humans fight wars.

Most astronomers and cosmologists, thinking on the far frontiers of modern philosophy and epistemology, believe there may be other life and perhaps even intelligent, self-aware life in the universe—if not in the Solar System, although that really remains yet to be proved negative—then among the stars. Travel to the stars is not impossible although the distances involved are enormous; advanced studies on accomplishing this long journey have been completed and show what must be done. Interstellar travel is not impossible, only extremely difficult with existing or projected technology.

Fifty years ago, the laser was not extremely difficult; it was impossible. But space flight, travel into the Earth-Moon system, was in the same status then as interstellar flight is today: extremely difficult with existing or projected technology.

Whether it is a hundred years in the future or five hundred years, someday human beings will expand beyond the closed system of the Solar System to the stars.

If they meet *something else* out there, that intelligent, self-aware species of extraterrestrials might be meaner and nastier, more covetous, more treacherous, and with a greater lust for power over everything than the worst despots, tyrants, and Attilas of human history on Earth.

The human race may then discover why it was born and tempered in the caldrons of wars on a small planet circling a middle-aged average star in a remote arm of the Milky Way galaxy.

Even that long-term thinking has the same goal as thinking about and planning for space war over the next fifty years.

It will be a great relief to be able to look up at the sky and the stars and not be afraid.

APPENDIX 1
Space-to-Earth Weapons

Weapon: Continuous wave high-energy laser.
Target: Terrestrial structures and vehicles.
Period: 1990–2000
Comment: HEL(CW) could be deployed in space by the late 1980's. Deployment in GEO impractical due to long ranges. LEO HEL(CW) could deliver 100 times solar flux in beam 1 microradian wide, but atmospheric effects could reduce intensity by factor of 5–15.

Weapon: Pulsed high-energy laser.
Target: Terrestrial structures and vehicles.
Period: 1980–2000, possibly infeasible
Comment: Level of capability increases with time. Use in GEO probably infeasible for Earth attacks because of ranges. In late 1990's, values are 20 megawatts output, beam width 1.5 microradians.

Weapon: Particle beam weapon.
Target: Terrestrial structures and vehicles.
Period: Infeasible
Comment: Unlikely to be used for space-to-Earth because of effects of interaction with atmosphere.

Weapon: Entry vehicle.
Target: Terrestrial structures.
Period: Late 1980's
Comment: Earth bombardment, second strike capability. Warhead not needed if large and fast enough. Capabilities increase with time.

Weapon: Space cruiser (hypersonic).
Target: Terrestrial structures.
Period: Late 1980's
Comment: Earth recon, strike, psychwar.

Weapon: Radio frequency transmitter.
Target: Radio frequency equipment.
Period: 1990–2000
Comment: Electronic warfare use on any frequency.

Weapon: Radio frequency transmitter.
Target: People.
Period: 1985–2025
Comment: Direct broadcast of propaganda.

Weapon: Radio frequency transmitter.
Target: Weather modification.
Period: Infeasible
Comment: Requires too much power.

Weapon: Radio frequency sensors.
Target: Radio frequency emissions.
Period: Present
Comment: Electronic and signal intelligence gathering.

Weapon: Optical/infrared sensors.
Target: Structures and vehicles.
Period: Present
Comment: Reconnaissance and surveillance.

Weapon: Radars.
Target: Structures and vehicles.
Period: 1985–1995
Comment: Reconnaissance and surveillance.

Weapon: Radio frequency and laser communications.
Target: People.
Period: Present
Comment: Military communications and control.

APPENDIX 2
Space-to-Space
Weapons

Weapon: Continuous wave high-energy laser.
Target: Spacecraft and missiles.
Period: 1985–1995
Comment: Level of capability increases with time. Could be deployed in space by late 1980's. Capabilities 10 megawatts and 1 microradian beam width, 3000 watts/square centimeter at 1000 kilometers suitable for ASAT, ABM self-defense, blockade.

Weapon: Pulsed high-energy laser.
Target: Spacecraft and missiles.
Period: 1985–1995
Comment: Level of capability increases with time. Electrically powered types suitable for GEO deployment because of solar electric power availability. Late 1990's: 20 megawatts output, 1.5 microradian beam width, 250 watts/square centimenter at 100 kilometers suitable for self-defense, attack nearby satellites, blockade. LEO deployment for ABM with power relay from SPS.

Weapon: Particle beam weapon (neutral hydrogen).
Target: Spacecraft and missiles.
Period: 1990–2000
Comment: 50–100 megawatts input required to deposit 100 calories per gram at 1000 kilometers. Power relay from GEO to LEO required for ABM use.

Weapon: Particle beam weapon (H+ or electron).
Target: Spacecraft and missiles.
Period: Infeasible
Comment: High intensity of less than fully neutralized beams don't

190

propagate well in vacuum. Geomagnetic anomalies make focus and aim difficult.

Weapon: Particle beam weapon (neutron or gamma ray).
Target: Spacecraft and missiles.
Period: Infeasible
Comment: Beam divergence too great.

Weapon: Orbital interceptors.
Target: Spacecraft.
Period: 1981
Comment: In development. Space torpedoes or mines. Nuclear or conventional warheads.

Weapon: Space cutters.
Target: Space vehicles.
Period: 1990's
Comment: Used for inspection, interception, pilot vehicles.

Weapon: Space cruisers.
Target: Space facilities and vehicles.
Period: 1990–1995
Comment: Deep-space inspection, interception, defense, attack.

Weapon: Nuclear detonations.
Target: Spacecraft.
Period: 1981
Comment: Weapons exist if deployed. May destroy attacker's systems by electromagnetic pulse.

Weapon: Space transportation vehicles.
Target: Spacecraft and nonspecific.
Period: 1981
Comment: ASAT carrier. Support, shelter, logistics.

Weapon: Radio frequency transmitter.
Target: Spacecraft.
Period: 1990
Comment: Electronic warfare only.

Weapon: Radio frequency sensors.
Target: Spacecraft and radio frequency emissions.

Period: 1985
Comment: Electronic intelligence, capability depends on receiver sensitivity at given frequency and signal processing ability.

Weapon: Optical and infrared sensors.
Target: Spacecraft.
Period: 1985
Comment: Reconnaissance and surveillance.

Weapon: Radar.
Target: Spacecraft.
Period: 1985
Comment: Reconnaissance and surveillance, tracking.

Weapon: Radio frequency and laser communication.
Target: Spacecraft.
Period: 1985
Comment: Military communications and control.

Weapon: Space facilities for CBW.
Target: People.
Period: May be infeasible
Comment: Chemical and biological warfare (CBW) facilities in separate modules to permit isolation and secrecy. May not offer advantages over Earth-based facilities.

APPENDIX 3
Earth-to-Space Weapons

Weapon: Continuous wave high-energy laser.
Target: Spacecraft.
Period: 1985
Comment: Level of capability increases with time. For the late 1980's, a plausible HEL(CW) is a chemical laser, 10 megawatt output, 4 meter mirror, beam width 1.5 microradians.

Weapon: Pulsed high-energy laser.
Target: Spacecraft.
Period: 1985
Comment: Level of capability increases with time. For the late 1980's, a plausible HEL(P) is a closed cycle carbon dioxide electrodynamic laser with 10 megawatts output, 4 meter mirror, beam width 3.5 microradians, rep rate a function of target characteristics and range.

Weapon: Particle beam weapon.
Target: Spacecraft.
Period: Infeasible
Comment: Neutral or pulsed charged beam considered infeasible because Earth's atmosphere interactions prevent ground-to-space or space-to-ground use.

Weapon: Orbital interceptor (ASAT)
Target: Spacecraft.
Period: 1982
Comment: Under development in USA. Conventional or nuclear warhead.

Weapon: Space transportation system.
Target: Nonspecific.
Period: 1990
Comment: Used for transportation of men and equipment including ASAT weapons.

Weapon: Launch sites.
Target: Nonspecific.
Period: Infeasible
Comment: Not a threat because facilities can be used for military and commercial purposes.

APPENDIX 4
Claims Versus Reality: Space Weapons

Claim: "All space facilities and spacecraft could be destroyed by an Earth-based laser."

Reality: The Earth's atmosphere disperses and attenuates HEL beams, and spacecraft can be "hardened" or protected against HEL beams. Space facilities in GEO are out of range of any HEL laser currently conceivable.

Claim: "A single small projectile properly placed can disable any space system."

Reality: By means of proper design, shielding, and component redundancy, most space systems can be made reasonably impervious to small projectiles although space transportation vehicles and facilities in low Earth orbit (LEO) will remain vulnerable. Space facilities will have to be shielded against micrometeorite damage in any event, and this sort of shielding is also effective against small projectile weapons.

Claim: "Objects in space are easy to hit and destroy with simple non-nuclear tactical rockets."

Reality: Nonnuclear intercept and kill in space is extremely difficult and requires very sophisticated homing devices. Very sophisticated and advanced rocket missiles are needed and nuclear warheads are required in order to justify the expense and the operational difficulties of the military deployment of such systems.

Claim: "Space-based lasers are small objects easy to conceal and use with no advance warning."

Reality: HEL weapons require very large power supplies, making such spacecraft very large and easily detected and tracked. The existence, orbits, and ownership of such spacecraft would be well known shortly after launching.

Claim: "Any huge military satellite can fall out of orbit if it's hit and damaged or if its propulsion system is disabled."

Reality: Once placed in orbit, a space facility or satellite will stay there with only small attitude control thrusters required to maintain and trim the orbit. If hit, it will remain in orbit, and any velocity changes that could possibly be effected by any ASAT might cause it to hit other objects in orbit over a period of time. But since there is negligible Earth's atmosphere at the altitude of most LEO satellites and facilities, a space facility or satellite can be placed in an orbit that does not decay because of atmospheric drag as Skylab did. Higher space facilities or satellites would not be affected at all because decay from GEO would require millions of years in the worst case.

Claim: "Any hit on a large space facility will result in it being ripped apart."

Reality: Space facilities will be designed to be damage tolerant in common with other large structures. For example, even the impact of a B-25 bomber didn't destroy the Empire State Building.

Claim: "Blast damage in space is similar to that on Earth. So shock waves from a small explosion can have devastating effects on large enclosed structures in space, meaning that living facilities in space are highly vulnerable to attack with small conventional warheads."

Reality: With no atmosphere surrounding space facilities, there is no medium for propagating the compression-expansion wave that magnifies the explosion's compression wave as it does on Earth. The explosive must be detonated close enough to a structure that the explosion's own blast wave creates the damage before it dissipates in the vacuum of space

APPENDIX 5
Space Systems' Vulnerabilities to Weapons

System Element	Subsystem Element	Vulnerabilities
Transportation	All	SMET, ASAT, Space cruiser
LEO Facilities	All	SMET, ASAT, Space cruiser, CBW
GEO Facilities	All	SMET, Space cruiser, CBW
Command and control centers	All	SMET, EW, CBW
Communicaton system	R-f and laser links	SMET, EW

APPENDIX 6
Defensive Space Weapons

Defensive weapon	Used Against
Antiballistic missiles (ABM)	Reentry vehicles, ASAT
Antisatellite vehicle (ASAT)	Earth-to-LEO vehicles, ASAT attackers, and Space cruisers
Counter-ASAT	ASAT
Decoys, chaff	ASAT
Dual keys	Inadvertent initiation of offensive systems
Electronic countermeasures	Electronic warfare
Encryption	Espionage & intelligence
Hardening and protective coatings	Directed energy weapons
Long range space surveillance	Space cruisers and ASAT
Maneuver	ASAT
Reduced observables	Surveillance, reconnaissance, ASAT
Reflectors and shields	Directed energy weapons

Bibliography

Ageton, Arthur A., *The Naval Officer's Guide.* New York: McGraw-Hill Book Company, Inc., 1951.

Bain, Claud N., "Power from Space by Laser," *Astronautics & Aeronautics,* Vol. 17, No. 3 (March 1979).

Billman, Kenneth W., "Radiation Energy Conversion in Space," *Astronautics & Aeronautics,* Vol. 17, No. 3 (March 1979).

Bretnor, Reginald, *Decisive Warfare, A Study in Military Theory.* Harrisburg, Pa: Stackpole Books, 1969.

———, *The Future at War,* 4 vols. New York: Ace Books, 1979–1980.

Churchill, Winston S., *The Second World War, Their Finest Hour.* Boston: Houghton Mifflin Company, 1949.

Clarke, Arthur C., *Profiles of the Future.* New York: Harper & Row Publishers, Inc., 1963.

Cole, Dandridge M., and Donald W. Cox, *Islands in Space, the Challenge of the Planetoids.* Philadelphia: Chilton Books, 1964.

Coon, Carleton S., *The Story of Man.* New York: Alfred A. Knopf, 1969.

Duelfer, Charles, "War and Space," *ANALOG* magazine, Vol. XCIX No. 5 (May 1979).

Dula, Arthur M., "Frontier Law 1977—Law of Outer Space," *Albertus Magnus, University of Houston College of Law Alumni Publication,* Vol. 1, No. 1 (December 1976/January 1977).

Durant, Will and Ariel, *The Lessons of History.* New York: Simon and Schuster, 1968.

Farago, Ladislas, *Patton: Ordeal and Triumph.* New York: Dell Publishing Company, Inc., 1963.

Ford, Brian J., *Allied Secret Weapons; The War of Science.* New York: Ballantine Books, Inc., 1971.

Gerry, Edward T., and John D. G. Rather, "The Laser Future," *Astronautics & Aeronautics,* Vol. 17, No. 3 (March 1979).

Glasstone, Samuel, ed., *The Effects of Nuclear Weapons.* Washington DC: Superintendent of Documents, 1962.

Haley, Andrew G., *Space Law and Government.* New York: Appleton-Century-Crofts, 1963.

Harper, George W., "Build Your Own A-Bomb and Wake Up the Neighborhood," *ANALOG* magazine, Vol. XCVIX No. 4 (April 1979).

Heinlein, Robert A., *The Moon Is a Harsh Mistress.* New York: G. P. Putnam's Sons, 1966.

———, *The Past Through Tomorrow.* New York: G. P. Putnam's Sons, 1967.

Hunter, Maxwell W., II, *Strategic Dynamics and Space-laser Weaponry.* San Carlos, Calif.: Privately published, 31 October 1977.

Josephy, Alvin M., Jr. editor, *The American Heritage History of World War I.* New York: American Heritage Publishing Company, 1964.

Kahn, Herman, *Thinking About the Unthinkable.* New York: Horizon Press, 1962.

Marshall, George C., *The Winning of the War in Europe and the Pacific.* New York: Simon and Schuster, 1945.

Nalos, Ervin J., "New Developments in Electromagnetic Energy Beaming," *Proceedings of the IEEE,* Vol. 66, No. 3 (March 1978).

Parkinson, C. Northcote, *East and West.* Boston: Houghton Mifflin Co., 1963.

Polmar, Norman, *Strategic Weapons: An Introduction.* New York: Crane, Russak & Co., Inc., 1975.

Salkeld, Robert, *War and Space.* Englewood Cliffs, NJ, Prentice-Hall, Inc., 1970.

Sänger, E., and Bredt, J., *Über einen Raketenantrieb für Fernbomber (A Rocket Drive for Long Range Bombers).* Ainring, Austria: Deutsche Luftfahrtforschung UM 3538, 1944; published in translation in the USA by Robert Cornog, Santa Barbara, Calif., 1952.

Smyth, H. D., *A General Account of the Development of Methods of Using Atomic Energy for Military Purposes Under the Auspices of the United States Government* ("The Smyth Report"). United States Army Corps of Engineers, 1945.

Stine, G. Harry, *The Third Industrial Revolution.* New York: Ace Books, 1979.

———, *The Space Enterprise.* New York: Ace Books, 1980.

Thomas, Craig, *Firefox.* New York: Holt, Rinehart and Winston, 1977.

Tombaugh, C. W., et al., *The Search for Small Natural Earth Satellites, Final Technical Report.* University Park, NM: New Mexico State University Physical Science Laboratory, 1959.

Vajk, J. Peter, et al., *On the Military Implications of a Satellite Power System.* Pleasanton, Calif.: Science Applications, Inc., April 1980.

Vajk, J. Peter, *Doomsday Has Been Cancelled.* Culver City, Calif.: Peace Press, 1978.

Vick, Charles P., "The Soviet Super Boosters," *Spaceflight,* Vol. 15

No. 3 (December 1973) and Vol 16 No. 12 (March 1974), British Interplanetary Society, London.

Wells, Herbert George, *The War of the Worlds, Seven Science Fiction Novels of H. G. Wells.* New York: Dover Publications, Inc.

——, *A Forecast of Space Technology, 1980–2000,* NASA SP-387, National Aeronautics and Space Administration, Washington DC 20546.

——, *Federal Aviation Regulations,* Section 307, 72 Statute 749, 49 US Code 1348.

——, *Satellite Power System Concept Development and Evaluation Program, Reference System Report.* US Department of Energy, Office of Energy Research, Washington DC 20545, DOE/ER-0023, October 1978.

——, "U.S. Pushes Development of Beam Weapons," *Aviation Week & Space Technology,* Vol. 109, No. 14 (2 October 1978).

——, "Key Beam Weapon Tests Slated," *Aviation Week & Space Technology,* Vol. 109, No. 15 (9 October 1978).

——, "Army Pushing New Weapons Effort," *Aviation Week & Space Technology,* Vol. 109, No. 16 (16 October 1978).

——, *Satellite Power System Concept Development and Evaluation Program, Preliminary Assessment,* U.S. Department of Energy, Office of Energy Research, Washington DC 20545, DOE/ER-0041, September 1979.

——, "Ariane Launcher in Kourou Test," *Aviation Week & Space Technology,* Vol. 112, No. 4 (28 January 1980).

——, "Technical Survey, Particle Beams, Laser Weapons," *Aviation Week & Space Technology,* Vol. 113, No. 4 (July 28), 1980; Vol. 113, No. 5 (4 August 1980).

——"Indian SLV-3 Booster is Launched . . . ," *Aviation Week & Space Technology,* Vol. 113, No. 8 (25 August 1980).

——, *STS Flight Assignment Baseline,* JSC-13000-4, Lyndon B. Johnson Space Center, Houston, Texas, 23 September 1980.

——, "Space-based Laser Battle Stations Seen," *Aviation Week & Space Technology,* Vol. 113, No. 23 (8 December 1980).

Index